STANDING NEXT TO HISTORY

STANDING NEXT TO HISTORY

TO HISTORY

★ ★ ★ ★

AN AGENT'S LIFE INSIDE

THE SECRET SERVICE

★ ★ ★ ★

JOSEPH PETRO

with JEFFREY ROBINSON

THOMAS DUNNE BOOKS
ST. MARTIN'S GRIFFIN ⚘ NEW YORK

THOMAS DUNNE BOOKS.
An imprint of St. Martin's Press.

STANDING NEXT TO HISTORY. Copyright © 2005 by Joseph Petro.
All rights reserved. Printed in the United States of America.
For information, address
St. Martin's Press, 175 Fifth Avenue, New York, N.Y. 10010.

www.stmartins.com

Book design by Gretchen Achilles

Library of Congress Cataloging-in-Publication Data

Petro, Joseph, 1944–
    Standing next to history : an agent's life inside the Secret Service /
by Joseph Petro with Jeffrey Robinson.
        p.   cm.
    ISBN 0-312-33221-1 (hc)
    ISBN 0-312-33222-X (pbk)
    EAN 978-0-312-33222-8
    1. Petro, Joseph, 1944– 2. United States. Secret Service—
Officials and employees—Biography. 3. Presidents—Protection—
United States. 4. Reagan, Ronald. I. Robinson, Jeffrey, 1945–
II. Title.

HV7911.P46A3   2005
363.28'3'092—dc22   2004056194

10 9 8 7 6 5

TO THE THREE MOST IMPORTANT WOMEN IN MY LIFE:

MY MOTHER, DOROTHY;

MY DAUGHTER, MICHELLE;

AND MY WIFE, SUSAN

CONTENTS

★ ★ ★ ★

STANDING NEXT TO HISTORY

PROLOGUE

The irony of doing a "spontaneous" presidential event is the amount of planning it requires.

The operations center for the Presidential Protective Division (PPD) is a suite of cramped offices on the ground floor of the majestic Executive Office Building (EOB)—once home to both the State and War departments—next door to the White House.

Referred to simply as "Room 10," ours was typical of EOB offices—a crowded maze of desks and filing cabinets and highly polished floors, where phones were always ringing and people were always shuffling in and out. Most of the president's staff is headquartered in the EOB and suffers those same crowded, hectic conditions, with the notable exception of the vice president, whose more spacious and serene official suite of offices is on the second floor.

I'd been working in Room 10 for the past year as assistant special agent in charge of PPD and, on that April morning in 1984, was busy sorting through duty schedules when Mike Deaver called from the West Wing. "Meet me on West Exec," the president's deputy chief of staff said. "We're taking a helicopter ride."

Deaver was one of Ronald Reagan's "triumvirate." He, along with chief of staff James Baker and counselor to the president Ed

Meese, made up the inner circle of the first administration, and, at that time, Deaver may have been the closest to the president. His office was next to the Oval Office, and had a door leading directly into it, making him the only member of staff who could enter unobserved. He oversaw the "Reagan image," a job he'd held since the California governor days. Years later, one newsmagazine would note that while Reagan cooked the steaks, it was Deaver who managed the sizzle. Another article suggested that if the first administration had been a film, Deaver's on-screen credit would have read "Directed By."

Grabbing my jacket, I hurried out of the building's side exit where it opens onto West Executive Avenue, the private street that separates the EOB from the White House. Senior staffers park their cars in West Exec, and that morning a four-door Chrysler sedan with a military driver was waiting for us. Deaver was just coming through the door of the West Wing, followed by Bill Henkel, head of the president's Advance Office. A cantankerous, no-nonsense guy who'd learned his trade in the Nixon White House, Henkel managed presidential trips and events. The three of us jumped into the car, and the driver headed out the gate for the Southeast Freeway. Before I could ask what was going on, Deaver announced, "Baltimore. Opening day. No one knows."

I had to smile. We were on the way to tell the owner of the Baltimore Orioles that the president had just invited himself to throw out the first ball of the season. To make that happen would take more than one hundred people.

On the ten-minute ride to Anacostia, the old Naval Air Station that is home to HMX—the Marine Corps detachment that flies the president's helicopters—Deaver outlined the particulars. The president would throw out the ball, spend the first inning in the Oriole dugout, and then we'd come home. The entire event would last only half an hour.

One of the "white tops"—a green and white Sikorsky H-3—

was waiting for us. Whenever the president is on board, it's designated Marine One, the same way that any plane the president flies on is designated Air Force One. For the three of us, the designation was less glamorous, just another HMX "plane." Despite the fact that it's a helicopter, for some odd reason in White House terminology helicopters are planes, and I have no idea why. We left from Anacostia because only Marine One takes off and lands at the White House. Not even the vice president in Marine Two can land there.

As we took off, I was on the phone to the Baltimore office of the Secret Service, asking them to have agents meet us at the landing zone. I then telephoned the Secret Service garage, which in those days was at the Washington Navy Yard, and told them we needed to get cars heading north right away. Baltimore is a forty-minute drive from Washington, and agents needed to be in place when Marine One landed with the president. The garage dispatched an armored limousine, several follow-up cars, and what we called an off-the-record car—a nondescript Lincoln Town Car—just in case we needed it. Finally, because we plan for any contingency, which in this case meant that the motorcade might not get to Baltimore in time, I phoned the field office again to station two extra cars at the landing zone.

Deaver, Henkel, and I then got into a discussion about where the president would stand when he threw out the ball. Deaver and Henkel wanted maximum visibility, to put him where the whole crowd could see him, which meant the pitcher's mound. For that same reason, the mound was my last choice. They wanted footage of the president on the evening news in front of an enthusiastic crowd because that's good for their business. But it wasn't good for the Secret Service. The president would be too exposed and too far from the safety of the dugout. I wanted him to step out of the dugout and throw it to home plate from there. Deaver and Henkel didn't like that. I offered the on-deck circle. They didn't like that either. We debated the possibilities, and eventually settled on third base.

I agreed because it was only another twenty feet or so farther away, and they agreed because he would still be visible to the crowd.

Generally speaking, unannounced short trips like this one are low risk. Since no one is expecting the president, it's unlikely that an assassin will be waiting for him. But there could be a bizarre spontaneous action by someone who just happens to have a gun. Even though it's a remote possibility, it cannot be ignored. What's more, the longer the president stays in view, the riskier it gets. People have time to think, to scheme, to realize there is an opportunity. To cover that threat, while we were flying to Baltimore, I phoned back to Washington, to brief Bob DeProspero—the agent in charge of PPD—and we decided to put the president in a bulletproof vest.

The security detail on duty at the White House was ready for the trip to Baltimore, because they're always ready to move at any time to go anywhere. In this case, all they needed to do was get the president on Marine One and fly up. What I didn't know was that the president had a few ideas of his own.

First, he wanted to warm up, and sent his staff scurrying around the White House for a baseball. I have no idea where they found one, except they did, and somewhere in the building they also found a glove. So, fifteen minutes before he climbed onto Marine One, the seventy-three-year-old Ronald Reagan went out to the Rose Garden with a staffer and had a catch. Then he put some money in his pocket.

Our landing zone in Baltimore was the Water Works, a fenced-in area across the street from Municipal Stadium. Half a dozen field agents had already secured it and were waiting for us with a small fleet of cars. No sooner had Mike, Bill, and I gotten out of the helicopter than it took off for the White House to pick up the president.

The game was an hour away, and crowds were beginning to arrive. The three of us—men in dark suits who'd just stepped off a marine helicopter—attracted attention as we hurried through the opening-day throng. Obviously, we didn't have tickets, so we needed to talk our way inside. I spotted a Baltimore police lieutenant, identified myself as a Secret Service agent, and explained that we needed to speak with Edward Bennett Williams, the Washington lawyer who owned the Orioles. The officer escorted us through the turnstiles and into the clubhouse, and we informed Williams that the president would be arriving.

With time running short, the three of us rushed through a series of briefings. I asked the Baltimore police to put extra personnel in place for crowd control, to block the route between the landing zone and the stadium, and to secure the area in front of the clubhouse entrance where we would park the president's car. I then walked the route the president would take from the clubhouse entrance to the dugout and back again. Although most of the crowd would be in the stadium when the president arrived, there were always people showing up late or mingling outside, and there could be no question of letting them get anywhere near him. So I double-checked that the streets and parking area were secure, then stationed several field agents behind the dugout and in the stands to watch the crowd. The head of publicity for the Orioles roped off an area behind third base for the press, while the team's head of security briefed his people. Mike stayed with Williams and his other guest, baseball commissioner Bowie Kuhn, while Bill and I hurried back to the landing zone, because, by this time, the president was on his way.

But the limousine and other cars weren't there yet. I got on the radio with the limousine driver, tried to work out how much longer he'd be, and realized that he might not get there in time. Sure enough, a few minutes later, three helicopters came into view.

Anyone who watches television news, seeing Marine One taking off and landing on the White House lawn, might get the impression that the president's helicopter flies alone. It doesn't. There are always at least two others with him, and sometimes more. At a minimum, there's one for the press, which may also have some White House staff on it, and one for the Secret Service. Each helicopter seats ten

to twelve people. The press and agents fly out of Anacostia and ren-
dezvous with Marine One in the air. During any flight, the three helicopters are always moving around and changing positions so that it
is difficult to identify Marine One.

In Baltimore, as soon as the press and agents were on the
ground, Marine One came in for a landing. That's when the cars
from Washington finally pulled up. But the limousine was low on
gas. For the most part, these specially built armored cars are not only
indefatigable, but are maintained daily. They don't even have flats,
because they have special tires with padded cells inside so that if one
loses air—due to a puncture or because someone shot at the tires—
they won't go flat for several miles. However, the limousines are gas
guzzlers, getting four miles to the gallon, and this one had just
driven all the way up from D.C. I wasn't sure we had enough gas to
get the president to the stadium and back again to the landing zone
and decided that while the president was at the game, the limousine
would be refueled. However, I wasn't comfortable sending the limousine to a gas station, so we got one of our agents to bring gas in.

The crowd outside the stadium saw the three official helicopters
landing and saw the police blocking off streets, and word spread that
the president was there. We got him quickly from the landing zone
into the clubhouse, where Williams and Kuhn welcomed him. The
Orioles backroom staff was there, too, along with manager Earl
Weaver and a few of the players. The president greeted them all—
we called this "the grip and grin"—and before the National Anthem
ended, he was in the dugout.

At one point, I found myself standing next to the Orioles' star
infielder, Cal Ripken, who didn't seem overjoyed that the president
was there. "Every time a president comes to one of our games," he
told me, "we lose." Ripken must have known what he was talking
about, because that day the Orioles lost to the White Sox 5–2.

When the stadium announcer told the crowd, "Ladies and gen-
tlemen, the president of the United States," the place erupted.

Ronald Reagan stepped out of the dugout with the team and greeted the crowd with his usual stage presence. Rick Dempsey, the Orioles catcher, waited at home plate as the president went to third base, wound up, threw the ball, and hit Dempsey's mitt. The crowd erupted again. Dempsey ran up to president and handed him the ball. The president worked the crowd for another few seconds before we ushered him safely back inside the dugout.

Had he planned to stay for the game, we would have moved him to the owner's box, where he would be less exposed to the crowd. But a single inning in the dugout, at least on this occasion, was acceptable. The president sat down on the bench in between Williams and Kuhn, the first batter stepped up to the plate, and, suddenly, Bill Henkel mentioned hot dogs. He told me the president would eat a hot dog so that the White House could have its "Picture of the Day." Okay, baseball and hot dogs go together, it's a traditional thing, and why shouldn't the president have a hot dog at a ball game? The answer is, because the president of the United States shouldn't be eating any food that the Secret Service doesn't control.

In principle, nothing edible gets near the president unless we know where it comes from and who has handled it. Even at state banquets, while it appears as that he is eating the same food as everyone else, his meal is cooked by White House stewards. If he's overseas, his stewards find out what's being served at the banquet and bring the ingredients with them from the United States. They even dress the same way the other waiters dress, in order to serve him without drawing attention to themselves. The hot dog wasn't anticipated, but Henkel wanted it, and apparently the president was looking forward to it. I radioed up to one of the agents on top of the dugout and asked him to select a hot dog vendor at random. He found an older guy and brought him down to the dugout. The vendor could see who his customers were, but didn't necessarily appreciate the fact that while he was waiting to mustard up a snack for the president, he was losing business back in the stands.

The Orioles retired the side, came up to bat, and we moved the vendor along the bench to the president, who looked up at him, grinned widely, and said, "Three hot dogs, please."

The vendor readied the hot dogs and handed one to the president, one to Williams, and one to Kuhn. The president gestured to Williams and Kuhn, "I'll take care of this," reached into his pocket, pulled out a five-dollar bill, handed it to the vendor, and said generously, "Keep the change."

The vendor took the money, stared for a moment, hesitated, then turned back to the president. "Sir. The hot dogs are two bucks apiece."

There was an awkward few seconds because the president didn't have any more money, but Henkel was very quick and slipped another five-dollar bill into the president's hand.

The president smiled again, handed the money to the vendor, and repeated, "Keep the change."

The inning ended, the president thanked everyone in the dugout, and we moved him back through the clubhouse to the cars. The freshly fueled limousine got him to the Water Works. We climbed into the plane and headed home.

The H-3 has only one cabin. There is a single seat for the president with a small writing table, and across from him a bench seat for two people. There are two bench seats behind that, one on each side, and a single seat at the rear, next to the radio equipment, which is where I usually sat. There is also a jump seat behind the cockpit for a second agent. There's a minifridge at the back with soft drinks— strictly self-serve—and a little tray with mints and gum. True to form, there were plenty of jelly beans on board. But that was no surprise because, in this administration, there were plenty of jelly beans everywhere.

Henkel and I were sitting together just behind the president, who was leaning over his desk, scribbling something on one of the

Marine One embossed note cards. I didn't pay much attention to what he was doing until he sat up, leaned back, and handed the card to Henkel.

It read, "Dear Bill, I owe you five dollars. Ronald Reagan."

CHAPTER ONE

★ ★ ★ ★

TAKING A BULLET

If you fail in this business, you could lose the president.

At no point did anyone ever say to me, your job is to take a bullet for the president of the United States.

Legend has it there's a blood oath that Secret Service agents take in which we swear to lay down our own life to save the president's. There is no such pledge, no such promise, and, maybe even more important, no such requirement. It's a myth, nothing more than part of the mystique that surrounds the Secret Service. Instead, the reality of the job—and this, perhaps, best defines the fundamental principle of the Secret Service—is to do absolutely everything possible to prevent such a decision from ever having to be made.

It goes without saying that protecting the president can be dangerous, and, yes, there may be a moment when, because of where we are, getting killed is a real possibility. But police officers face that same possibility every day. So, too, firemen, soldiers, sailors, and pilots. Danger is hardly unique to the Secret Service. Because no one ever knows for sure how he or she will react in a life-threatening situation, we try to leave nothing to chance. We practice assassinations at speeches and at rallies and in motorcades, getting in and out of the car. We don't use professional drivers; we train our own agents to drive the presidential limousine because that driver is the most important person in the motorcade. Armored to our specifications, the limousine is much heavier than a regular car and a lot harder to drive. It doesn't respond the way a standard Cadillac limousine would respond. In an emergency, the driver may have to do something—break through a barricade or execute a J-turn—and even though there is always a supervisor sitting next to him, there might be a few seconds when the life of the president hangs on the driver's instinctive reaction. So we work a lot of assassination scenarios around cars, all of them authentically played out with presidential limousines and crowds and explosives, and with mock assassins firing guns.

However, the classic scenario for an "attack on the principal" (AOP) is the rope line, where the president shakes hands over the simple barrier that separates him from the crowd. It's a very dangerous time, because you don't always know who's in the crowd. Even if you've controlled access by putting everyone through a metal detector—known as a magnetometer—you cannot trust the machine to pick up everything. In theory, the metal detector should spot a gun. But there's always the possibility that someone can get through with an explosive device or something simple, like a pen, with which he plans to stab the president. So you look for anomalies, for something that doesn't fit, for the man who's not smiling, for the woman who's wearing a heavy coat on a warm day, for someone who appears unusually nervous.

The level of crowd emotion is always high when the president is near enough to touch, and agents need to see that emotion reflected in everyone's eyes. I would stand within a hand's reach of him, ready to grab him around the waist and yank him away, all the time looking into eyes for a stare that told me the person wasn't happy to see the president up close. And I would also be looking at hands, for the person who wasn't trying to shake hands with the president. Anyone whose hands were in his pockets was someone I needed to worry about. That's why there were agents in front of the president, and behind him, too, looking into eyes and saying to people in the crowd, "Let me see your hands, please. . . . Hands, please. Let me see your hands."

It's not a perfect science, but rather a technique that can be learned and perfected with practice, which is why the Secret Service teaches it and why we practice it over and over and over again. Agents on the president's detail, and on the vice president's detail, too, spend two weeks out of every two months at the Secret Service training center at Beltsville, Maryland, going through realistic situations that have been specifically designed to create instinctive reactions to a single second's madness.

Although the Beltsville facility was pretty basic when I first went through there in 1971, today it is a small town—much like a movie set—with city blocks featuring façades of office buildings and hotels. They have a series of roads for motorcades and a Boeing 707 to work scenarios involving airplanes. As a supervisor I'd go out there every couple of months to train with the details. On one occasion, with an agent named Frank Larkin playing the president, I was working a rope line, exactly the way I did many times with Ronald Reagan as he shook hands with people in the crowd. Suddenly, someone started firing at us, and the crowd panicked. Instinctively, I grabbed Frank, threw him into the back of the limousine, and we took off. It's the most basic technique in the manual—called "cover and evacuate"—because it's the best thing to do. You cover the president, get him into the car, and evacuate him from the scene, leaving the shift agents to take care of the scene itself.

Once we were safely out of the way, I turned around to say something to Frank, but he was sprawled across the rear seat with blood pouring out of his mouth and down the front of his suit. I froze. Having served in combat, having seen the results of shootings, having seen blood, I know about the effect of shock. In some cases it lasts for a few seconds, in some cases it lasts longer. For the most part it depends on how dramatic the shooting is and how often you've seen such things. In this case, the shock of seeing blood, which I hadn't expected, lasted only a split second. It turned out that Hollywood blood packs were the latest addition to the training. I blurted out, "You scared the hell out of me. I thought you were really hurt." That was the idea.

Prior to the assassinations of John and Robert Kennedy, the Secret Service didn't run a lot of complex assassination scenarios. But by the 1970s, we had Beltsville and were going through them regularly, training agents to act instinctively, which is not necessarily the same as doing what comes naturally. For example, most people duck when they hear gunshots. It's the predictable response of policemen and soldiers. They get down low to protect themselves before returning fire. But Secret Service agents need to do just the opposite, which is an unnatural reaction. When shots are fired, we're trained to pull our weapon, stand up straight, and return fire. Instead of protecting ourselves, we turn ourselves into a larger target. That's one reason why all of our weapons training is done standing up. We don't do any prone shooting.

If you study the film footage of the Reagan assassination attempt in 1981, what you see is agents standing up while the president's military aide is diving to the ground. This is not a criticism of the army, because that's what the aide had been trained to do. He responded to his training by hitting the ground; the agents responded to theirs by standing tall. If I heard shots today, I'm sure that I would stand up, at least until I realized that's not a good thing for me to be doing at this point in my life, at which time, I hope, it wouldn't take me long to get back down.

Our training put a lot of emphasis on shooting. I wasn't a particularly good shot in the navy, where I found that with automatic weapons I could just spray an area and let the weapon do the work. But I became a marksman in the Secret Service because there was so much weapons training. Agents are required to qualify with their handgun once a month—mine was a .357 Magnum, but the service now uses 9mm semiautomatics—and with the Uzi submachine gun and the shotgun once a quarter. Handgun qualification was done at a small range in the basement of the U.S. Post Office on Pennsylvania Avenue, while the quarterly qualification was an eight-hour ordeal at Beltsville, when an agent was put through all the various judgmental courses. The best of those was called Hogan's Alley, which is a city street where pop-up targets suddenly appear and you have to shoot the bad guys and not shoot the good guys and have only have a fraction of a second to decide who's who. It's terrific training. So the Secret Service made us all good shots, which was a necessity for agents. If we ever found ourselves shooting into a crowd, we had to hit our target.

Our sidearm wasn't the only thing we always carried. There was a speed loader for the revolver, giving us more bullets, the radio and the famous earpiece, an armored vest—all agents were required to wear the vest whenever we were with a protectee—and handcuffs. All agents were required to have them, too, although I admit that when I was with the president, I never bothered. I figured that if he and I found ourselves in a position where I needed to handcuff someone, we were in the wrong place and needed to get out of there fast.

Another important aspect of Secret Service training is medical emergencies, which pose the highest risk to the president. We become experts in "ten-minute medicine." We learn to stabilize someone for ten minutes because, by design, wherever we travel with the president, we are never more than ten minutes away from professional medical attention. Whether the emergency is a heart attack or a stroke, a shooting, a broken leg, or an automobile accident, we train to keep someone alive for ten minutes. We can't perform a tracheotomy, but we can clear an airspace to keep that person breathing until someone arrives on the scene who can perform a tracheotomy. We are trained in cardiopulmonary resuscitation and on defibrillators, which weren't as easy to use then as they are now. In my day we spent as much time cursing the dummies as we did defibrillating them. Today defibrillators are very compact and so easy to operate that we call them "agent-proof."

Legislation creating the Secret Service was on Abraham Lincoln's desk waiting to be signed on the night he was assassinated. In those days, a reported one-third of the currency then in circulation in the United States was counterfeit, and Lincoln's idea was to create the nation's first federal law-enforcement agency, housed in the Treasury Department, to protect all the financial instruments of the United States. Today, in addition to preventing counterfeiting and the theft or forging of government checks, our investigative mission includes protecting against fraud involving credit cards, computers, ATMs, and electronic transfers. Over the years, the Secret Service investigated the Teapot Dome scandal, numerous government land frauds, the machinations of the Ku Klux Klan, and espionage activities during the Spanish-American War. In 1908, the government moved nine Secret Service "operatives" out of Treasury and put them in the Justice Department. This new corps of federal agents worked directly for the attorney general and would eventually become the nucleus of the Federal Bureau of Investigation.

The most significant change in the mission of the Secret Service came in 1901. In the aftermath of the assassination of President William McKinley—the third president to be killed in thirty-six years—Congress directed the Secret Service to protect the president. Today, protection is the Secret Service's primary responsibility. In addition to the president and vice president, the service protects their spouses and their immediate families, former officeholders, and visiting heads of state. Following the Robert Kennedy assassination, which took place during the 1968 primary election campaign, the mission was expanded to protect presidential candidates as well.

Because the president can order the Secret Service to protect anyone under threat, there have been times when we've protected cabinet officers, the national security advisor, and the White House chief of staff. On a couple of occasions, after threats were made against Senator Ted Kennedy, President Reagan ordered us to protect him. We have also protected the Declaration of Independence and the Constitution, the Gutenberg Bible, and the most famous painting in the world, the Mona Lisa, when it was exhibited in the United States in 1962–1963.

It's important to note that the protection afforded the president and the vice president is statutory. They have no choice in the matter. They cannot simply decide one day that they don't want to be protected. I suppose a president could say, I don't like this particular agent, and transfer him out, but that doesn't really happen—although I've heard stories about Lyndon Johnson getting angry with agents and shouting at them, "You're fired." Many of those same agents were fired by Johnson five and six times.

In the end, the Secret Service can only provide as much protection as the protectee is willing to accept. How close in we get, or how far away we stand, depends entirely on circumstance. I joined President Reagan's detail two years after he'd been shot, at a time when everyone was extremely concerned about him. We raised the bar to protect him, and he went along with that, sometimes to the point of actually overriding the advice of his staff.

For instance, when it was announced that he would address the United Nations in September 1986, the staff decided that after the president's speech, he should walk from the podium into the General Assembly and sit with the U.S. delegation during the next speech. From a public relations viewpoint, it was a fine idea. But from a security viewpoint, it was quite the opposite. We had no control over who would be in the room, nor could we put magnetometers at the doors, which meant that anybody could come in carrying anything they wanted, including a weapon. And we had reason for concern: Only five months before, President Reagan had ordered the bombing of Libya, and the U.S. delegation sat almost directly in front of the Libyan delegation. There was simply no way we were going to place him in that kind of danger. But the staff was insistent that this could be done safely and refused to accept our evaluation that it could not. We went round and round over this, until, finally, it became necessary to see the president.

We didn't have a scheduled appointment that day, so Bill Henkel and I stood outside the Oval Office and waited for a break between meetings. Vice President George Bush and chief of staff Don Regan were there when we walked in. The president wasn't expecting to see me. He turned to Regan with a worried look on his face. "What's this meeting about?"

Regan told him. "A security issue."

Immediately, the president said, "You already know how I'm going to come out on this one."

Bill explained the situation, and I told him why we were very much against his sitting with the U.S. delegation. "With diplomatic immunity, anybody can bring weapons into the General Assembly. What's more, the Libyan delegation would be right behind you."

The president shrugged. "Maybe this is something George should do."

Everybody laughed, and Vice President Bush said, "Sure, I'll even paint a big bull's-eye on my back."

And that was the end of that. The president came down on the side of the Secret Service. He did not sit with the delegation.

No, the job is not about a blood oath to stop a bullet. It's about doing everything humanly possible to avoid finding yourself in a situation where you have to make that decision. It's about always controlling the environment and wrapping the president in a cocoon of safety. That begins with our "three perimeter" philosophy. We set up a series of boundaries. The outer perimeter is usually a show of force by uniformed police manning barricades. Their job is to keep people at a safe distance from the president. Inside that, we set up a middle perimeter, which is made up of Secret Service agents and uniformed police standing post. We put them at doors and in hallways, around the building to encircle it, and on rooftops. Their job is to make certain that anyone who might have somehow managed to get beyond the outer perimeter can get no farther. Included here is a major deterrent called the CAT—the Secret Service's Counter Assault Team—a group of men so heavily armed with automatic weapons and other arms that they could just about take over a small country. Then there is an inner perimeter, which is the Secret Service detail immediately surrounding the president. They see to it that anyone who, against the odds, has gotten through the outer and middle perimeters is now stopped. The three-perimeter concept is the same fundamental principle whether the president is attending a rally with fifteen thousand people or on a golf course with three other people. There are always perimeters.

Inside those perimeters we "create an atmosphere" that permeates every inch of every event. When we step off an elevator with the president, there should be a "clean" hallway, not one in which clusters of people are milling about. The only person we want to see is the advance agent who's going to lead us to the suite. When the hallway is clean and there's no noise and it's dignified, we know that everything is under control. We want every place to be quiet, dignified, and secure, just like the hallway outside the Oval Office, where everyone thinks, "I shouldn't be here," and where everyone whispers.

The more effectively we micromanage the environment, the more effectively we can protect the president. We work with his staff to control where he goes, how he gets there, who gets close to him, and how close that person gets. And all the time we look for irregularities. That's why we study assassinations, to see where those anomalies were missed. We sit in classrooms and run films back and forth, just like a football team going over game films, trying to see what happened and how it happened and how it could have been prevented. We study every assassination and every attempted assassination, wherever it happened, to learn from the mistakes of others, and from our own mistakes. And when we talk about our own mistakes, at the top of the list is Dallas, November 1963.

We study the assassination of John F. Kennedy endlessly. I long ago lost count of how many times I've seen the Zapruder film. I have no wish to get bogged down in conspiracy theories, but I will say I have never seen any evidence that Lee Harvey Oswald did not kill President Kennedy. I've read the books and gone through the theories that say Oswald did not act alone, but the assassination we study has Oswald perched on the southeast corner of the sixth floor of the Texas School Book Depository overlooking Dealey Plaza. What happened that day was the result of a series of breakdowns, on several levels.

The presidential limousine in which Kennedy rode was a Lincoln convertible with a removable protective bubble top. The agents with the president wanted to keep the bubble top on, and that would have saved John Kennedy's life. But it was a beautiful day, and someone decided to take the bubble top off. There is reason to believe that the president himself made that decision.

There was also talk about putting agents on the back of the limousine. There was a running board that could be extended past the rear bumper. It's possible that if agents had been standing on it, they might have blocked Oswald's line of sight. It's speculative, but at least Oswald's angle of attack would have been different with agents between him and the president. Then, even if the first shot had been successful, he probably would not have managed to fire a lethal second shot from the rear because the agents on the running board would have reacted immediately to cover the president. As I read the *Warren Commission Report,* it seems that the president was the one who said, No agents on the back of the car.

The third breakdown was in the choice of a parade route through downtown Dallas, where thousands of windows could have provided an assassin a vantage point. Compounding matters, the parade route was publicized in advance. Today, we don't publicize parade routes, although that, in and of itself, is not protection. But in Dallas that morning, everybody knew where the president would be and when he would be there.

The fourth breakdown was in not properly sweeping Dealey Plaza. It was an obviously dangerous place. The Texas School Book Depository provided one of several good spots for a sniper. It was also the last building on the route having a vantage point of the motorcade.

When I went to see Dealey Plaza for myself some years after the assassination, I was amazed at how short the distance was from Oswald's hiding place to the president's limousine. Nor had I realized until then that the fatal shot was not a marksman's sweep across the plaza from left to right, but linear, meaning up and down. The motorcade was moving away from the depository, so the target was always in a straight line. Oswald also had a scope, which made the target very big. While I don't know how advanced his weapons training was in the military, I do know that anybody who'd served in the military and had reasonable rifle skills could have hit the president. The shot was much easier than most people realize. There was speculation just after the assassination that Oswald's rifle—it had a bolt action—could not be fired three times in rapid succession, but it can be, and many people have since shown that it can.

In the final analysis, though, what matters most to the Secret Service is that we lost the president. We failed. And in my mind, it was a failure of negotiation. The bubble top was a negotiation. Had the agents pushed harder to put it on the limousine, would they have saved the president? Undoubtedly. So I'd often wonder, How hard do I have to push? I'd ask myself, If something happens, will it be because I did not push enough? I constantly worried when I was responsible for the president. There was a persistent uneasiness always churning just below the surface wherever we went anywhere with him. And that uneasiness would torment me on foreign trips. My counterpart in some other country would try to assure me, "We're responsible for the president's safety while he's here." I'd have to tell him that he might think he is responsible, but if something happened to the president, anywhere in the world, the Secret Service would have to answer to Congress and to the American people. Our responsibility is simply not negotiable.

The assassination of Robert Kennedy illustrates the significant difference between a bodyguard and a protective detail. On June 5, 1968, Kennedy finished a campaign speech in the ballroom of the Ambassador Hotel in Los Angeles and was heading out of the hotel through a pantry next to the kitchen. His bodyguard, L.A. Rams football star Rosie Grier, was there primarily to protect him from overenthusiastic crowds, not to prevent an assassination. Would Bobby Kennedy have been murdered by Sirhan Sirhan if he'd had Secret Service protection? The answer is a qualified no. Had Secret Service agents been around, Sirhan Sirhan would have had to change his tactic. Without the Secret Service, Bobby Kennedy was much more vulnerable.

Dr. Martin Luther King Jr. was murdered on April 4, 1968, on the second-floor balcony of the Lorraine Motel in Memphis, Tennessee. In this case, agents might have been a deterrent to assassination, but the problem was the balcony and the fact that it's not easy to protect someone from a sniper. No one with Dr. King was looking at windows, as agents would have. But then, agents would not have put him in a second-floor room where the only way in and out was along an open balcony. We would have kept him on the ground floor, where we could control physical and visual access to him. A lot of the decisions that were made by Dr. King and his staff would not have been made by Secret Service agents.

The attack on Pope John Paul II in St. Peter's Square on May 13, 1981, is a classic case of dealing with an assassin who is willing to give up his own life. It's tough to defend against someone who is willing to die—as we've seen all too often since September 11—chances are he can get close enough to his target to be a very serious threat. Mehmet Ali Agca was just another face in a crowd of nearly a hundred thousand people that day, until he got within point-blank range and fired several times. The pope was in a wide-open car with Vatican security officers forming an inner perimeter around him. But there were no effective middle or outer perimeters, making it impossible to protect him in that crowd.

The attempted murder of Alabama governor George Wallace in May 1972 is another case we've studied closely. As a candidate for president, Wallace was attending a political rally at a shopping center in Laurel, Maryland. He spoke to the small crowd from behind a bulletproof shield, but then moved away from the podium to shake hands in the crowd. Suddenly, a twenty-two-year-old man named Arthur Bremer appeared with a .38 and got off five shots. All five hit Wallace, who was crippled for life. Three other people were also wounded, including agent Nick Zarvos, who took a bullet in the neck. Looking at the films, you see that, as soon as Bremer fired, agents dived for him, because that's what they were trained to do. They expected that, if there was a problem, it would come from the crowd and that there would be a gun. In those days, crowds weren't subjected to magnetometers. After the shooting, Bremer's diary was found. In it he wrote that he'd tried to kill Richard Nixon but could never get close enough because the Secret Service was always in the way.

How many times does that happen? We don't know. How many times do people think about doing something but stop because there are Secret Service agents between them and their target? More than we will ever know.

There were two attempts on the life of President Gerald Ford. The first occurred in Sacramento, California, on September 5, 1975, when a strange woman named Lynette "Squeaky" Fromme—a follower of mass murderer Charles Manson—broke through a crowd and pointed a handgun at the president. My friend Larry Buendorf was working the rope line right where Fromme was standing. He spotted the .45 coming out of her coat pocket, and lunged for it. He got his thumb between the hammer and the firing pin so that when she pulled the trigger, the gun didn't fire. He wrestled her to the ground as other agents arrived. By that time, the president was in the car and out of there. Fromme got close because we didn't run people through metal detectors during those years.

Seventeen days later, in San Francisco, the president was just coming out of the St. Francis Hotel to get into the limousine when Sara Jane Moore fired off a round from across the street. The bullet missed the president and lodged in the wall of the hotel. Ironically, the night before the attack, Moore had been interviewed by the Secret Service because she'd written a threatening letter. After talking to her, an agent determined that she wasn't dangerous.

A few weeks after that, President Ford was giving a speech in an auditorium at the University of Michigan, with balloons in the room, and one of the balloons popped. Ford immediately ducked behind the podium as agents stood up and reached for their weapons. One agent was unfairly criticized in the media for reacting like that, but he did what he was trained to do. Everybody reacted properly. Even Ford was criticized for being so edgy, but a bursting balloon can sound just like a .22.

We study those assassinations, along with the murders of John Lennon, Indira Gandhi, Benigno Aquino, and Anwar Sadat, to name a few. But it was the attempt on Ronald Reagan that significantly changed the way we protect the president.

On March 30, 1981, the seventy-year-old president had been in office for just seventy days. After he spoke to a labor union group at the Hilton Hotel on Connecticut Avenue in downtown Washington, agents escorted him out through the special "presidents only" door at the side of the main door and onto the street. A rope line had been set up between that private entrance and the hotel entrance to keep reporters back. But a twenty-five-year-old man named John

Hinckley had made his way into the press group and had a .22-caliber revolver in his pocket. Just as the president got to the limousine and raised his left arm to wave at the reporters fifteen feet away, Hinckley squeezed off five shots.

One bullet hit press secretary James Brady in the forehead. Another hit District of Columbia police officer Thomas Delahanty in the neck. A third hit agent Tim McCarthy in the chest as he turned and stood up straight to put himself in front of the president. Whether Tim had time to decide that he would sacrifice himself for the president, I don't know, but he was where he was supposed to be, doing what he was trained to do—act instinctively. It all happened so fast that it's hard to imagine that Tim, or anyone else, had time to think. Mayhem had broken out in under two seconds.

The back doors on that particular presidential limousine opened to the rear, which is the opposite of a regular vehicle. The president reached out to catch himself, and at precisely that moment a bullet ricocheted through the opening between the door and the structure of the car. It was a totally freakish shot, because the president was actually behind the armored door. As Hinckley was firing, Jerry Parr, the agent in charge of PPD, and Ray Shaddick, who was the shift supervisor, shoved the president into the car. He landed heavily on the transmission riser in the middle of the floor of the limousine just as Parr piled on top of him and Ray slammed the door shut. The car sped off for the White House.

In the wake of the attempt, there was much publicity about how Hinckley had become obsessed with actress Jodie Foster after seeing her in the 1976 film *Taxi Driver*. To impress her, he decided to mimic the film's main character—played by Robert De Niro—who plots to kill a presidential candidate. It was later disclosed that, in October 1980, Hinckley had been arrested at Nashville airport with three handguns in his luggage on the same day that President Jimmy Carter was in town. More than twenty years after his attempted murder of the president, it has been revealed that Hinckley is still obsessed with Foster and, for a while, exchanged correspondence with serial killer Ted Bundy. To the chagrin of the Secret Service, Hinckley has now been allowed out of his mental institution on a day-release program. I am not alone in believing that Hinckley only escaped life in prison on a technicality—his insanity plea—and am not pleased that he's out there somewhere, walking the streets, for several hours at a stretch.

Secret Service agents on the scene, and Jerry Parr in particular, used their training to save the president's life. In the limousine Jerry started running his hands around the president's chest, back, and shoulders feeling for blood. When he didn't find any, his first thought was that, luckily, the president had escaped serious injury. That's when deep-red, frothy blood started flowing out of the president's mouth. Jerry yelled to the driver to go to George Washington University Hospital, because from his training, Jerry knew blood that color indicated a lung injury.

The motorcade instantly diverted. The hospital was alerted by radio that the president was on his way, and the limousine arrived within a couple of minutes. It was hectic and traumatic, but everything worked precisely the way it was supposed to, exactly the way we had trained to make it work. Especially Jerry Parr's reaction. Had he not understood the significance of the blood, he would not have realized the extent of the president's injuries, and Ronald Reagan surely would have died.

CHAPTER TWO

★ ★ ★ ★

ON THE ROAD

There is no time to think when all hell breaks loose, but there is plenty of time to prepare for it.

The critical question is, What if?

When I was with the president, I asked myself that question constantly. I would sit on a stage or on a dais or I'd be walking with him, always watching the audience, always within arm's reach should I need to grab him, always asking myself, What if? And the answer to that question carries with it a substantial burden that agents didn't face fifty years ago because, these days, everything the president does in public is videotaped. Somewhere there is always a camera running, just in case, even in the motorcade when one of the news crews is allowed to stick a camera out of the top of a press van. Agents know that if we are forced to react, whatever we do will be studied again and again. It will be dissected by Congress and the media nanosecond by nanosecond. So the thoughts at the front of my mind had to be, What if a shot goes off, how should I react? What if something happens, where's the fastest way to safety? What if all hell breaks out, what should I do?

To have answers at hand, every aspect of every event needs to be planned, reviewed, and rehearsed. We build into every event all the possible permutations and contingencies for any crisis. On paper that's easy. In practice there are real conflicts between what the president's staff wants the president to do, what the media expects of the president, and what the Secret Service feels it must do to protect the president. The staff is looking for controlled public access to the president, the media wants total access to the president regardless of the public, and we would prefer that no one at all gets too close to him. Too often, we get caught in the middle of those battles, and it's the Secret Service that takes the blame when one side or the other isn't happy.

It presents a difficult balancing act. The trick is to get everyone's issues resolved early on, to define the conflicting objectives, and to find solutions to all the problems—genuine and potential—long before the president comes into view. The difference, then, between a good advance agent and a great advance agent is how well he or she anticipates the unexpected. It can be something benign, such as the president needing to go to the bathroom. But you have to know where the bathroom is and have an agent already there so that when you arrive with the president, the place is secure. Or there could be a minor emergency. Say the president cuts himself and starts bleeding, or he takes ill, as George H.W. Bush did at a dinner in Japan. You need to arrange for a secure place where you can take the president so that a doctor can deal with the problem. Or there could be a very serious emergency, like a shooting or a heart attack or a stroke. You need to know the fastest route to the proper hospital from every point along the route—not just any hospital, but one equipped to deal with trauma, which may not be the nearest—and then you need a "hospital agent" already stationed there to coordinate the president's emergency arrival. The measure of great advance agents is that they are always able to deal with any interruption to the schedule, on a scale from zero to ten, because they've taken every conceivable interruption into account and made plans to deal with it.

With so much at stake, the advance process—the planning for

any presidential appearance—has become a science. I witnessed the Nixon, Ford, and Carter White Houses as a young agent, and later the White House of George H.W. Bush, and I can say that none of them did it with the dexterity, competence, and talent of the Reagan White House. Much of the credit for that goes to Mike Deaver and Bill Henkel.

Deaver was the pragmatic visionary who could predict issues and know where he needed to focus. A short, thin, balding, quiet man—a keen observer of all things around him—he had an absolute grasp of what made sense for Ronald Reagan. He had a terrific sense of an event and knew how to create a positive atmosphere around it. He was one of the two men who called the president "Governor"— the other was a ranch hand—and the president liked that greeting. You could see that there was a deep affection between them. What's more, Deaver and President Reagan could read each other's brain waves. Fiercely loyal, Deaver had a deep understanding of the president that allowed him, in a measured and philosophical way, to sculpt the Ronald Reagan image. It was Deaver, for example, who came up with the "Picture of the Day" concept. Wherever the president went, Deaver was always looking for a special setting so that one picture a day would help to shape and perpetuate the image. Deaver never missed a trick.

Bill Henkel was different. He was just as demanding as Deaver—and as smart, perceptive, and visually adept as Deaver— but he had more of an ego and was much more volatile. A natty dresser who'd played football in high school and college, Bill learned his lessons the hard way, in the Nixon White House. He had joined the staff in 1970, at the age of twenty-nine, as an assistant in the advance office, and within two years he was running it. The following year he was promoted to special assistant to the president. Nixon made his now infamous 1972 trip to North Carolina for a Billy Graham revival while on Bill's watch. The war in Vietnam was raging, and Henkel, acting on orders, instructed the Secret Service to keep protesters out of the event. So agents at the doors "profiled" people coming through, allowing in well-dressed men and women and turning away anyone who looked like a possible problem. Shortly after the event, a huge lawsuit was filed against Nixon, Henkel, and the Republican Party for discrimination. Because the Secret Service had carried out Henkel's orders, we got sued, too. Years later, when I was working for the director of the Secret Service, the suit was still in progress.

After working for Nixon, Bill served for a few years as deputy assistant secretary of commerce before going to Wall Street. By the time he returned to the White House in 1982 to take up his old post as special assistant to the president and director of the Presidential Advance Office, Henkel was streetwise and savvy, while still maintaining some of the old Nixon gruffness.

We locked horns the first time we worked together on a preadvance trip to Kansas City in April 1983. The president was going to appear at a high school on the outskirts of town. All presidents like to visit high schools because students always show a lot of energy and enthusiasm, which makes for good footage on the evening news. Playing off that, Bill intended to put a group of students on the stage behind the president. That's not something the Secret Service likes, because it's very distracting for the agents. We can't realistically be expected to watch everyone in front of the president and behind him at the same time. We want the audience in front of us and a clear escape route behind us. We don't want to trample over anyone trying to get out of the place.

As thirty of us on the preadvance trip stood around in the middle of a high school gym, Bill went on about students behind the president until I piped up. "I'm not sure that's such a good idea."

Henkel flew into a rage. "We will do whatever we want to." And his tirade lasted several minutes.

I didn't appreciate the public berating, so as we were getting ready to leave, I said that I needed to speak with him privately. We went out a nearby door, which led to a loading dock behind the gym. There, next to the Dumpsters, I told him that I found his behavior inappropriate and that it was no way for us to begin a relationship. I'm not sure he expected to be spoken to that way. But once I'd made my point, I calmly explained why it wasn't a good idea to have all these kids behind the president. Decidedly uneasy out there with me, Bill said he merely wanted a picture with colorful images that come from a crowd behind the president. I suggested that he didn't need hundreds of people, that he could get the same effect with forty people by putting the high school band behind the president. They were kids in brightly colored uniforms, and they had instruments to carry, which meant they'd be fairly static. I said, "That would be manageable," Bill said, "I can live with that," and he got his picture.

Over the next four years, Bill and I worked advance trips around the world, ate a lot of meals together, and shared a lot of down time together. He reminded me often of how I'd invited him out on that loading dock next to the garbage cans. But that's how we came to understand that we could always negotiate. When politics and protection clashed, we could always find a compromise. On those occasions when Bill went off on a tangent, making all sorts of demands, I never questioned him in front of other people. We'd talk about it alone, off to the side, where he'd explain what he wanted to achieve, and with the president's safety foremost in my mind, I'd find a way to do it. The most dangerous thing I can think of that any president has done for a photo op was George W. Bush in 2003, landing a jet on an aircraft carrier. I have to assume that the Secret Service strongly objected to it. I would have, because it was a very dangerous stunt and posed a totally unnecessary risk.

Short of anything like that, if Bill Henkel had wanted the president to walk across the Brooklyn Bridge at high noon, it would be okay with us, as long as everyone understood the implications: we'd shut down the Brooklyn Bridge six hours ahead of time; we'd make sure every window in every building on both sides of the bridge was closed; we'd need hundreds of policemen to help us do this; and he would be the one to take the heat from the predictable outcry, "Why did you close down the Brooklyn Bridge and gridlock New York traffic?" As long as he understood what this was going to entail and still wanted to do it, we'd make it happen. Luckily, when faced with anything even remotely close to that, Henkel's cool head would prevail and he'd say, Forget it, let's do something else.

A few months after Kansas City, having established the tone for our relationship, we set out together for a trip throughout the Pacific. The president was scheduled to make an autumn 1983 visit to Japan, Korea, and other locations, so ten weeks before his departure, we did "the survey," the first of three long and stressful trips that need to take place before the president travels overseas.

Bill and Mike Deaver, along with Mark Weinberg, who was assistant press secretary, U.S. Army major Casey Bower, who was one of the president's military aides, Jeannie Bull, from the State Department, someone from the National Security Council, an Air Force One pilot who needed to check out airports, a speechwriter who was looking to get the feel of the venues, and I flew out of Andrews Air Force Base on the most famous of the White House Boeing 707s—tail number 26000. That was John Kennedy's Air Force One, the plane that took him to Dallas and brought his body home and on which Lyndon Johnson was sworn in as president of the United States. The first few times I flew on that plane, I thought about the emotional and historical significance of it. But after a while it was just another airplane, and as part of this group, we flew hundreds of thousands of miles on it.

It was identical to the president's plane, which bore the tail number 27000 and was nicknamed the *Spirit of '76.* In fact, 26000 was the backup. To the right, as you walked in the front door, there was a communications station where the White House Communications Agency (WHCA) made sure the president could speak on the phone from the plane to anyone in the world, and that everyone on the plane could get in touch with the White House. Along the corridor, which ran down the right side of the plane, the first compartment on the left belonged to the president. It was just large enough for facing sofas that turned into beds, a desk, some chairs, and a private bath. On 26000, even though he wasn't there, we still considered his quarters off-limits, and none of us went up there.

Right behind the president's cabin, there was a conference room with a round table, some nice armchairs, and a small television where we played movies that were hard to watch and, because of the engine noise, difficult to hear. Behind that was a small compartment with a table for four and a table for six that was used by the staff, and then there was the Secret Service compartment with two tables. On one side, at the rear of the plane, there were ten seats for the press, and on the other there was a galley where our food was prepared. There was also a small galley up forward, just behind the cockpit, which was where stewards prepared the president's meals. There were seats for only forty-two people.

Our flights on 26000 were usually very long, and all too often, because we crammed so much into those trips, flying time was our only down time. We heard each other's war stories a hundred times, and the best of them belonged to Bill Henkel. He'd been on a Moscow trip with Nixon, staying in guest quarters at the Kremlin. Jeannie Bull was on that trip, too, and confirmed the story. One night after work, they all got together in one of the rooms for a nightcap and started looking around the room to see if they could find the listening device that they knew the KGB had invariably planted somewhere. They looked under the lamps and under the tables and finally pulled back the rug to find something very strange. It was a brass plate held in place by a screw. Having decided that this was the bug, they took it apart to see what it looked like. They used a coin to unscrew the cover, and all of a sudden they heard a huge crash, as the chandelier in the room below came loose from its fixture and fell to the floor.

After we got bored with war stories, we got into the habit of playing Trivial Pursuit and charades. Jeannie was my Trivial Pursuit partner, and together we knew a lot of trivial stuff. She was the State Department administration person who handled all the logistics for White House trips. It's a little-known fact that the State Department pays for these trips. It's an even more obscure fact that the president has a passport. It was Jeannie who turned over the president's passport, and all our passports, to immigration control wherever we landed and saw to it that the formalities of a visit were properly dealt with. It's a bureaucratic procedure, but everybody's passport has to get processed. Jeannie skillfully handled the endless administrative tasks associated with these visits. But as far as we were concerned, her most important task on these advance trips was the trunk that became known as "Chez Jean-nay." It followed us on every trip—except when we were with the president—and was our own portable cocktail bar. We made sure it was the first thing off the airplane and was delivered promptly to Jeannie's room. She'd only open the trunk in the evenings, especially those nights when we'd fly in late from somewhere else and not have anything scheduled until the next day. Once it was open, we would have some drinks and the next game of charades could begin. Those evenings and those games helped to create a cohesiveness among us. On the plane, between games and war stories, we ironed out all the issues. We came to understand what everyone in the group needed to do, and that made solving problems among ourselves easier. We represented different entities and had our own agendas, and sometimes those objectives clashed, but we blended into a pretty solid team, and the results showed in the quality of the Reagan White House advances.

On that first trip together we stopped in Hawaii, then went on to Guam, where Air Force One would refuel with the president. At the far end of the Anderson Air Force Base runway were four B-52s on round-the-clock alert, with engines running, pilots in ready rooms nearby, and bomb bays loaded with nuclear weapons. Those huge planes just sat there, wings drooping like vultures, awaiting the command that we all prayed would never come. This was still the days of the cold war, and those B-52s were part of America's front-line deterrence. No matter how many times I flew into or out of Guam, they were always there, and seeing them always provided a sobering moment.

Otherwise, Anderson AFB was a treat, a far cry from the naval stations I'd known during the Vietnam war. The navy doesn't live as well as the air force, and a four-star general there once told me why. "When we get an appropriation from Congress to build an air force base," he said, "we build the Officers' Club, the Enlisted Men's Club, the NCO Club, the commissary, the movie theater, and all the other creature comforts. Then we go back to Congress for a supplemental to build the runway. What can they say?" He was probably being facetious, although I've never been sure, because from what I know about how the government pays for things, it might well have worked like that.

From Guam we flew to Tokyo to meet with the host committee, the foreign ministry people, and representatives from the Imperial Palace. There's always a lot of backdoor maneuvering on survey trips because the staff wants events where the president will be extremely visible, and the Secret Service wants to limit his exposure to safe sites. This is also where we have our first run-in with the host country. The Japanese are always difficult, because they know what they want and have their own ideas about how to get it. This part of the trip was going to be a state visit, which meant it was protocol driven, and when it comes to protocol, the Japanese are especially rigid. They came to our meetings prepared with books that spelled out exactly how everything was supposed to happen—the president would use Akasaka Palace as his residence; the emperor would greet him there on the first night; the president would dine with the emperor at the Imperial Palace the following night, and so forth. We viewed the sites, decided they could work, then studied the routes from the airport to Akasaka

Palace and from Akasaka Palace to the emperor's palace. Included in the plans was an obligatory stop at the highly revered Meiji Shrine, in the heart of Tokyo, which honors the emperor who opened Japan to the forces of modernization in 1868. I didn't know it yet, but the shrine was going to become a huge problem.

After Tokyo we flew to Seoul. The Korean leg of the president's trip was also a state visit, but Mrs. Reagan had mentioned to Mike Deaver that she was nervous about the president going there, so we became very restrictive about what we would let him do. To begin with, we wouldn't do anything in public or in the open air. Even the arrival ceremonies at Kimpo Airport would happen inside the terminal. The Koreans didn't like that. Not only was this unprecedented, they saw it as a reflection of their ability to provide safety for the president. They argued, but we refused to budge.

Without consulting us, the Koreans had decided that the president would stay at the brand-new Chosun Hotel. They didn't like it when we informed them that that wasn't going to happen either.

We have inherent issues with hotels. Given a choice, we prefer not to use a hotel if it can be avoided. In many hotels, the presidential or royal suite is up high, which always worried me. If something happened, we might not be able to get him out quickly enough. As a young agent, I remember being told never to put a protectee above the ninth floor, because that's the maximum height a hook and ladder can reach. But the president isn't going to stay in a single room, and there may not be any large suites below the ninth floor. There are times when the president is forced to share a hotel with guests who are not associated with the visit, which means we have to segregate the entourage as best as we can from the general public. It's better when the official entourage is so large that we can take over the entire hotel. Even then hotels are risky. Anytime we stayed in one with President Reagan, I was uneasy. On those occasions, we'd take over three entire floors, put him on the middle floor, and put staff and agents on the floors above and below. Not even that alleviated my concerns, because I still worried about rooms four or five floors below. Making matters more difficult, hotel managers don't much like us. We're a major disruption to their business. We shut down elevators, we close off corridors, we block entrances and exits, we station people all over the place, inside and out, and totally unsettle the service staff. So for everybody's sake, especially ours, we eventually decided that because we could do an event with the president just about anywhere in the States and still get back to the White House that same evening, that's what we would do. The exceptions were late events in New York and trips to the West Coast.

Overseas, using hotels is almost always avoidable, and the president rarely stays in one. Our first choice is usually our ambassador's residence. They're generally comfortable enough for him and secure enough for us. I'm sure some presidents have stayed in foreign hotels, but I never stayed in one with President Reagan, and letting him stay at the Chosun was completely out of the question. The presidential suite was in the midst of renovation, and all the walls were down. It was bad enough that everyone knew the president was coming—which offered too many people too much time to make plans—but there was no way we could control what was being put into those walls. Anyone could hide anything in there, from listening devices to explosives, and we might not find it until it was too late. So the Koreans were politely advised that the president would stay at our ambassador's residence.

From there we moved on to an event that the staff insisted would be the highlight of the trip—the president's visit to Camp Liberty, along the demilitarized zone on the border with North Korea, the American outpost closest to the communist north. The idea was to let the president look across no-man's-land toward Panmunjom. Needless to say, everyone was extremely nervous about this, because it posed a genuine risk to his safety. Despite our insistence that we would not do outdoor visits, here we were doing an outdoor visit within firing range of the North Korean army. The event particularly irked our Korean hosts, who were deeply insulted that we didn't trust them to protect the president in the south, and now we were making him a fitting target for their communist enemies in the north.

Of course, taking the president to the DMZ didn't mean we were going to allow the North Koreans to take potshots at him. So, from the moment we arrived on that survey trip, we set about guaranteeing that the president would be virtually invisible from the north side of the DMZ. We scouted lookout points until we settled on one that was close, but not the closest, then made plans to camouflage everything. The army didn't have enough camouflage netting in Korea, so they commandeered it from all over the Far East—literally by the ton—and strung it on every telephone pole and on every tree. By the time we arrived with the president, they'd covered everything with netting, completely concealing the view from North Korea.

From Korea we went to Indonesia, and there we ran into insurmountable problems. Deaver wasn't happy about the political environment. Suharto was still in power, and we were concerned that the Indonesians were demanding too much control. We sat down with the Indonesian general in charge of security, who insisted that we use their cars. He pointed out that they'd bought their limousines from Cadillac and had them armored at Hess and Eisenhart in Cincinnati, the same outfit that armored our Cadillacs. For the Indonesians, this was obviously an issue of credibility, honor, and pride. For us, it was not negotiable.

When the president travels, we bring our own cars—especially the limousines—because that's where the president can safely speak with someone. We don't trust any place else, not even an ambassador's residence, as there is always the risk of listening devices. We control the limousines all the time and can guarantee privacy. They comfortably seat four people, but handle up to six, with two bench seats facing each other in the back. For those of us over six feet tall, there isn't a lot of room in the front seat because of all the communications equipment between the supervising agent and the driver. There is a glass partition that can be raised to give the president privacy if he wants it, but in my four years of sitting in the right front seat of the president's limousine, and three years sitting in the same seat of the vice president's limousine, the glass partition was never up. Which is just as well, because in an emergency the agent in front might need to get into the back fast. We practice climbing over that front seat, an awkward movement if you're very tall.

I tried to explain to the Indonesian general why we needed to use our own cars, but he took a tough stance. When I told him about our communications equipment, he wanted us to install it in their car. When I mentioned tires and drivers, he insisted, "Our tires are the same as yours, and our drivers are equally well trained, and you can have your person in the car with him." As a matter of course, we always put local license plates on the cars wherever we go—whether it's Indiana or Italy—and I explained that to the general as well. I said that the cars would have Indonesian plates, so that if the object of the exercise was to show the people that we were using Indonesian limousines, the license plates would do the trick. But he was intractable. By the time we were on the plane for the Philippines, Indonesia was getting scratched from the president's itinerary. Although I don't think the cars were the only reason for canceling the visit. Interestingly enough, two years later, we took the president to Bali, and this time our cars came along. I can only surmise that the Indonesians believed our cars would be less of an issue in Bali than in Jakarta, their capital.

There were problems in the Philippines, too. Ferdinand and Imelda Marcos were soon to leave for exile in Hawaii, and the man who had intended to lead the country, Benigno Aquino, had just returned to Manila, only to be shot on arrival at the airport. Security was on the top of the agenda for our discussions with our ambassador and his staff at a working dinner on our first night there. We left our hotel on our way to that dinner, got caught in downtown traffic, and that's when I heard an all too recognizable sound—one I can never forget—shots being fired from an M-16 rifle. From where we sat we could just see a policeman shooting into a taxicab. The street was a mess. The embassy driver got us out of there fast. Ultimately the decision was made to cancel Manila.

Our final stop was Bangkok, which went smoothly, except for one moment when, according to Mike Deaver, I personally set back United States-Thai relations. On our first morning there, I was standing at the window of my room watching the river twenty stories below, totally intrigued and fascinated by the water taxis, boats, and junks moving chaotically up- and downstream, when I spotted a PBR, the same type of river gunboat that I'd skippered in the navy in Vietnam. The Thais were using this one to escort the royal barge, which was carrying our little group to the palace. I went to the dock with one of our embassy people who spoke Thai, told the officer in command of the PBR that I'd served on them during the war, and asked permission to come aboard. It had been fourteen years since I'd stood on the deck of a PBR, and I felt a flood of memories and nostalgia. While the others climbed onto the barge, the captain asked me if I'd like to drive the PBR to the palace. I pulled her out into the river, the royal barge pulled out too, and our small flotilla headed upstream.

It was no problem for me to drive her, but these boats need to be maintained properly, and when they're not, all sorts of things go wrong. This one was in horrible condition and, sure enough, no more than a hundred yards from the dock, the pin connecting the Jacuzzi water pump to the diesel engine snapped. We lost power, and, just like that, my starboard engine shut down. We arrived at the palace ten minutes after the barge, which gave Deaver more than enough time to remind everybody that I'd knocked out half the Thai fleet.

The second of the three trips preceding a presidential visit takes place one month before he leaves the White House and is called "the preadvance."

This time a much a larger group goes and includes several people from the White House press office, television producers, a video production guy, and a still photographer. The Secret Service also adds to the entourage the lead advance agent for each country. On this trip we retraced our steps, again starting in Hawaii, going through Guam to Japan and Korea. With Indonesia and the Philippines out, we went from Korea to Thailand. By design, the preadvance is a much more granular exercise. We no longer ask, Where? We start to ask, How? It's all about establishing parameters for timing, motorcades, distances, routes.

Three weeks later, which is one week before the president leaves Washington, the actual advance team goes in to do all the nitty-gritty detail work. The Secret Service team now includes the lead agent, site agents, intelligence agents, and the transportation people, who lock down everything concerning the motorcades. The White House sends site people, press advance, and logistics people. The military teams do advance work for the planes and the helicopters. WHCA has enough folks to hook up all the telephones and communications. The residences where the president will stay are swept and secured twenty-four hours ahead of his arrival. Every site where he stops is swept and secured on the day of the visit, as close to his actual arrival time as possible. By this point, if the survey and preadvance have been done properly, all that's left to do is to work out the logistics: where we're going to put agents, where the cars will be parked, where the airplane will be parked, how we're going to feed people.

But this time problems awaited us in Tokyo. To begin with, the Japanese announced that they intended to add cars to the middle of the motorcade. They'd decided that our Secret Service follow-up car—which contains the shift leader and the working agents, and normally travels right behind the limousine—should be two cars back so that they could put their own people in the car immediately behind the president. We said no, and explained why until we were blue in the face. Next, they balked at our concerns over the visit to the Meiji Shrine. There had just been an incident at the Martyrs Mausoleum in Rangoon, Burma, where a bomb had exploded, killing seventeen people, including four South Korean cabinet ministers on an official visit. My feeling was that if the Rangoon incident was an indication of rising political unrest in the Far East, exposing the president to a public shrine was not a good idea. The Japanese said it was a must stop. I worried that they would be so respectful of the shrine, they wouldn't want to disturb it and therefore wouldn't search it well enough. There was no way we could cancel the visit to the shrine, so we insisted that it had to be swept by a Secret Service team. The Japanese said no. We tentatively settled on the idea that the Secret Service would, instead, be permitted to watch the Japanese security sweep the shrine. We also wanted to run everyone through metal detectors at all of the president's events, including the visit to the shrine. That, too, was met with resistance.

There wasn't time to resolve those issues on the advance, so, three days before the actual visit, Bill Henkel and I returned to Japan. I probably would have gone back there anyway before the president, because it's always a good idea to have a supervisor on the ground, rested and fresh, when he lands. With the visit occuring in a few days, however, it was unusual to have still outstanding issues.

Bill and I sat down with ten people from the Japanese government and stayed at the table for the entire three days trying to negotiate ourselves out of what had become a major impasse. The stumbling block was the head of the national police, a little man in his fifties, heavyset with thinning black hair, named Motoishi. He didn't appreciate our interfering in his security sweep of the shrine, wasn't going to let us run everyone attending any presidential event through magnetometers—he said that, anyway, "magging" members of the press was illegal—and insisted that our follow-up car give way to his own cars in the motorcades. At all times, the Japanese contingent remained polite, but no matter how long we sat there, no matter what we said, and no matter how hard we tried to reason with him, Mr. Motoishi remained unmovable.

I left the room every so often to report back to Washington that we were still deadlocked. Bill and I also kept our ambassador to Japan informed. Mike Mansfield, formerly a U.S. senator from Montana and majority leader of the Senate, had been appointed by Jimmy Carter in 1977. He was seventy-four years old at the time, and perhaps President Carter felt this was a suitable reward for a man on his way out of public life. But Mansfield was a legendary figure. Ronald Reagan reappointed him, and he served in Tokyo until 1989 at the age of eighty-six—longer, older, and arguably more efficient than any previous U.S. ambassador to Japan.

By noon of the third day, Bill and I conceded that our marathon stalemate with Mr. Motoishi had gone on long enough. We went to brief Ambassador Mansfield, who decided that the situation was critical enough to wake Mike Deaver, Secret Service director John Simpson, and Bob DeProspero, who was now head of PPD. It was the middle of the night in Washington, and the president was due to leave the White House in six hours.

After hearing the ambassador explain the problem, Deaver came straight to the point. "If these issues aren't resolved, we're not coming." That was a pretty dramatic moment. Mansfield hung up, looked at Bill and me, reached for the phone, and dialed Prime Minister Yasuhiro Nakasone's office. He said he needed to see the PM at once, and was told to be at his residence in an hour.

Despite the ticking clock—the president was now five hours away from takeoff—the prime minister escorted us through all the usual niceties, including tea. The ambassador outlined the problem, and I went into specifics. I said there were three issues: the bomb sweep of the Meiji Shrine, the use of magnetometers for everyone attending the event there—including the press—and the position of the follow-up car in the motorcade. When I was done, the ambassador informed the PM, "I'm afraid that if we are not able to work out these issues right away, the trip could be in some jeopardy."

Nakasone got visibly upset. He kept dropping sugar cubes into his teacup but instead of stirring them gently, he started mashing them ferociously with the flat side of his spoon. He needed this trip to bolster his waning political popularity, and having it canceled at the last minute would be a personal disaster. Suddenly he grabbed a handful of pencils, lined them up on the coffee table, announced that they were cars in the motorcade, and tried to come to an agreement with me about where the follow-up could be. I clarified why each car is positioned the way it is, but he continued moving pencils until there was really nothing else to say. That's when he rang for his secretary of the cabinet—the number-two man in his government—and ordered him to assemble a group of insiders to meet with us immediately to resolve these issues. Within five minutes, we were escorted out of his office and into a nearby conference room, where, sitting around the table, I was shocked to find many of the same characters I'd been dealing with for three days, including Mr. Motoishi.

He came up to me and very aggressively demanded, "How could you do this to me?" I'd gone over his head, and he took it as an insult.

I reminded him, "I told you this was serious, and you didn't believe me."

We sat down with the cabinet secretary now at the head of the table and began what had to be the final meeting. It got a little heated, but the weight of the prime minister's office did the trick, and with just four hours to go before the president took off from Washington, they agreed we could observe the sweep of the shrine and could use magnetometers. In turn, I compromised, allowing them to save face on the position of the follow-up car. We telephoned Deaver to say it was settled, and the president left the White House on schedule. That night I fell asleep reminding myself I just discussed the intricacies of motorcade philosophy with the prime minister of Japan.

The next morning I got up believing that the worst was over. I got to the airport early to do a final check on the arrival arrangements and was assured that everyone understood what was going to happen, that everything was all right. The president would get off Air Force One, stand at the bottom of the steps for the usual ceremonies, then walk about fifty yards to the waiting Marine One helicopter, which would fly him to the Akasaka Palace. In situations like that, we drive the limousine parallel to the president's walk, and even refer to it as "the parallel car." It stays a few feet away from him on the tarmac, rolling at his walking pace, close enough so that if something happens, we have a place to put him and, if need be, a way to evacuate the scene. It had all been explained to the Japanese during the survey and preadvance trips and had never been an issue. Until now. With Air Force One no more than ten minutes out, our advance agent ran up to me, frantic, because the police would not allow the limousine through the gate.

Looking around, I spotted a slightly smug Mr. Motoishi. I walked over to him and said politely, "There must be a mistake. The parallel car is supposed to be on the tarmac."

He shook his head emphatically, "No car."

I reminded him, "But we've already agreed..."

He repeated, "No car."

I didn't know if this was just his ego talking—some sort of payback for the day before—or if he thought he had some logical reason. Either way, I didn't care. This was a clear challenge to us, and if I allowed it to happen, it would undermine all of the agreements we'd made for the rest of the trip. I said to him, point-blank, "Mr. Motoishi, if the car is not out here on the tarmac, the president is not getting off the airplane." He glared at me, gave a sharp intake of breath—which the Japanese do to show displeasure—and I showed him how displeased I was by turning my back and walking away.

Out of his earshot, I got on my radio and called up to DeProspero on Air Force One. "I'll explain this to you when you get on the
ground, but I need you to keep the president on the plane for three
minutes after the door opens."

This is not the way these things are supposed to happen, and the
door opening is significant. When the president arrives, they crack
the main cabin door while the staff, agents, and press hurry off the
rear of the plane. That takes about five minutes. Once everyone is
ready, the main door is pushed open, "Ruffles and Flourishes" is
played, and the band strikes up "Hail to the Chief." That's when the
president emerges. And that was the point where I wanted Bob to
keep him out of sight and to start the three-minute countdown.

Mr. Motoishi was fifty feet down the tarmac from me as the
gleaming white and blue 707 came into view. We watched it land
and then taxi up to where we were all waiting. As the president was
due at ten o'clock sharp, the plane blocked precisely at 10:00:00. Air
Force One pilots take great pride in "meeting the block time" to the
second. I know from being on the plane with President Reagan that
whenever he landed, he'd watch the atomic clock on the bulkhead in
the front compartment, waiting for the final lurch into the blocks.
On those rare occasions when the plane touched down a few moments late, we'd taxi at ninety miles an hour to hit the blocks on
time. If we landed a few moments early, we'd taxi at five miles an
hour to block precisely. Air Force One is, to say the very least, an on-
time airline.

So the president's plane blocked at ten o'clock sharp, the front
door cracked open, and the staff, agents, and press hurried out the
back. Some of the agents came up to where I was standing, and in
the middle of what was an extremely stressful few minutes, a warm
feeling swept over me. Our guys were there, and the shift leader,
Rick Wright, started barking orders. You go here, you go there. I told
myself, the cavalry has arrived. But the parallel car still hadn't.

Everybody was ready for the president. There were little girls with flowers and a line of dignitaries waiting to greet him at the bottom of the steps. Then, suddenly, the front door was flung open. The band played "Ruffles and Flourishes," went straight into "Hail to the Chief," and . . . nothing happened. The president didn't appear.

Out of the corner of my eye, I could see that Mr. Motoishi was very nervous, pacing along the tarmac. I refused to look straight at him because I wanted to make it clear that we had nothing to discuss. It was a very long three minutes. No one on the tarmac knew what was wrong or why the president had not yet left the plane. Except for me and Mr. Motoishi.

Then Mr. Motoishi blinked. He nodded to someone, the parallel car rolled into position, and at that very instant a beaming Ronald Reagan stepped through the door.

★ ★ ★ ★

CHAPTER THREE

PROTECTING PEOPLE
YOU LIKE

Life at the White House is fairly routine for the Secret Service. The president comes to work and goes home. It's a four-minute walk. But when he leaves the building, everything changes.

If you fire a handgun at the White House while standing on Pennsylvania Avenue, you've committed a crime that falls under the authority of the Washington Metropolitan Police and you will be arrested by them. If you step onto the sidewalk in front of the White House and do the same thing, you answer to the United States Park Police and will be arrested by them. If you jump the fence, you are under the jurisdiction of the Secret Service and will be arrested by our Uniformed Division (UD). But if you stand on Pennsylvania Avenue and fire a shot, then run onto the sidewalk and fire a second shot, and then jump the fence, it's not clear who has jurisdiction. You will be arrested, and arrested very quickly, but which group prosecutes the case remains a question.

The gate that surrounds the White House and its lawns is the outer perimeter. The Uniformed Division, which works inside the gate, forms the middle perimeter. Once known as the White

House Police, they are also responsible for the canine corps, which is bomb dogs for sweeps of cars and in buildings; the countersniper division, which places officers on rooftops with automatic weapons and precision sights; our shooting ranges and our weapons training; and all the electronic protection for the White House, the EOB, and the vice president's residence, which includes alarms, motion detectors, closed-circuit television cameras, and so forth. They also set up and run our magnetometers. The equipment they use is top of the line, but in the end the equipment is just tools. You need people with eyes paying attention to protect the president. You need to put people between the president and danger.

Accordingly, if someone tries to come over the fence, bells and whistles go off everywhere, and the UD responds with weapons drawn. The fence jumper is usually intercepted by the time he hits the ground. Depending on where the president is, the Secret Service detail inside the White House—being the inner perimeter—might move in on him a little closer. But there's no chance that anyone coming over a fence is going to get near the building, because before he gets close, he'll be stopped. But then, people who jump the fence are, generally speaking, not assassins. They are people who want to get caught, or shot, or both. They are people looking for attention.

And even if someone manages to get close to the building— which he couldn't—he'd never get inside, because all the doors and windows are locked.

And even if someone gets inside—which he couldn't—he'd never get inside the Oval Office, because those doors are also always locked. What's more, none of the four doors to the Oval Office open like regular doors. There's a trick to it. That also applies to the doors on the limousine. They don't work like regular car doors, and unless you know to open them, they simply won't open. Anyway, there are always so many people around the White House with weapons that getting close to the president isn't something that's going to happen.

Although fence jumpers are not a daily occurrence, they show up more regularly than most people know and only make the papers when someone is shot on the White House lawn. Still, there are contingency plans for everything, even the impossible. The president is briefed on what to anticipate if something happens and knows where he will be taken. In the hours immediately following 9/11, President Bush was moved to a secret location where he was safe. On several occasions, Vice President Cheney has also been moved. These contingencies are practiced and rehearsed.

There are two operational command posts at the White House. The UD runs a big, hi-tech command post. That's where they have all the alarms and security cameras. The Secret Service command post is officially called W-16, but code-named "Horsepower," and is on the ground floor of the West Wing. It's a rectangular office that runs along the wall on the south side, partially under the Cabinet Room and partially under the Oval Office. When I worked in that room, my mother would tell people, "My son's desk is ten feet from the president's. Vertically."

The doctor's office, which is really just an examining room, is on the ground floor of the residence, next to the Map Room. They can't do any major procedures there, but the White House is only four minutes from George Washington University Hospital. The photographer's office is down the hall from W-16, next to the barber shop. That's one chair, just for the president, with the barber coming in from his own shop.

For the record, there is a little-known third command post at the White House. It's a tiny room on the ground floor of the residence, right behind the elevator on the north side of the hallway, across from the Diplomatic Reception Room. Normally it is used by the first lady's detail, but when the president is upstairs in the residence, the night shift moves over there. Its code name is Staircase.

Official code names are assigned by WHCA, which is an army agency staffed by the Signal Corps. They began to be used in the days when our communications were not scrambled, and the Secret Service didn't want to attract unwanted attention by saying the word "president" over a radio. I'm not really sure why WHCA still uses code names, because, since the mideighties, all of our transmissions are encrypted. Code names are usually two-syllable words, easy to pronounce, and somehow—at least in someone's mind—are supposed to fit the person or place. President Reagan was "Rawhide" and Mrs. Reagan was "Rainbow." The president's limousine was "Stagecoach," and the follow-up car was "Halfback." Personally, I always thought they were a little silly. I can honestly say that at no time during my Secret Service career did I ever get on a radio and announce, "This is Stagecoach with Rawhide and Rainbow . . ." or anything even remotely similar. If I said, "This is Petro," everyone knew who I was, where I was, and who I was with. But code names took on a romantic air when it was revealed that John Kennedy was "Lancer" and Jackie was "Lace." Shades of Camelot.

When we first started protecting Nelson Rockefeller and his wife, the vice president's code name was "Sandstorm," and Mrs. Rockefeller's was "Shooting Star." Within a few days someone realized the latter wasn't such a good name, because in a broken transmission all you might hear was the word "shooting," and that could inadvertently set off a chain reaction and an awful lot of problems. So they changed her code name to "Stardust." These days, lists of WHCA code names can be found on the Internet. If you look carefully, you'll see that everyone in the president's family has a code name starting with the same letter, so that Richard Nixon was "Searchlight" and Pat Nixon was "Starlight"; Gerald Ford was "Passkey" and Betty Ford was "Pinafore"; Jimmy Carter was "Deacon" and Rosalynn Carter was "Dancer"; George Herbert Walker Bush was "Timberwolf" and Barbara Bush was "Tranquility." Visitors we protected also got code names. Prince Charles was "Unicorn," his mother Queen Elizabeth II was "Kittyhawk," Frank Sinatra was "Napoleon," and my all-time fa-vorite was Pope John Paul II, whose code name was "Halo."

In addition to screening every person who comes into the White House, the Secret Service has procedures for screening every item that comes in, too. I won't go into detail, for obvious reasons, but suffice it to say that everything is inspected off-site, including all the food that regularly gets sent to the president. At Thanksgiving and Christmas, for instance, people send him cured hams, turkeys, cakes, cookies, and puddings. Sadly, all of it must be destroyed. We can't trust unprotected or unsolicited food.

The only letters or packages that actually get brought into the White House have been looked at and secured. That said, if the president's daughter wants to send him a birthday card, there's a way for her to do that. Same thing with phone calls. The president has private lines and private addresses.

There is still a bowling alley in the basement of the White House, but the indoor swimming pool has been covered—Richard Nixon did that—and today it's the press briefing room. There is a trapdoor in the floor of the room, and through it you can see the tiles of the old pool. I doubt that it is deliberate, but the way the press briefing room is designed, reporters sit at the shallow end of the pool and the press spokesperson stands on the podium at the deep end. If that wasn't done purposely, it probably should have been.

Some years after Richard Nixon covered the indoor pool, Gerald Ford had an outdoor pool built on the south grounds, next to the tennis court. Both are well hidden, so you can't easily see them. I re-call the Reagans using the pool occasionally, but never the tennis court. President Reagan did work out, and there is a small gym up-stairs at the residence. After he was shot, he went through a long se-ries of exercises to strengthen his upper body and used to brag that he'd added an inch to his chest. This was a man in his seventies, and in very good shape.

This was also a man who never carried anything in his pockets. When he remembered, the president might sometimes bring a pair of glasses with him, but I held his jacket often enough to know that his pockets were empty. With the exception of that five-dollar bill he brought to the Orioles game to pay for hot dogs, he never carried money. I have no idea where he got the five dollars. He must have had money stashed somewhere, because if he'd have asked for money, someone would have warned him that five wasn't enough. On those rare occasions when he wanted to buy something, there was always somebody to arrange for the payment.

He wasn't allowed to drive—except for the Jeep he kept at the ranch—and someone else always opened the doors he went through, so there was no reason for him to carry keys. As far as I know, the only thing that President Reagan ever had with him was a handkerchief and a little plastic-coated card with instructions on how to implement the nuclear codes. The White House Military Office had briefed him before his inauguration in January 1981 on what's known as "the football." It's a briefcase containing things I can't discuss that is never far from him. Along with the military aide who carries the football, the other person who is never far from the president's side is the doctor.

There's a story told, which I can't substantiate, that during his first briefing on the "football," President Reagan said, "Where's the button that I push?" I wasn't there, so I don't know if he said it, but it sounds like his sense of humor. Anybody who thinks that he said such things in earnest doesn't know the man. He took his duties seriously, but he was always telling stories and always happy to see the people around him laugh. I read not long ago that for two weeks in 1954 he worked in Las Vegas as a stand-up comic. Because he had such a wonderful sense of humor, there were times when people chose not to tell him certain things. Like about the national Christmas tree.

Presidents traditionally light the tree on the Ellipse, a quarter of a mile south of the White House. But following the assassination attempt and the bombing of the marine barracks in Beirut in October 1983, we rearranged some of President Reagan's events. We didn't want him exposed, the way he would be at the Ellipse, so it was decided that he would host the tree-lighting ceremony from the south grounds of the White House. WHCA built a podium with a big switch on top of it and set it up just in front of the steps, so that the president could watch the tree light up when he threw the switch.

On my first Christmas there, which was only two months after the Beirut bombing, I stepped out onto the south lawn a few minutes before I brought the president out, to see where the press would be and where the carolers would be and where they wanted the president to stand. I noticed the WHCA officer putting the podium on the lawn and what caught my eye was that I couldn't see the wire leading from the switch down to the tree. I walked around for a moment looking for it, then quietly asked, "Where's the wire to the tree?"

The WHCA officer replied, "There isn't one."

"So how does it turn the lights on all the way down at the Ellipse?"

"It doesn't," he said. "It's a dead switch. When the president pulls the switch, I radio down to one of our guys at the tree to say, turn on the lights. That's when he plugs them in."

I said, "What happens if the president pulls the switch and the radio doesn't work?"

The fellow from WHCA assured me, "We test it nine times and have a backup radio to make certain it will work."

I'm sure that the president didn't know. The switch looked like a switch, it worked like a switch, I assumed it was a real switch, and he would have assumed that, too. The reason no one told him was, perhaps, because he would have played games with the switch. He would have pulled it halfway and watched the lights come on before he made the connection. No one would have trusted him not to have fun with it.

* * *

Can you successfully protect someone you don't like? The answer is, definitely, yes. At various times I protected Yassir Arafat and Fidel Castro and did my best for them, just as I did my best for Ronald and Nancy Reagan, whom I did like. We take our responsibilities seriously regardless of who we're protecting. Years ago I saw a T-shirt with the Secret Service logo and the words "You elect 'em, we protect 'em," and that's the way it works. It doesn't matter whether we agree with a protectee's politics, whether the protectee is a Republican or a Democrat or the Communist leader of Cuba. I can swear that had I not liked Ronald Reagan, I would have still done everything in my power to protect him in exactly the way that I did.

Accepting that, if you like a protectee sometimes it means you are more sensitive to him or her as a person. The graciousness that the Reagans always showed the agents was returned to them in kind. Typical was the case of two female agents on one occasion when the president attended an annual "boys only" dinner hosted by his pal Paul Laxalt.

A former governor and three-term United States senator from Nevada, Laxalt's yearly, black-tie affair at the Georgetown Club on Wisconsin Avenue was a popular night out. The room was small, packed with a hundred men dining on Rocky Mountain oysters—lamb's testicles—and, in true guy's-night-out spirit, telling off-color jokes. I'd accompanied the president there a few times, always with an all-male detail. I was scheduled to work it again one year when I realized that, for the first time, two women were on the shift. Barbara Riggs, who eventually became assistant director of the Secret Service, and Shawn Campbell, another outstanding agent, were to come with us. I admired them both, but I wasn't sure that it was wise to have female agents in the room. I didn't know, nor did I particularly care, whether any of the other men at the dinner would be bothered by their presence, but I knew it would be awkward for the president. This was a man who held doors for women and stood up when a woman walked into a room. I never heard him utter a foul word, nor did I ever hear him tell an off-color joke, even at the Laxalt dinners.

In principle, I could have had Barbara and Shawn assigned to other duties for the evening. In practice, it was not the proper thing to do. Many women in the Secret Service believed that they should be expected to do, and that they themselves should expect to do, anything a male agent does. Rightly so. In this case, the best thing would be to explain the situation to them and see how they felt about it. But Barbara and Shawn beat me to it. Barbara came to me to say, "We know what this event is tonight, and Shawn and I think it's probably a good idea if we stay out with the motorcade." It was a classy and dignified way to handle the matter. They could have insisted on going into the room, but they liked the president enough to respect his feelings.

Although the president was always personable with the agents, he did not get personal. He knew faces, but he wasn't someone who made it a point to memorize everyone's name. He referred to us as "the fellas," which included the female agents, and it was rare to find one of "the fellas" who didn't like him. There was a way to approach him, and when it was done properly, and when there was time for such things, he was receptive to being approached. I took him to the barbershop one morning and realized, while waiting for him, that he'd never seen our command post. I alerted the guys to straighten up the place, and when his hair was cut, I asked the president, "Would you like to see W-16?" He said he'd love to.

There's a small area just inside the door with a couch, and off to the left, separated by a little counter, there's a U-shaped section with all the alarms, telephones, monitors, and other communications equipment. It's manned twenty-four hours a day, seven days a week, regardless of whether the president is in the White House or not. There's a large cabinet where we keep weapons and, beyond that, a small office where I sometimes worked. The president was his normal gracious self, saying hello to the agents on duty and listening attentively to what everyone said. The room was decorated with vintage Secret Service photographs of previous presidents with agents, and he looked at all of them. At the back, under the staircase, there were two other things I wanted him to see. So just before we left, I said, "Mr. President, I want to show you where the guys keep their equipment." He must have thought to himself, Why do I have to see this?

He spotted what I wanted him to see as soon as we turned the corner: one was a poster of an ad from *Look* magazine in which the actor Ronald Reagan was a model for a shirt company, and the other was a popular poster at that time showing Sylvester Stallone's body with Ronald Reagan's head and the caption "Ronbo." He'd never seen the Ronbo before, and he loved it.

Upstairs in his own office, there was a sign on his desk that comes pretty close to summing him up. It read: "There is no limit to what a man can do or where he can go if he doesn't mind who gets the credit." To that I would add, he was an old-school kind of guy. He would often work in the residence in the early morning, but would always come down to the Oval Office at nine. One morning in particular, I was waiting upstairs by the elevator and the door to the residence was ajar. It was perhaps three minutes to nine, and I could see him pacing up and down the middle corridor of the second floor, looking at his watch. For him, nine meant precisely nine.

On those mornings when I'd walk with him from the residence, he followed the same routine. I'd open the Oval Office door for him and hold it, because he always came right back out. He'd go to his desk and reach into the lower right-hand drawer. I don't know who it was, but somebody kept that drawer filled with nuts. He'd take a handful, then come back out onto the portico and spread the nuts around for the squirrels. (In January 1989, when he left the Oval Office for the last time, he placed a note for the squirrels to watch out for the Bushes' dog.)

It was difficult not to like him. He was warm, he listened to what people had to say, and he genuinely liked people. He was a man whose natural ease made everything seem normal, and he was never too busy to make the people around him feel special. And it was rare to find anybody he didn't like. The only person I can think of who wound up on both lists—a man who didn't care for Ronald Reagan and a man whom Ronald Reagan didn't particularly care for—was French president, François Mitterand.

Diplomatic interaction is often intertwined with personalities, and if the personalities don't like each other, their countries are not going far together. You see it in government, just as you see it in business. Whether it's working out a nuclear nonproliferation treaty or trying to hire a driver for an executive, chemistry matters. And there didn't appear to be enough of the right chemistry with François Mitterand. He was aloof, and though he was never disrespectful, he always gave us the impression that he didn't much care for Americans.

In spring 1986, we were together at a G-7 economic summit in Japan. As deputy agent in charge of PPD, I was in the limousine with the president, going from our ambassador's residence, where he was staying, to the plenary session at the Akasaka Palace. We were riding in a standard presidential motorcade of around twenty-six cars. There's a pilot car that is five minutes ahead and a route car that is three minutes ahead. Then there are motorcycle outriders, followed by the lead car, the protocol car, and two limousines. In the old days we put only one in the motorcade—the spare car would be an off-the-record Town Car—but we changed that after the assassination attempt, using two identical limousines to halve the odds if someone tried to attack the president. Behind the limousines is a follow-up car with shift agents, then two or three cars for the senior White House staff, and then the CAT car, with agents in battle gear and carrying automatic weapons. Behind them are a few more staff cars, then three or four press vans, a local ambulance, the WHCA car, and a bunch of tail cars, followed by more motorcycles. Everyone is linked by Secret Service radio, which is vital when something unexpected happens, which it did in Japan.

The police always block off the streets and cross streets we're traveling, but in Japan they also block the parallel streets on either side of the motorcade route, which causes havoc with downtown traffic. Still, we were moving along at a fairly good thirty-five-mile-an-hour clip when the president leaned toward the front right seat and asked, "Joe, has President Mitterand arrived at the palace?"

I said I'd find out and got on the radio. Ten seconds later I told the president, "No, he hasn't arrived yet."

Protocol dictated that the G-7 leaders arrive in reverse order of seniority. That meant, Mitterand should arrive sixth and Ronald Reagan should arrive last. Even though the president never took too much interest in these things, at least not that I'd ever noticed, he seemed unusually aware of protocol that morning. Having been annoyed by Mitterand a few times in the past, especially Mitterand's habit of always arriving late and keeping everyone waiting, the president decided he wasn't going to put up with it this time. When I said that Mitterand hadn't arrived yet, he said, "Slow down the motorcade."

I stared at him for a second, thought to myself, this is going to be interesting, nodded, "Yes, sir," got on the radio, and told the agent in the lead car, "Slow down the motorcade."

Now, this is not an insignificant matter. Dozens of streets were blocked ahead of us and parallel to us, and, I assumed, Tokyo rush-hour traffic had already come to a standstill. Slowing down to ten miles an hour wasn't going to help, but that's what we did.

We rolled along like that for a couple of minutes before the president wanted to know: "Has he arrived?"

I got on the radio again, was told, "Not yet," and related that to the president. Decidedly not pleased, he now said, "Joe, stop the motorcade."

I looked back at him and thought, This is really going to be interesting. I got on my radio and repeated his order, "Stop the motorcade."

For the Japanese, who don't deal with change well even in minimal things, this was major. By coincidence, when I told the lead car to stop the motorcade, we were within a block of the New Otani Hotel, where some of the G-7 leaders, their staffs, and the press were staying. The Japanese police, knowing that the hotel had been secured for the summit and that the parking lot was sealed off, made a very good decision to pull the entire motorcade into the parking lot. As we rolled to a halt, agents in the follow-up car jumped out and surrounded the limousine. And there we sat.

Turning around to tell the president that we would both remain in the car, I spotted the inimitable Helen Thomas—doyenne of the White House correspondents—getting out of a press van and sprinting toward the limousine. She didn't get very far before agents escorted her back to the van. But stopping a motorcade like this was unprecedented, and she, along with the other reporters, clearly thought something was very wrong. The obvious assumption was that the president was involved in a medical emergency. The doctor was also out of his car and coming toward us. I got a message to him that there was nothing to worry about, then told the shift leader, "Keep everybody in the cars. Don't let anybody out."

Locking down the press didn't please them, and they quickly turned hostile. Thomas demanded to know what was going on and refused to understand why she couldn't get out of the van to find out for herself. If the president was not well, she knew, this was a major story. And she wasn't alone in thinking that. None of the media appreciated the Secret Service telling them they had to stay put, but they did stay put because they didn't have a choice, and so did the rest of the motorcade.

The Japanese police were still blocking traffic through most of Tokyo, but there was nothing I could do about that. I was too busy on the radio trying to find out where the Mitterand motorcade was.

The president was soon getting anxious, too, asking repeatedly, "What's going on?"

When I finally had an answer for him it was "Mitterand hasn't even left his hotel."

The president mumbled something under his breath, then said, "Let's go."

I gave the order to load back up, and off we went to the Akasaka Palace.

There is a regular routine for the arrival of the presidential limousine. The supervisor sitting in the front right seat stays in the car with the president until the agents in the follow-up secure the area and surround the limousine. There's no rush to get the president out of the car. Even on those occasions when we pulled into a protected site—such as an underground garage or one of those specially constructed tents that we use to mask an arrival site—I would never get out of the car myself until everybody else was ready. Only after I made certain that everybody was in place would I open the door to let the president out.

Now, at the palace, when I opened the car, Jim Kuhn was waiting for us. He had worked for Henkel as part of his advance team until 1985, when the president appointed him to be his aide. A really good guy, with a terrific sense of humor, Jim handled all of the president's personal business. By arrangement with the Japanese, only the American president and the French president were permitted to have an agent with them upstairs. But the Japanese also agreed to allow Jim to go upstairs, too. So Jim and I accompanied the president to the room where the plenary session was taking place. We stayed with him as he walked around the big conference table shaking hands with the other leaders. Everyone was there except Mitterand.

The press pool was in the room taping the arrivals. President Reagan took his place and sat down, and I positioned myself immediately behind him, intent on staying there until the press left.

The president began reading some documents. A few minutes later, Mitterand made his grand entrance. He, too, walked around the conference table saying hello to the other leaders, each of whom stood up to greet him—except Ronald Reagan. The president kept his eyes glued to the papers he was reading until Mitterand walked up to him and extended his hand. The president suddenly looked up, as if he'd been surprised, said, "Oh," but stayed seated while he shook Mitterand's hand. I'm sure Mitterand got the message. Jim and I certainly did.

The press left, Jim and I left, and the doors were closed. A small detail of Japanese police, together with the French security officer who'd accompanied Mitterand, were already in the anteroom when Jim and I got there. Fifteen or twenty minutes later, the doors to the conference room flew open, and Mitterand came through on his way to the bathroom. Instantly, everyone in the anteroom jumped to their feet, except Jim and me. We just sat there as Mitterand walked past. He looked at us, and so did the French security guy hurrying after him.

We were amused by our boyish sense of "follow-the-leader," but the question now became, What are we going to do when Mitterand comes back? I was the one who said, "We need to be consistent. If we stand now, we give in."

So Jim and I agreed we would just sit there. And sure enough, a few moments later, when Mitterand headed back into the conference room, everyone else in the anteroom jumped to his feet, except for us. That earned us a very unfriendly glare from the French president.

When the meeting ended, Jim climbed into the limousine with the president for the trip to the New Otani, where there was a luncheon. As the motorcade moved through Tokyo, Jim and I told the president what we'd done. Or, more correctly, what we hadn't done.

"In fact," Jim admitted, "it happened not once but twice. And you didn't stand up either."

His hearty laugh and the twinkle in his eyes was the president's way of saying, "Way to go, fellas."

Reagan had been in that morning meeting for several hours and hadn't gone to the men's room, and I knew that once he got into the luncheon, neither of us would have a chance for another several hours. So just before we arrived at the hotel, I asked the president if he wanted to make a stop. He said he did, and I radioed ahead. This time we arrived last, because the Japanese were controlling all the motorcades from the palace and Mitterand had no control over when he showed up.

The first thing I spotted when we pulled up to the front door were hundreds of Japanese police, in plainclothes, all over the place. It was too many people, and we couldn't be sure who they all were. Someone could have gotten into the middle of this group and the Japanese police might not know them either. The area was too crowded, and it wasn't supposed to be like that. So I asked the president to wait in the car until I got out and looked around. In front of me was a sea of black-haired men in dark blue suits. I waited several seconds before opening the president's door. He was also surprised to see so many people at the arrival site and wanted to know, "Are these all police?"

I said, "Yes, sir, they are."

He whispered in my ear, "If a firecracker goes off, we're dead."

We stepped inside the hotel, and an agent steered us to the men's room, just off to the side of the lobby. It was already secured. Normally, I would go in with him to assure myself that it was empty, then step out. But this time, I also had to use the bathroom. He walked up to the urinal, and I started thinking to myself, What do I do now? Once he was ready, he wouldn't look to see where I was; he'd wash his hands, assume I was with him, and leave. So I went up to him at the urinal and said, "Mr. President, would you do me a favor?"

He turned to me with a startled look, as if to say, What could you possibly want me to do at this moment? "Joe?"

I said, "Would you please wait for me?"

His face lit up. "Oh . . . sure."

It doesn't sound like much, but I don't know how many other presidents would have reacted the same way. He was a considerate man, and in his mind, just because he was president of the United States, that didn't mean he couldn't wait a few seconds for another guy and even laugh about it.

Throughout those years with him, I collected dozens of photographs of us together. But the one I would have loved to have is one from the back, of the two of us, standing there in that men's room.

CHAPTER FOUR

★ ★ ★ ★

THE TWO OF THEM

While he was the most powerful man in the world, they were the most visible couple in the world.

Nancy Reagan was a class act.

Some people at the White House feared her, and behind her back they chided her concerns about the president, belittling them with the expression, "mommy watch." I think it might have been coined by the then chief of staff, Don Regan, who did not get along with Mrs. Reagan. Other books have described his feelings about her and her feelings about him, but I don't know what went on between them. I do know, however, that Don Regan wasn't particularly well liked by many people at the White House.

Personally, I found the term "mommy watch" distasteful. Yes, she was very protective of her husband. Yes, she was profoundly loyal to him. And yes, she was deeply involved in everything that he did. But her concern for his safety is an understandable reaction to the fact that her husband had been shot and nearly killed. I never found her unreasonable, never found her intimidating, and never saw her show her temper. In fact, the Nancy Reagan I got to know was a warm, considerate person, exactly like her husband.

Michael Deaver later wrote that the secret to dealing with Mrs. Reagan was "Treat her like a human being, and most important, tell the truth."

It never dawned on me that there was any other way. In my dealings with her she was always accommodating, easy to get along with, and always a lady. There were stories in the press describing her as extremely difficult, and perhaps with some people she was, but I never saw that. Whenever she expressed herself to me, particularly about the president's safety, her views were reasonable. She would tell me what she wanted—as when she wanted her husband to wear the armored vest—and it was usually in line with my own thinking.

President Reagan never liked wearing the vest—no president does—because it's heavy, cumbersome, and uncomfortable. Had he been wearing it when John Hinckley shot him, it might not have prevented his injuries because of the way the vest wraps around the chest and where the bullet hit him. But there were times when we'd insist on it, and there were times when she'd insist on it, and he'd always comply. He would complain about it and say, "I hate this," but he would be complaining while he was taking off his shirt. It wasn't as if he was asked to wear it at every event. I think we were fairly judicious in our requests, and over the course of four years it might have happened only a dozen times. And I certainly couldn't blame him for not liking it, because I hated it, too. Agents on the detail were required to wear the vest every time we left the White House with the president. It's made of Kevlar and weighs around four pounds, although after a few hours on a hot day it feels more like a hundred pounds.

His armored coat was another matter. When I first came onto the detail, the president was wearing a London Fog trench coat that had an armored lining. It didn't fit him well and didn't look very presidential. None of us liked it, including Mrs. Reagan. But he kept it and wore it because it did the job. I finally suggested that the Secret Service buy him a cashmere topcoat, and Mrs. Reagan liked that idea.

So I went to a very fine men's store in Washington, bought one off the rack—44 long—and arranged with the manager to have his tailor sew in the armored lining that we provided. When it was ready, I brought the store manager and his tailor to the White House, and upstairs into the private residence, for a fitting. While the tailor was making his chalk marks, I glanced toward the president's closet and noticed his suits—about fifteen of them—hanging there, each of them carefully separated by an inch or two. The president saw what I was looking at and proudly explained that he would select a different suit every day, going right down the line until he got to the end, and then he would start at the beginning all over again. He explained, "I wear them in order, and the only time I go out of order is when I need a suit for a big event and a brown suit is up. I skip the brown suit and go to the next one, a blue or a black suit."

A few of the suits were specially made slightly large to wear over the armored vest, but all of his clothes were beautiful. He looked really great in this coat, which was heavy, but he was strong enough to handle it, and that's the coat he wore to the inaugural in 1985. The one thing I will say that struck me odd about his dress sense was that President Reagan never wore an undershirt. But then, a lot of men don't. Maybe it's a California thing. Years later I read stories about him never updating his wardrobe, hoarding clothes until they were threadbare. If he did, none of them were hanging in that closet that night. Nor did he ever wear them while I was around. He had beautifully tailored clothes and looked good in everything, even a T-shirt and jeans.

I also read somewhere that he was a superstitious man. Bill Henkel told me that he always carried a lucky charm, but I never saw it. Some people say that he knocked on wood—I guess sometimes he might have—and that he made a habit of tossing salt over his shoulder. But I never saw that either. They also say that he never walked under ladders, which I guess is true.

Over those years, too, you couldn't help but read criticism in the press about Mrs. Reagan. She was a better dresser than he was, but as he was admired for it, there were times when she was criticized for it. Early on in the first administration, Mrs. Reagan was labeled by some factions in the media as little more than a California socialite whose main interests were designer clothes and the adoration of her husband. Well into the second administration they were still writing about "the gaze"—that special look she always had whenever she watched her husband make a speech—and still chastising her for borrowing gowns from designer friends. Maybe criticism just goes along with the role. Mrs. Reagan herself has since become very philosophical about it. More than sixteen years after leaving the White House, she told Katie Couric on NBC's *Today* show, "I'd been first lady of California for eight years and I thought well, surely, you know, I've seen it. The, 'it' can't get any worse than this, but it did and it does. I mean, you're really, really in a fishbowl."

Throughout her years in that fishbowl, there were reports in the media that her poll numbers—her popularity in the country—were never anywhere near as high as Jackie Kennedy's, and were, in fact, among the lowest of any modern first lady. And yet, for three of those eight years, Nancy Reagan was voted the most admired woman in America.

First ladies have their own Secret Service detail, and that's a tough assignment. It's not as high profile as the president's, but then there are different considerations. For instance, the probability of assassination is lower whereas the probability of some kind of kidnapping is higher. Being on a smaller detail means that agents get closer to their protectee. It concerned me as a supervisor that some agents had a tendency to get too close. The same problem can work in reverse, too, that spouses can get attached to their agents.

One of Mrs. Reagan's junior agents ingratiated himself to her by doing little favors, helping her when he wasn't expected to help, paying attention to her concerns when they really weren't any concern of the Secret Service. There's a film called *Guarding Tess* that describes the bond between a former first lady and her agents pretty well. Keeping professional distance is not always easy, and lots of agents work hard to maintain that distance. It's important for agents to understand the concept and to accept the fact that the protectee is not their friend. Some agents want to get close and think it is in their best interest as a way to progress professionally. It's a no-win situation for the agent in question, and a no-win situation for the other agents, because it creates an unhealthy work atmosphere.

This junior agent never did anything that might be labeled inappropriate for a friend to do, but he wasn't the first lady's friend, he was there to protect her. I spent the better part of a year and a half trying to transfer him. It wasn't easy. The first lady didn't want him to leave. The closer he got to her, the more inclined she was to say, I like him, I've been with him long enough that he knows how I like to do things and I don't want to break in someone else. So I'd arrange to get him moved to another assignment, he'd drop a hint to her that he might be transferred, she'd express her concern about his leaving, and he'd stay. When I eventually moved him away, it didn't please either one of them, but it was the right thing to do.

The job of first lady is a full-time occupation, and Mrs. Reagan worked very hard at that job. From her office in the East Wing, she launched and managed her Just Say No campaign against drug abuse in young people, which took her to sixty-five cities in thirty-three states. In 1985 she hosted a conference at the White House for first ladies from seventeen nations to help focus their attention on drug and alcohol abuse problems. She worked to support the Foster Grandparent Program, stressed education through the Nancy Reagan Foundation, and introduced young performers to the American public through a public television series *In Performance at the White House.*

Unlike some modern first ladies, Mrs. Reagan didn't do a lot of personal things like shopping. But even if she had wanted to, Mrs. Reagan couldn't shop often because she was so recognizable.

In theory, taking the first lady out of the White House on her own is a surveillance job. But on those few occasions when I was aware that Mrs. Reagan went out for an afternoon like that, it usually turned into more than anyone had bargained for because she would invariably attract a huge crowd.

Although we never had this problem with her, one of the difficulties of shopping with a protectee is deciding what happens with the shopping bags. Agents don't carry packages. They aren't there for that purpose and can't do their work if their arms are encumbered. Not all protectees understand this issue. I remember there were concerns when we started protecting Vice President Nelson Rockefeller. We worried that he might treat us like servants, and get out of the car and leave his bags for us to carry. But Rockefeller never did that. He carried his own bags and never expected us to carry anything. Not every protectee was as considerate. Several would leave their bags for us, and our response was just to walk away, leaving the protectee to find a staff guy to carry them.

I mention this because it is an issue. Some agents think they can win over a protectee—and this gets back to those agents protecting a spouse—when they help with shopping bags or luggage. Others vehemently refuse, under any circumstance, to carry anything for a protectee. I always took the position that we were not supposed to do it, and shouldn't if it interfered at all with our operational readiness. At the same time, there were instances when common courtesy and common sense prevailed. The Reagans never expected us to carry anything for them, but when we pulled into the ranch and they got out of the car with four bags, I wouldn't just walk away. The president would always pick up one suitcase, but he couldn't take all four at once, and Mrs. Reagan would always take her bag, so I would pick up the other two and put them inside the door. It was either that, which took three seconds, or leave the bags sitting by the car. It was no big deal, but that was really the only circumstance with the president where something like that happened. If the bags were, say, on the tarmac as we were getting onto Air Force One, I wouldn't touch them, nor would any of the other agents.

When Nancy Davis married "Dutch" Reagan in 1952, some people in Hollywood knew him as "One-Take Reagan," a tribute to his unswerving ability to get a scene right the first time. Just how good an actor he actually was I'll leave for others to decide. At the inaugural gala in 1981, the new president and first lady were sitting in large chairs on a stage facing the audience while Frank Sinatra hosted the celebrations. At one point "Old Blue Eyes" looked out at the huge crowd, turned to the president, and told him, "Ronnie, if you could have drawn a crowd like this when you were an actor, you wouldn't have had to get into politics."

His one-take abilities never left him. Every week or so he would do a series of tapings with a TelePrompTer. All presidents do them, to wish someone happy birthday, or congratulate someone on an anniversary. This president would sit there and do half a dozen of them, straight off the TelePrompTer, and not miss a word. I never saw him do a second take. But he had a secret. I remember standing behind him many times as he gave speeches. His notes, on little half sheets of paper, were filled with pencil underlines and perpendicular lines where he was reminding himself to stop or to add emphasis. Ever the seasoned actor, he regarded his speech notes and TelePrompTer tapings just like movie scripts. He marked them up and rehearsed them so that he was sure to get it right the first time.

At the White House, we only occasionally saw some of the Reagans' famous friends from those Hollywood days. When the Reagans threw Bob Hope an eightieth birthday party at the Kennedy Center, Hope stayed the night in the Lincoln Bedroom. Of all their chums, Hope was the most pompous, the most unfriendly, and the most dissimilar from them.

It was in California where they rekindled old friendships. Not so much at their ranch in Santa Barbara—Audrey Hepburn, gorgeously elegant in white Levi's and a white shirt, was one of the few friends to visit them there—but in Los Angeles and Palm Springs. Their trips west depended entirely on the president's schedule, but the schedule was usually arranged with certain California stops in mind—a week at Easter, three weeks in the summer, and a week or two in the fall and winter. The trip at Christmas was the one especially reserved for seeing friends.

Yet, traditionally, they always celebrated Christmas Day at the White House. Knowing that they would be spending ten days on the West Coast, the Reagans made a point of being in Washington on December 25, deliberately, so that the staff and agents could be at home with their own families. A day or two later, we'd head for Los Angeles, to the Century Plaza Hotel. Then, on the thirtieth, we'd move on to Palm Springs so that the Reagans could spend New Year's Eve with Walter and Leonore Annenberg. He was the publisher of Triangle Publications, which included the *Philadelphia Inquirer,* the *Daily News, TV Guide,* and the *Daily Racing Form.* He was also ambassador to Great Britain. Mrs. Annenberg was the administration's chief of protocol. It was on this trip that the president played his annual round of golf. The Annenbergs had a private course encircling their estate. The president never played particularly well, although he was a good enough athlete to have played better golf. But that would have meant playing more often, and after an abandoned round at Augusta National in 1983, he refused to do that.

The president had been at Augusta in October of that year with Secretary of State George Shultz and a couple of other people when a guy in a pickup truck crashed through an exterior gate, charged into the pro shop with a gun, fired a round into the ceiling, and took a bunch of hostages. Word quickly reached the agents with the president, and he was moved off the course to a safe place.

One of the pro shop hostages was Lanny Wyles, the staff advance. Another was Dave Fisher, then the president's personal aide.

When the man with the gun demanded to see the president, Lanny and Dave persuaded him to free the other hostages. Dave then suggested that he could relay the man's message directly to the president, so the man let Dave leave, much to the chagrin of Lanny, who was now the only hostage. Agents on the scene soon got involved, and the man surrendered. The incident received almost no press coverage because it happened the day after the bombing of the marine barracks in Beirut and the day of the U.S. invasion of Grenada. But the president was so disturbed by the incident that he never played golf again on any course except the Annenbergs'. He said that he was giving up golf purposely because he was concerned about putting other people at unnecessary risk. His exact words were "Playing golf is not worth the chance that someone could get killed."

The president's one round of golf a year was followed by a gala New Year's Eve party at which everybody, from the catering staff to all of the Reagans' Hollywood pals, was subjected to our magnetometers. The only people who ever got close to them in Palm Springs without being magged were the agents on the detail, the Annenbergs, and once, but only once, five teenagers.

We were just arriving at the Annenbergs' front gate for our two-day visit when the president spotted the teenagers holding up a placard that read "Please stop and say hello, Mr. President." He leaned forward and asked, "Joe, do you think I can stop and say hi to the kids?"

The easiest thing would have been to say no. He would have understood and just waved at them. But I knew he'd like this, so I made the instant decision to stop the motorcade. As soon as we stopped, the detail agents were on the ground surrounding the limousine. I asked the president to wait in the car for a moment, then got out to satisfy myself that it was safe. There was no one else around, except those kids and us. We had police cars parked sideways at the entrance, had cops and agents everywhere, and there were no high buildings. I opened the back door and the president stepped out, but I left the door open and made sure he stayed right there next to it. He shook hands with the kids and signed their placard. Mrs. Reagan slid across the seat and said hello. The entire stop lasted two minutes. The kids, of course, never thought he would do it, and they were ecstatic. One of the White House photographers rushed around, took a couple of pictures, and then the president got back into the car. He waved good-bye, and in no time we were rolling onto the property. It's arguable whether or not I should have made that stop. I'm sure those kids will never forget it. He might have remembered that moment for a long time, too. Anyway, how often is the president able to do things like that? I know it meant something to him because, when we got back into the car, the president leaned forward and said, "Thank you, Joe."

There were two occasions when, at Mrs. Reagan's behest, I secretly moved the two of them.

In 1986 we were at the Century Plaza and the Reagans were in the market for a house. Mrs. Reagan's great friend Betsy Bloomingdale—of New York department store fame—was handling everything for them. It had to be kept a secret because if word got out that the house was for the Reagans, the price would shoot up. It was on this trip that Mrs. Bloomingdale told Mrs. Reagan she'd found someplace great, which was the house in Bel Air that they moved into when he left office.

Mrs. Reagan came to me and said, "The president and I are going to see a house, and I don't want anybody to know we're going there." I appreciated her concerns, but getting the president and the first lady out of the Century Plaza and moving them around Los Angeles without anybody finding out was not an easy thing to do.

First I needed to cover the national security base so that nobody would think that the president was out of reach. I phoned Don Regan, who was on the golf course, and said, if you need the president, call the command post. Next, I needed to get the president's stewards off the floor, because they worked inside his suite. I told them that the president was going to have a private meeting and sent them down-stairs. That left the president and first lady alone in the top-floor suite, with the Secret Service detail, the military aide, the doctor, and the WHCA officer. At the same time, I'd arranged for two armored off-the-record cars and one unmarked police car to wait for us in the base-ment garage, but I did not tell the police why I needed their car or where we were going.

The military aide, the doctor, the WHCA officer, the shift agents, and I escorted the Reagans down a back elevator and into the garage. None of the hotel staff saw us leave. Better still, the press didn't get wind of it either. If they'd known what we were up to, they would have blown the story about the new house.

Once we got into the cars, and formed our little unmarked mo-torcade, we headed to Bel Air. The windows in those cars are tinted, but not totally blacked out, so I had to warn the president, "Please don't wave to anybody." We pulled into traffic, stopped at lights, and watched people walk by. We were as nondescript as possible. He didn't wave, and nobody ever realized that the president and Mrs. Reagan were in the backseat.

Arriving at the house, I hurried the Reagans inside, where Mrs. Bloomingdale was waiting for them. We walked in and out of all the rooms, and at one point the president said, "I'd like to see the base-ment." It's the kind of thing that guys do, so the president, Mrs. Bloomingdale, and I went downstairs. He checked out the empty basement, then wondered out loud, "Is it oil or gas heat?" I had to stop myself from laughing because I could see from his expression that he was serious. I have no idea what possible difference it could make, except maybe he thought it was one of those questions he needed to ask. But then, for those ten minutes, he wasn't the presi-dent of the United States, he was just a guy buying a house.

Once the Reagans had seen the house, we left Mrs. Blooming-dale there, got back into the cars, and returned to the hotel, stopping at lights, the same way we'd come. We got the Reagans upstairs to the suite, and not even the press secretary knew they'd been gone.

The second time I sneaked them away from the press, I wasn't quite so lucky.

It was Sunday, over the Fourth of July weekend 1986, and we were at Camp David. Just before we boarded the helicopter for the flight to the White House, Mrs. Reagan said quietly to me, "I'd like to see you in the residence after we land."

We arrived on the south lawn at around two o'clock that afternoon and I followed them upstairs. When the president went into the residence, Mrs. Reagan told me that she and the president were going to have dinner that night at the Jockey Club to celebrate her birthday with two old friends, Charles and Mary Jane Wick. Mrs. Reagan now said, very emphatically, "This is a private dinner, just the four of us and I don't want anyone to know about this. No press. No one."

The Wicks had been their neighbors in California back in the fifties. He was a former bandleader, producer of the 1961 film *Snow White and the Three Stooges,* and had been cochairman of the 1981 Presidential Inaugural Committee. As soon as Reagan was installed in the White House, he appointed Wick to run the United States Information Agency and Radio Free Europe. Mrs. Wick was part of Mrs. Reagan's inner circle of pals, which included Betsy Bloomingdale.

Getting the Reagans out of a hotel without anybody knowing it was one thing. Getting them out of the White House without anybody knowing was a real trick. Back downstairs, I told the shift that I would be out for a little while. Then I got into my car and drove to the Jockey Club, which is in the Ritz-Carlton Hotel on Massachusetts Avenue. The place was empty, and I had to walk around to find the maître d'. I identified myself and asked him if he had a dinner reservation that evening in the name of Charles Wick.

He confirmed that he did. "A table for four at seven-thirty."

I asked, "Do you know who the other two people are?" He said he didn't, and I said, "Sit down." I told him that President and Mrs. Reagan would be joining the Wicks and warned him that this had to be absolutely private. I said, "If this information leaves here and the press finds out about this, we're not coming." I made him understand that a press leak would be taken very seriously.

In the end, my anxieties were unwarranted, because the man was very cooperative. He showed me how the Jockey Club was divided into three sections and how he could set the third section aside for that single table of four. It was perfect, because it was at the rear and was hidden by a large row of plants, so that nobody else in the restaurant could see who was dining there. Best of all, there was a back door, so they could get in and out without anyone else seeing them. I looked out the back door and found a fire escape leading down to a service bay and a parking lot. I liked that because we could stage the cars there without attracting attention.

The maître d' and I worked out all the arrangements. Because WHCA wouldn't have time to install a separate phone line in, I told him that a WHCA officer would have to sit in his office literally holding the phone with the line open for as long as the president was there. He said that was no problem. I then told him I'd need a few other tables for dinner that evening, preferably in the middle section, so that agents, the military aide, and the doctor would be within a few feet of the president. I said I'd also need an agent in the kitchen. None of that was a problem either.

Returning to the White House, I assured Mrs. Reagan that everything was arranged, and even warned her not to wear heels that night because she'd have to climb up a fire escape. I phoned Don Regan at home, explained that I was taking the president and Mrs. Reagan out that night and said, "I can't tell you where we're going, but if you need to get in touch, call W-16." He didn't ask any questions.

The motorcade would be two armored off-the-record cars, but instead of having them waiting for us at the West Wing, I had them meet us at the East Wing entrance, about as far away as I could possibly get from the press offices. I then briefed the doctor, the military aide, and the WHCA officer. I explained that the Reagans were going to have dinner at the Jockey Club, that the military aide had to change into civilian clothes, and that they couldn't call anybody or tell anybody about this because if word got out, we would all get fired. I assured them that I'd made all the correct arrangements and that there was nothing to worry about. And I reiterated several times, "Don't tell anybody."

I briefed the agents on the detail, explaining the evening and telling them how we would get the president and first lady out of the White House, into the restaurant, out of the restaurant, and back to the White House. I sent one agent over to the hotel to sit in the lobby, sent two more over to the restaurant to have dinner, and sent another agent into the kitchen. I contacted the Washington police and our CAT teams and arranged backup.

At 7:15, I brought the president and the first lady down from the residence. As we stepped off the elevator, he instinctively turned to the right, toward the West Wing. I said, "No, Mr. President, this way, please," and led them out the door of the East Wing. We got into the first of the two off-the-record cars, the detail agents got into the second car, and with two unmarked police cars, pulled out onto Pennsylvania Avenue. As I had in Los Angeles, I reminded the president, "Please just sit back and don't wave to anybody."

But this time he stared at me with a very concerned expression and asked, "Is something going on that I don't know about?"

I didn't want to blow the surprise, so I looked at Mrs. Reagan. She read my thoughts and said to her husband, "This is my idea, Ronnie."

We made our way through Sunday night Washington traffic and arrived unseen at the rear of the Ritz-Carlton. We climbed the fire escape and stepped into the back section of the restaurant where the Wicks were waiting.

Toward the end of their meal, the maître d' came up to me to say, "We've had people come into this restaurant, dine and leave, and never realize that the president was there."

When the meal was over, we left by the fire escape, got into the cars, and headed back to the White House. I decided that instead of sneaking in through the East Wing, we might as well just drive through the Northwest Gate. I was mildly concerned that word might have leaked out that the president was missing from the White House and that there could be cameras waiting for us, but it was too late for the press to spoil Mrs. Reagan's birthday surprise. As it turned out, no one saw us.

I was home by eleven o'clock, and within fifteen minutes my Signal phone rang. That's a direct line from the White House and on the end of it was a seriously unhappy press secretary, Larry Speakes. He demanded to know, "How could you do this? You've violated a very strict agreement that we have with the press about taking the president out of the White House without a press pool coming along."

My response was "This was Mrs. Reagan's idea. Complain to her."

Fifteen minutes later, a very peeved Mark Weinberg, who was Larry's deputy and my good friend, called to say, "You should have told me. We should've known."

I reminded him, "If I'd told you, you would have been obliged to tell Larry. No one knew. I couldn't tell anyone."

The next morning, I arrived at work to discover that Larry and Mark weren't the only ones angry with me. The entire White House press corps was fuming, too. In my own mind, I knew that we never took any unnecessary risks with the president and the first lady that night. They were always in an armored car, we had plenty of protection and backup, nobody knew we were leaving, nobody knew where we were going, and we had enough contingency plans in place that we could respond to anything. To this day I am convinced that no one dining in the restaurant ever knew we were there. So I decided to write off everyone's fury as just part of the deal. But the media was so annoyed that they demanded a meeting with the president, and his secretary put it on the schedule for six that evening. It took place in the Green Room on the first floor of the residence. I wasn't personally worried, because I had two things going for me: The dinner was Mrs. Reagan's idea, and all I did was make it happen safely; and I had the president to defuse the situation.

He was unbelievably good at this sort of thing, and handled it perfectly. The reporters walked out of the room chuckling, although Bill Plante of CBS News turned toward the president with one final admonition. "Please, Mr. President, in the future, treat us like your American Express card. Don't leave home without us."

CHAPTER FIVE

★ ★ ★ ★

JUST A KID FROM
ALLENTOWN

On November 22, 1963, John Kerry was a sophomore at Yale University in New Haven, Connecticut; Ronald Reagan was finishing his last film in Hollywood, an adaptation of Ernest Hemingway's short story "The Killers"; and I was packing to leave for a football game.

'd never heard of John Kerry. I had, of course, seen Ronald Reagan in the movies and on television. But in my wildest dreams, as I packed an overnight suitcase, I could never have guessed how that Friday afternoon in Dallas would change my life forever and, to some small extent, mix mine with theirs.

I was just a kid from Allentown, Pennsylvania, gone to the big city—Philadelphia—on a football scholarship to Temple University. We were playing the final game of the 1963 season at Gettysburg on Saturday, and the team bus was scheduled to leave in an hour. At around 12:40, I was in my dorm room when I heard on the radio that shots had been fired at the president's limousine in Dallas. The announcement that the president was dead came as we were boarding the bus.

Like most people, I spent the weekend glued to the television, watching the events that followed in the wake of the assassination. I listened intently to descriptions of Secret Service agent Clint Hill jumping onto the rear bumper of the president's Lincoln convertible, then scrambling up the trunk to get to Mrs. Kennedy. I watched reporters describe how, two cars back, Rufus Youngblood had thrown Vice President Lyndon Johnson to the floor of his limousine and fallen across him. I read how Secret Service drivers in the president's limousine, and in the vice president's limousine, and in the follow-up cars had sped away to Parkland Memorial Hospital.

In the months following the Kennedy assassination, I read everything I could about that day in Dallas and about the Secret Service.

Two years later, my final game as Temple's quarterback was at Hofstra, on Long Island. It was not only the last time I put on my lucky number 12 jersey but also one of my most memorable games, for all the wrong reasons. We kicked off, they did nothing with their first possession, and we took over. I got us inside the twenty-yard line, called a "sprint out left," and ran the ball myself to the three, where I got knocked out of bounds, then tackled. I never came back onto the field. My right hand was badly broken, we lost the game, and that was the end of my college football career. But it didn't appear that it was going to be the end of my playing days. Around Thanksgiving, I received a phone call from the Cleveland Browns to say they'd drafted me as a defensive back. I graduated on June 17, 1966, and was looking forward to training camp in July, when, the next day, I received a letter which famously began "Greetings from the President of the United States."

Once the initial shock of getting drafted by the army wore off, I called the Browns' coach, Blanton Collier, to tell him the bad news. He said, "Let me work on it," and phoned me back a few hours later to announce that I'd just been enrolled as a graduate student at Case Western Reserve University in Cleveland. As such,

I would be deferred from military service. Three days later, my no-tice to report for an army physical was rescinded. On July 1, I joined the other rookies in Hiram, Ohio. Ten days into camp I got another induction notice. The draft board had suddenly decided to take everyone who'd already had a four-year deferment, and that put an end to my career with the Browns. As of August 3, I was to become a soldier. Instead, I rushed to a navy recruiter, and by the time my date with the army arrived, I was in the navy pipeline for Aviation Officer Candidate School.

It was the same year John Kerry enlisted in the navy and Ronald Reagan became governor of California.

My orders said that I was to report for training at Pensacola, Florida, by 1800 hours on October 3. I figured getting there an hour and a half early would give me a chance to look around. The film *An Officer and a Gentleman* hadn't yet been made, but that's what this place was like, and if I'd seen the film, I wouldn't have arrived at 4:30. Instead of looking around, a marine drill instructor decided I should spend the time doing push-ups.

The first four weeks were challenging, but my dreams were crushed when I couldn't pass an eye test for flight training. I was transferred to Officer Candidate School at Newport, Rhode Island, and sixteen weeks later was commissioned an ensign. I didn't know it then, but John Kerry was there at the same time, although he was a few classes ahead of me.

My first ship was the USS *Plymouth Rock,* a landing ship dock out of Little Creek, Virginia. Shortly after I joined the crew, we got a new skipper who'd just come back from Vietnam, where he'd been in charge of the Riverine Forces—large river assault boats. One night in the wardroom he was showing slides of his experi-ences, and up came a slide of a PBR, a river patrol boat just like those in the movie *Apocalypse Now.* They were much smaller than the Riverines, only thirty-one feet long, with a crew of four. It was love at first sight. I said to myself, That's what I want to do. As soon as he finished showing us his slides, I asked the skipper, "How do I get on PBRs?"

It took eight months to get off the *Plymouth Rock,* but on my twenty-fifth birthday, March 28, 1969, I arrived at Mare Island, in Vallejo, California, for PBR school. There were fifty enlisted men and four officers in my class, one of whom was an Annapolis grad named John Poe. He had a wife and two young children in San Diego, and every weekend for the next twelve weeks he'd fly down there to be with them. John and I got to be great pals, and because I was single and could always find use for a car over the weekend, I'd drop him off at the airport on Friday night and use his convertible until it was time to pick him up on Sunday night.

We trained with Navy Seals in the sloughs of the Sacramento River, which were similar to but more difficult to maneuver in than the canals of Vietnam. I didn't know it then, but for every Navy Seal who died in Vietnam, five PBR sailors were killed in combat. From there we went to Whidbey Island, Washington, for SERE, survival-evasion-resistance-escape, which is prison-camp training. They put us on a mountain, in the cold and snow, gave us a parachute and a knife, and left us there to forage for food. John and I bunked together under the parachute. After that they took us to another mountain, gave us a coordinate, and challenged us to get to "Friendly Village." If we made it, they said, we could have an apple and an orange before being taken to prison camp. If we got caught on the way down, we would be taken straight to the camp.

Everybody was on his own this time, trying to avoid Asian navy guys with AK-47s going through the woods hunting us down. I was in good shape in those days, so I could run and made it to Friendly Village. I got my apple and my orange, and was then hauled off to prison camp. That was the most intimidating experience I've ever been through. They put us all in prison garb, locked us away in little boxes, fed us gruel, threw cold water on us, deprived us of sleep, hit us, knocked us down, made us move rocks, and constantly shouted at us. We quickly lost track of time, and it seemed as if we were there forever. Anyone who escaped got an apple and an orange. I tried several times, but it was too hard to get out of there. Somehow, one guy a few classes before ours escaped fifteen times. He was later shot down in Vietnam, and thanks to this training, he was one of the few pilots to make his way safely out of the north.

They never told us how long this was going to last, which was part of the torture, and for all that any of us knew, this misery could go on for weeks. On what I think might have been the third or fourth day, they lined us up, and the camp commander started ranting and raving. Out of the corner of my eye I saw someone hauling down the North Vietnamese flag and sending up the American flag, and then they played the National Anthem. All the guards saluted us, and we all broke down in tears. The training taught us the trauma of being captured, reinforced the idea that we really didn't want that to happen, and made every one of us believe that, if it did happen, we had to depend on our buddies.

As soon as we got back to the base, John Poe and I went to the Officers' Club, and, for some unfathomable reason, we were the only two people in the bar that night. He loved the Beatles song "Hey Jude," so we drank margaritas, fed the jukebox, and played it over and over and over again.

From Whidbey Island they sent us to San Diego for Vietnamese language training. That's where I met John's wife and kids and presented him with a shiny 45-rpm copy of "Hey Jude."

On my last night in the States, June 9, 1969, I went to the Coronado Beach Hotel, by myself, and blew what little money I had on a great meal and a bottle of wine. The next morning I was standing at the base bus stop, because I couldn't afford a cab to the airport, when an older couple pulled up in a car and insisted on driving me. I guess they knew where I was going. I flew to San Francisco, took a bus to Travis Air Force Base, phoned my parents to say good-bye and spent several hours in the Officers' Club looking at a group of young marine lieutenants, wondering how many of them would be coming home alive. From there I flew to Hawaii, then to Subic Bay, Manila, and on to Tan Son Nhut Air Force Base in Saigon, where I was assigned to quarters that had been bombed the day before. The next morning my name was on a list for assignment to River Division 512 in Tra Cu. I decided that was good luck in a way. I was wearing number 12 again.

It was a long helicopter ride up to Tra Cu, a navy advanced tactical support base on the Vam Co Dong River, which paralleled the Cambodian border. The Vam Co Dong and the Vam Co Tay outlined the parrot's beak of Cambodia, which is where a huge American invasion occurred a year later. River Division 512 was part of an operation called Giant Slingshot, and these guys were getting hit every night. It was a very bad place to be, so close to the enemy that you could see their camps across the border in Cambodia. I shared a hooch with a fellow patrol officer named Bill Waters. Every now and then the navy would send us a film, and every now and then Bill's mother would send him one of those popcorn shakers that you hold over an open flame. To run the film we had to shut off most of the electricity in the camp. Bill and I would sit there in our hooch watching it, cooking his mother's popcorn. It was as near to being home as we could get.

Within a couple of weeks 512 was moved south to Chau Doc on the Bassac River, a few hundred yards from Cambodia. Our patrol area was now the Vinh Te Canal, which was even worse than the Vam Co Dong.

A few weeks later I got orders to River Division 534, which had lost officers and needed replacements. I was back on the Vam Co Dong, four miles south of Tra Cu in Ben Luc, and now there was no number 12. I spent a few months there before our division got sent north to Go Dau Ha—we got into two big firefights on the way—

The job is not about taking a bullet for the president, it's about doing absolutely everything possible to prevent that decision from ever having to be made.
(White House)

ABOVE LEFT My parents, Joseph and Dorothy, in Wildwood, New Jersey, 1941.

ABOVE RIGHT Playing football for Temple, 1964.

The officers of 512—with me are Jack Geraghty (c) and Bill Waters (r), Chau Doc, Vietnam, 1969.

TOP River Patrol Division 512, Vinh Te Canal, Vietnam, 1969. *(U.S. Navy)*

LEFT My PBR.

BELOW Undercover in 1971, with agents Holly Hoffschmidt and Rick Zaino, as we investigated John Kerry's Vietnam Veterans Against the War.

ABOVE My first presidential inaugural, 1973. That's President Nixon waving from the car. I'm in a dark topcoat, two blocks behind him on the right, standing next to a lot of other post standers in dark topcoats. *(U.S. Secret Service)*

RIGHT Working a rope line in 1975 with Vice President Nelson Rockefeller, one of the most decent men I've ever met. *(White House)*

RIGHT Returning from Camp David to the south grounds of the White House in Marine One, with President and Mrs. Reagan. *(White House)*

Whenever the president left the Oval Office, the Secret Service was there, this time along with Vice President George H. W. Bush and Chief of Staff Don Regan. *(White House)*

With President and Mrs. Reagan in Tianamin Square, Beijing, China, 1984. *(White House)*

LEFT Throwing out the first ball on opening day in Baltimore, 1986. That's the day President Reagan decided to buy three hotdogs. *(White House)*

BELOW Moments before Mikhail Gorbachev arrived for the opening of the Geneva summit, Bill Henkel (in trench coat) suggested to President Reagan that he not wear his topcoat when he greets the Russian leader. The president agreed, and what appeared to be a trivial concession came to set the tone for the rest of the summit. Staff advance person Grey Terry (far left) and Don Regan are also pictured. *(White House)*

BOTTOM In Geneva President Reagan invited Mikhail Gorbachev to walk with him to a boathouse down by the lake. To the far right of the photo is Mikhail Dukacheyev. Henkel is in the white coat next to him. *(White House)*

The *Challenger* disaster so deeply touched us all, but none more than the president and first lady during the memorial service in Houston, 1986. *(White House)*

Sometimes standing next to history meant getting in the way of the secretary of defense (Casper Weinberger) when he wanted to take a picture of the president in Grenada, 1986. *(White House)*

RIGHT President Reagan rode big thoroughbreds, and rode them well. I had to take lessons to keep up. *(White House)*

ABOVE At the ranch in Santa Barbara, the rules were simple: We tacked our horses, the president tacked his. That's agent Barbara Riggs with us. *(White House)*

RIGHT The ranch was the only place we let President Reagan drive. *(White House)*

TOP AND RIGHT Agents Barbara Riggs and Karen Toll "cutting costs" at the Reagan ranch, as part of our April Fool's joke with the president. He and I are laughing about it.*(J. Barletta)*

President Reagan is as gracious as ever with my daughter Michelle at Fess (Davy Crockett) Parker's annual barbecue, 1985. *(White House)*

ABOVE When I took President Reagan on a tour of W-16, the Secret Service command post directly under the Oval Office, he was fascinated with our collection of early presidential protection photos. That's where he also saw, for the first time, the famous poster with his face on Sylvester Stallone's body captioned, "Ronbo." *(White House)*

BELOW LEFT President Reagan couldn't resist playing to a crowd. *(White House)*

BELOW RIGHT Sometimes in the winter, especially when that crowd was the press, he couldn't resist a snowball. *(White House)*

RIGHT While he was the most powerful man in the world, they were the most visible couple in the world. *(White House)*

BELOW My last flight on Air Force One, when the president came back to the Secret Service compartment to say thank you. *(White House)*

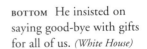

BOTTOM He insisted on saying good-bye with gifts for all of us. *(White House)*

LEFT INSET It took nearly ten months to set up the pope's tour, working daily with Agent Rich Miller (c) and my friend Monsignor Bob Lynch (r).

ABOVE Limousines and our redesigned popemobile roll off an Air Force C-5A, one of the six planes that came with us to every city. *(U.S. Secret Service)*

ABOVE We protected the pope the same way we protected the president, but the Church created a dynamic we weren't used to. *(The Vatican)*

LEFT The Holy Father and President Reagan meeting in Miami, 1987. *(White House)*

LEFT The storm that disrupted the outdoor mass in Miami was so violent that, had the pope not come off the stage when I asked him to, we were prepared to carry him off. *(Miami Herald)*

TOP RIGHT No amount of training could have fully prepared us for the raw emotion and abundant enthusiasm we had to deal with wherever we went with the pope. *(Washington Post)*

LEFT There was only one "incident" when a woman broke through the barriers along the parade route in San Antonio. The agents reacted immediately and appropriately. I'm in the front seat of the popemobile. *(The Vatican)*

ABOVE My daughter Michelle receiving a very special holy communion, Detroit, 1987. *(The Vatican)*

RIGHT Our eighth and final flight together on Shepherd One. *(The Vatican)*

Colorado River, Grand Canyon, 1990. While Vice President Dan Quayle (front right) is busy paddling, that's me in the front left, along with two other agents, pulling Mrs. Quayle out of the water. *(White House)*

The funeral for the Indian prime minister, Rajiv Gandhi, in 1991 was a particularly stressful event for the Secret Service. In addition to the heat and enormous crowds, there were guns everywhere, including three seats from the vice president on Yassir Arafat's hip. *(White House)*

Quayle liked the crowds while I worried about them.

You always remember your last game. I will always remember my last rope line.
(White House)

At the president's eightieth birthday in Los Angeles Mrs. Reagan asked about my daughter and about life back in Washington. I told her how much we missed her and Mr. Reagan.
(White House)

Susan and I at Camp Hiawatha, Kezar Falls, Maine, 1994.

The way I will always remember him. *(White House)*

and joined John Poe's River Division 592. But within a week or so, we were down from twenty boats to four and had taken a lot of casualties. John's executive officer, Lt. Philip Thomas Smith, of Austin, Texas, was due to leave, and his replacement, Lt. Andy Arje, was due to arrive. But the night before, one of the chief petty officers got sick, and Lt. Smith volunteered to take his patrol. His boat took fire and he was killed. The next morning, as Andy Arje stepped off the helicopter, sailors were loading a body bag on it. Andy asked me, Who's that? I hated to tell him it was the guy he was replacing, but I did. Andy went out that night, took fire, and suffered a slight wound. He went out the next night and got wounded again. Two days there, replacing a guy who got killed, and Andy had two Purple Hearts. A few nights later, my boats got into a firefight with the Viet Cong coming across the river. I was later awarded a Bronze Star. The paperwork attached to it said it was for that night and a few similar nights. But all I was doing was trying not to get myself or any member of my crew killed. In my head, the paperwork should have read, "For perfect attendance." Because all the time, deep down inside, I never thought I was going to get out of there alive.

Eventually they moved us back to Ben Luc, and before long, President Nixon's Vietnamization program kicked in, which meant we were going to turn our PBRs over to the Vietnamese. As soon as we handed the boats to them in October 1969, my career with Division 534 ended, and I got orders back to 512, where I hooked up again with Bill Waters and his mother's popcorn.

On November 23, 1969, there was a full moon with clear skies making the nighttime visibility excellent. Although the enemy rarely undertook major operations in moonlight, everyone in the division was on edge because, seventeen days earlier, one of our boat captains, Quartermaster First Class Jimmy Cain from Fort Worth, Texas, had been killed. That had been a cloudy night.

I was on patrol in the same part of the Vinh Te Canal where Jimmy died, just west of Chau Doc. Our mission was to interdict the movement of North Vietnamese and Viet Cong crossing the border. "Interdict" was a fancy military term meaning shoot them before they shoot you. Lack of rainfall had lowered the water level of the canal well below the bank, making it impossible for us to use the weapons on our boats. I had to position our ambush on the north bank of the canal in a heavily wooded area.

Some weeks earlier I had made a deal with a Special Forces sergeant, trading C rations for a 90 mm recoilless rifle. It was a big gun and gave our small group of two boats and nine men a little extra sense of security. The navy was equally concerned that we could be overrun—it had already happened several times to other crews—so they assigned to us six Cambodian mercenaries. That added considerably to our defensive capability, assuming they remained on our side. If they had not yet received their latest paycheck, we couldn't be totally sure of their loyalty.

After placing movement sensors around our position, in an effort to prevent anyone from sneaking up on us, I huddled behind a mound of dirt next to one of the mercenaries. There were North Vietnamese base camps less than a mile from us, just across the rice paddies, and in the quiet of the night I could hear them signaling back and forth using sticks to bang out some form of Morse-like code. There were also times when they played twangy Vietnamese music on loudspeakers, which, to our Western ears, was very annoying.

Waiting for something to happen, I looked skyward. The night was brilliant and that full moon was sharply in focus. Nine days before, Apollo 12 had blasted off from Florida, and as I stared at the moon, I realized that Charles Conrad and Alan Bean were somewhere on the surface. My mind focused on them, and I slowly forgot where I was and what I was doing there. I stared at the moon and thought about my lifelong fascination with flight, and my own recently shattered dream of flying for the navy.

Before long, the Cambodian mercenary wanted to know why I was watching the moon. In a mixture of English, Cambodian, and

Vietnamese, I tried to explain that while we were lying on the soft wet ground of a Southeast Asian jungle, two Americans were up there. He understood the irony of the moment, because in broken English he asked, "If your country can accomplish such an unbelievable task as putting a man on the moon, what in the world are you doing here with me, in this mud, waiting for the enemy to approach?" It was the first time I questioned my being in Vietnam. And to this day, each time I see a full moon, I think back to that night and wonder if I will ever come to terms with the experiences of that year. Sadly, the prospect of that, even all these years later, seems as distant and remote as the dark side of the moon.

Most guys on PBRs had similar experiences. Mine was not at all unique. I know that because we spent a lot of time sitting around and talking about our experiences on patrol. One of the names I remember coming up every now and then was John Kerry. He was on PCFs, called Swift Boats. Initially, we patrolled rivers and the bigger PCFs were on coastal patrol. As the war progressed, the PBRs moved farther in, and so did the PCFs. By the time we were working along the Cambodian border, the PCFs were on the major rivers. I knew a few guys who knew Kerry, but I didn't meet him. At least, not then.

One year after I arrived in Vietnam, I was on a flight back to San Francisco. That year in combat taught me a lot about myself and also showed me that life is truly random and circumstantial. I came back a very different person. It wasn't until we flew past the Golden Gate Bridge, and the pilot tipped his wings, that I really understood that I was one of the lucky ones. I was home alive.

That was June 1970. I didn't know what I wanted to do regarding a career, so I spent some time visiting friends, went down to the Jersey shore to be with my parents, and eventually made my way back home to Allentown. Then, out of the blue, I received a call from the Philadelphia Eagles. A players' strike in the National Football League had just been announced, the Eagles had twenty-six rookies coming to camp, and they needed a quarterback. It seemed like an eternity since I'd put on a football helmet, and I wasn't sure that I still had the right stuff, but the coach of the Eagles said, Come to Franklin Field tomorrow, spend some time with us, and if it works, we'll take you to training camp. As soon as I hung up, I phoned my old friend, Jack Callaghan, who'd played quarterback at Rutgers. I told him to meet me at nearby Muhlenberg College, and for the first time in four years, I gripped a football.

The next day, I spent a couple of hours at Franklin Field throwing passes to receivers. At the end of the session, the great Eagles wide receiver Pete Retzlaff, who was then the general manager, came up to me to say that he remembered me from college and invited me to camp. In those days, rookies didn't get paid. They only got $12 a day. Pete said he was going to offer me $200 a week plus per diem, but didn't want any of the other rookies to know about it. That was a lot of money in those days, certainly $200 a week more than I was making at the time, so I said sure.

Not being in shape to play football meant that the Eagles' training camp was a lot tougher for me than it was for the rest of the rookies, and it took several days before I started feeling good about being there. I had no idea whether I'd make the team, but I knew that when the strike ended, Norm Snead, the regular quarterback, would step into his old job. So I started thinking about what would happen if I didn't get to play. My father had an old school friend named Leo Cramsey who worked for the State Department, and he suggested I look into a career there. I got permission from the Eagles to leave for a day and went to Washington to see Leo, but just as I got there, Leo was on his way to Guatemala. With nothing else to do, I called on another friend of my dad's, Jack Yohe, who worked for the Federal Aviation Administration. His offices were across the street from the Hilton Hotel on Connecticut Avenue, the same place where Ronald Reagan would be shot. Jack and I chatted about football until he asked me what I wanted to do. When I confessed that I didn't know, he wondered, "How about the Secret Service?"

I told him I'd thought about it when I was in college, but never looked into how to start the process. Jack had a friend named Bob Snow, who was then the agent in charge of the special investigations division. His offices were at Secret Service headquarters, and on Jack's advice, I went to see him. Bob was a sharp young guy whose enthusiasm for the Secret Service rubbed off on me. I mentioned that I was currently at the Eagles' training camp, and he offered to arrange an appointment for me with the agent in charge of the Philadelphia field office.

At the end of August, the players strike ended, Norm Snead returned as first-string quarterback, and George Mira returned as his backup. I found myself standing around a lot. I concluded that even if I made the team, I'd have to wait three or four years before Snead and Mira moved on. Sadly, I came to accept that at the age of twenty-six, I probably didn't have much of a future with the Eagles. I went to Retzlaff and said, Thanks anyway but I've missed my time. He paid me all my money and even added an extra $200.

The Secret Service was now my priority. I drove down to Philadelphia for my interview. I thought it went well, and was told, We'll be in touch. As long as I was in town, I went up to Temple to see one of my old teammates, Frank Massino, who was on the coaching staff. They had a new head coach, Wayne Hardin, who'd just come from coaching at Annapolis. I'd never met him but, of course, knew of his terrific reputation. I was sitting with Massino and another old teammate, Earl Cleghorn, when Hardin walked in, said hello, and asked what I was doing these days. I told him I was home from Vietnam, that I was waiting to hear from the Secret Service, and had just left the Eagles' training camp. Just like that, he offered, "I need a quarterback coach. How would you like to work for me?"

I spent the next four and a half months coaching for Hardin, and wishing I could have played for him, because he was an outstanding coach and would have made me a much better quarterback.

I loved every minute of being back in the game, with one very notable exception.

About a week after I started, the whole team got together at preseason training camp in Valley Forge. I was on the field when I glanced over to the sidelines and spotted Andy Arje. I knew the look on his face, and we stared at each other for a very long time. When I walked over to him, we didn't even shake hands. All he said was "It's John."

I took the rest of the day off. John Poe could have left Vietnam in June, when I did, but he had extended for two months to be an admiral's aide in Saigon. The night before he was supposed to leave, he went out and had a couple of beers, and on his way back to his quarters, he got mugged. He was taken to a field hospital where the doctors felt he should spend a few more days. The flights out of Saigon for home usually left at six or seven in the morning, and if you missed yours, you could wait a week or two before getting onto another manifest. John decided he wasn't going to miss the plane, so he got out of bed and walked out of the hospital. A little while later he collapsed and died from a blood clot.

My friend John Poe was thirty-one.

By the beginning of 1971, I was phoning the Secret Service field office almost every day. But it was weeks before anyone said, "You're hired." From start to finish, getting in had been a six-month ordeal. On the evening of February 21, I phoned my cousin Jim Martin, who was an FBI agent, and told him, "I start tomorrow. What should I wear?"

He answered, "Lead off with a white shirt."

It's advice I've never forgotten. On the morning of February 22, that's exactly what I did. Since then, whenever I do anything for the first time, I always lead off with a white shirt.

I reported in to the Philadelphia Field Office and for the first few days did nothing more than sit around and read the manuals. Then they took me downstairs to the firing range to qualify with a service revolver. The agent who was "babysitting" me thought of himself as a hotshot, and just before taking me to the range, he asked in front of the whole staff, "Petro, you ever use a weapon?" I said I had. Playing the macho wise guy, he smirked, "Ever kill anybody?"

Instead of answering him directly, I stared for a moment, then said, "I got back from Vietnam last year."

He never taunted me again.

That week someone handed me a badge and someone else issued me a .357 Magnum. These days you go into training and don't get the badge and the gun until you graduate. That's not how it worked then, and just like that, I was a full-fledged special agent in the United States Secret Service.

It was a couple of weeks later before I got shipped off to the Treasury Law Enforcement Training Center in Washington. Again, it was different then than it is now; in those days they grouped all of the Treasury agents together. Only six of us were there from the Secret Service, and three of those guys became my lifelong friends: Bob Hast, Phil Kiefer, and Earl Devaney. The classes covered the basics of law enforcement, search and seizure, and how to arrest people. At the same time, Bob Hast introduced me to a young woman from Pennsylvania named Barbara Coccia, and we started dating.

After graduation, I returned to Philadelphia for a few weeks, then came back to Washington for Secret Service school. They were trying to get as many agents as possible through the protective courses before the 1972 presidential election campaign, so my class was the first one where we only did protective training. They planned to bring us back later for the investigative courses.

As a new agent on protective duty, I was a lowly post stander, one of dozens of agents who formed the second perimeter around a site. We never got close to the president because his detail came with him and left with him. We manned checkpoints at doors, entranceways, exits, and hallways, a physical presence wherever the Secret Service needed to display a physical presence. It's a very necessary thing, and the vital middle part of our "three perimeter" strategy.

I saw President Nixon's Secret Service detail on several occasions and thought to myself, these are impressive guys. They knew what they were doing, and everything happened very fast. The president was whisked in, and he was whisked out. I wouldn't learn for some time how a detail reflects the personality of the protectee and that this bunch was not only very aggressive, but also disturbingly arrogant.

The first time I personally encountered that arrogance was in Akron, Ohio. For some strange reason, Nixon was staying at a Holiday Inn. I was one of the post standers surrounding the hotel. The agent in charge of the site informed us that protesters across the street were carrying a North Vietnamese flag and ordered another agent and me to take it away from them. The other young agent was also a Vietnam veteran. I looked at him, then back at the agent in charge and asked, "Why?"

He answered, "Because it's an embarrassment to the president."

I thought to myself, Those protesters have a right to be doing what they are doing. It didn't matter that I'd fought against that flag for a year. Taking the flag away from them was wrong, and I said so to the agent in charge. In the end, nobody would do it.

The war had created an enormous amount of emotion in the United States—running the gamut from extreme hawk to extreme dove—and one of the people who came to national prominence during that time was John Kerry.

Thirty-three years later, after he had secured the Democratic nomination for president in the 2004 race, CNN revealed that the FBI had placed Kerry under surveillance. He'd returned home from Vietnam to take his stance as national spokesman for Vietnam Veterans Against the War (VVAW). The story of how undercover FBI agents shadowed Kerry in 1971 came to light when a historian obtained some twenty thousand pages of FBI files on the VVAW.

According to press reports, they revealed how Richard Nixon saw the VVAW as a major threat to the United States and, at one point, actually feared that Kerry's group might be plotting an armed coup d'état. What didn't come out in the CNN reports was that the Secret Service had been called in on this, too.

I'd just graduated from the protective course and had returned to Philadelphia to work for Myron "Mike" Weinstein, who was then agent in charge in Philadelphia and would later became deputy director of the Secret Service. He called me into his office to say the service was looking for some agents recently home from Vietnam to do an undercover assignment in Washington. Two days later I was back in D.C., partnered with Rick Zaino, who'd been in the army in Vietnam, and Holly Huffschmidt, who'd been a nurse in Vietnam. She was also one of the first female agents in the Secret Service. Our assignment was to infiltrate the VVAW.

Here I was, only two years after hearing John Kerry's name in Vietnam, trying to get inside his organization. Unlike Richard Nixon and the FBI, we weren't concerned with him. Instead, we were acting on intelligence about certain group members who might otherwise be planning to use the VVAW as a front for violent actions against the president of the United States.

Rick, Holly, and I donned our old greens and grew our hair. Rick and I also grew beards. The three of us were moved into the Park Central Hotel, which was, bizarrely, right across from Secret Service headquarters. They must have gotten a good rate. But it meant that we had to sneak in and out of the back of the hotel because we didn't want our fellow protesters to see us staying there. We joined Kerry's group and over the course of the next two months, we became protesters. Rick, Holly, and I had fake names and fake driver's licenses. I used Joe, but my last name was my mother's maiden name. Because we were legitimate veterans, we could talk the talk and tell our own stories. No one in the Secret Service seemed to worry that we might run into someone we'd served with over there. But then, almost three million men and women had served in Vietnam, so I guess the odds of that happening were pretty slim.

I met Kerry a couple of times, talked to him about PBRs and PCFs, and remember thinking that he was a very good speaker, that he had a real presence, and that he clearly had political aspirations. Honestly, I thought to myself at the time, this guy is going to run for president.

We handed out leaflets in front of the White House and went to meetings in bars and churches. We only really got two instructions from the Secret Service. The first was what to do if we got arrested. The Washington police had a habit of beating up protesters before they yanked them away, but we had a secret signal. When the cops started swinging their billy clubs, we were supposed to cross our hands in front of us. In theory, they'd all been briefed that anybody who did that was a good guy. Luckily, we never had to test that theory.

The second instruction was to check in a couple of times a day with our control agent, Rad Jones, which we could do easily from pay phones. However, I'm not sure how much anyone back at headquarters truly understood about what we were going through because one day, during a huge protest at the Washington Monument, Jones announced that he'd set up a meeting for us with an undercover FBI agent. Holly stayed with the protesters while Rick and I strolled close enough to the meeting point to spot a guy in khaki slacks, a button-down white shirt, wing-tip shoes, and a windbreaker. Everyone for miles around looked scruffy, except this guy. I said to Rick, There is no way we're going over there, and that was the extent of our meeting with the FBI.

In the end, we managed to identify a couple of guys who were nasty, but the organization itself did not appear to be involved in any violent activities.

Back in Philadelphia, I asked Mr. Weinstein—who was a great

boss and a wonderful person, but very intimidating to me at the time—if I could keep my long hair and beard. He said he didn't mind, except that I knew he did. And the way he told me he did was typical of him. One day, he happened to mention a temporary assignment available in Florida protecting the prime minister of Jamaica, Michael Manley. It was only four days, but the weather in Miami was great, and it would be particularly easy because Mr. Manley intended to spend most of his time in his hotel suite. I said I'd take it. He said, "Great, but you'll have to shave and get a haircut."

Freshly trimmed, I spent four days at a nice hotel in Miami as part of the detail protecting Manley, who made one speech and never came out of his suite after that. Food for two went into his room, empty trays came out of his room, and we never saw him again until the day he left.

I returned to Washington for investigation school, which was four weeks of learning how to deal with counterfeiting and check-forging cases. Without a doubt, counterfeiting is the sexy side of our investigative function. The theft and forging of government checks is decidedly less glamorous. Because I was the new kid on the block in Philadelphia, I was assigned to the check squad, which is, all too often, a lot of down and dirty stuff. I spent months knocking on doors, dealing with drug addicts, looking for government check forgers. The counterfeiting guys thumbed their noses, but the check squad was great fun, and I stayed on it for three years. In tandem with a U.S. postal inspector named Ryland Saxby, I averaged sixty to seventy arrests a year, which is a lot, and I guess the highlight of those three years was when I arrested Johnny Sample.

Sample played eleven seasons in the National Football League, with Baltimore, Pittsburgh, and Washington, and won himself a championship ring in 1969 as the New York Jets left cornerback in their Super Bowl III upset of the Colts. Sample, however, was considered a troublemaker for much of his career and didn't do a lot to change his image when he wrote a book titled *Confessions of a Dirty Ballplayer.* By the early 1970s, he owned a travel agency in West Philadelphia, through which he was running stolen government checks. Another agent and I went out to interview him, and I admit that I was somewhat flattered when he said he remembered me playing football at Temple. Over the next few weeks I interviewed him several more times, and we struck up a rapport. That didn't stop me, however, from handing the U.S. attorney enough evidence to warrant an arrest.

Because of Sample's tough reputation—and he was a very physical guy—some people in our office were nervous about hauling him in. So six of us, well armed, drove out to his travel agency prepared for the worst. My mistake was having told the others about how well Johnny and I got along. They elected me to go inside and break the news to him.

As I walked into his office, Johnny gave me a big greeting. "Hey, man, sit down." Getting comfortable wasn't a good idea, so I said, "No, Johnny, I can't sit down because you and I have to go outside. I'm afraid I have to put the cuffs on you." He wasn't pleased about it, but he let me do it. The next day when we took him to his arraignment, some photographers shot a picture of Johnny and me together. The caption referred to both of us as football players, and actually mentioned that I'd played at Temple. It was a good picture, and I still have it, but it put an abrupt end to any undercover work. Johnny was convicted and sentenced to three years' probation. In 1974 he violated probation and served one year in Allenwood.

Another big case I got involved with was in 1973. Basketball star Kareem Abdul-Jabbar owned a town house in Washington that he'd lent to his friend Hamaas Abdul Khaalis, the leader of the Hanafi sect of Muslims. Khaalis was involved in a political battle with Elijah Muhammad, the leader of the Black Muslims, when gunmen showed up at the town house—neither Abdul-Jabbar nor Khaalis was there—and murdered five people, including four children. Two women were severely wounded and left for dead. Not long afterward, one of my check-case informants said that some of men involved in those murders were holed up on the sixteenth floor of a tenement on Diamond Street—he indicated Apartment G—and warned that they had weapons with them. I alerted the Philadelphia police homicide squad and assured them that our informant was reliable. Based on that, they got a warrant to break down the door.

As the informant was ours, Saxby and I went along. The police hit the apartment with a SWAT team, stormed in with weapons drawn, and scared the hell out of four little old ladies. That's when someone noticed a Black Muslim symbol next door on Apartment H. I frantically tried to phone my informant while some Philadelphia cops rushed off to get a new warrant. We had the building surrounded, so no one was going to get in or get out, and there we waited until the second warrant arrived. When it did, the police hit Apartment H, and, sure enough, inside were four guys with weapons. Unfortunately, no one ever connected those weapons with the Washington murders, but it was a good collar, and the police knew that some of those guys had been involved.

A few weeks later, my informant came up with the name of the triggerman for the murders, plus a phone number in Chicago where he could be located. He asked if he could have some money for his trouble. I took his information upstairs to the FBI, handed them the triggerman's name and phone number, and added that they needed to pay my informant. An agent asked how much. I suggested a couple of thousand dollars. He said yeah, sure, and I assumed that meant the bureau would take care of it. Several weeks went by and I heard nothing, until I read in the newspaper that the guy in Chicago had been caught. So I went upstairs again to remind the agent that they owed my informant two grand. He confirmed that they'd arrested the triggerman, but insisted that they'd nabbed him on the street and not in the apartment, which meant they didn't owe my informant anything. I said, Hold on a second, he led you right to the guy; if all you had to do was sit there and wait until he came out, you still owe my informant his money. The bureau never did pay up.

CHAPTER SIX

★ ★ ★ ★

ROCKY

A year after winning reelection in 1972, Vice President Spiro Agnew was forced to resign for taking $29,500 in bribes. Under the terms of the Twenty-fifth Amendment to the Constitution, President Nixon appointed Congressman Gerald Ford of Michigan to serve as vice president.

The most polite word I can use to describe post standing is "routine." Officially, no one says it can be downright dead-boring, but it can be downright dead-boring. Although not all posts are created equal. It's not too bad standing just inside the front door of a nice hotel, it's another thing to be stuck outside somewhere at night during a snowstorm, or in the corner of a noisy, smoky kitchen, or on a loading dock next to the garbage cans.

Every few weeks my check investigations would be put on hold and I'd be shipped off somewhere to stand post. They were forgettable experiences, with a few exceptions. I was a post stander at Richard Nixon's inauguration in 1973, positioned on the corner of Ninth Street and Pennsylvania Avenue in the freezing cold for six hours. There's a famous panoramic photo of the inaugural parade taken from a rooftop. In the background of that photo, as the motorcade made its way along the avenue, there's a guy in a black overcoat standing in the street in front of the Justice Department. That's me.

The weather was warmer when I was a post stander in New Orleans for a Nixon visit, but that's when he famously shoved his press secretary, Ron Ziegler, down a ramp. And I was a post stander for Vice President Spiro Agnew one night in San Juan, Puerto Rico. A dozen of us were assigned to eleven posts outside the San Juan Hilton. It was hot, there were mosquitoes, and I was miserable. We stayed at each post for half an hour, then rotated to the next one, until we had made one full circuit and earned a half-hour break. As I came in after my circuit, somebody in the command post said, "The vice president's coming back. We need you on the roof." So my half-hour break was spent on the roof, after which I had to start another five-and-a-half-hour circuit. The lead advance agent for that visit was Dick Stiener. He and I would next work together twenty-four years later, for the Travelers Group.

During the 1972 presidential primary campaign season, I was assigned to the detail protecting Maine senator Edmund Muskie, who was making his bid for the Democratic nomination. He was a terrific guy. Because the detail was small, those of us who were very junior got to do a lot of things that are usually reserved for more senior agents, like advance work. My first trip was to St. Louis with an experienced agent. In those days, budget requirements forced agents to room together, and this one snored. I don't mean he made a little noise, I mean this guy could snore for his country; he was famous throughout the Secret Service. By midnight, he was making sounds like a locomotive. My only recourse was to get out of bed, go downstairs, and rent myself another room. It cost forty dollars, which was a lot of money for me. Still, I learned about advances during those six weeks, and the knowledge served me well later on.

The other memorable thing that happened during that detail was that I got married.

It was a Wednesday afternoon when Barbara and I decided to get married, and two days later, on June 23, 1972, we did. The ceremony was held at eleven o'clock at St. Mary's Church in Alexandria, Virginia. We had lunch at a restaurant afterward, and because I was working from four to twelve, I had to leave at 2:30. Two days later, I was off to Miami to do Muskie's advance for the Democratic convention. That was how our marriage began, and I guess we both saw right away that with all the traveling I had to do, it was going to be difficult.

One of the guys with me on the Muskie detail was Cliff Dietrich, and his death was a low point in my early career. We have had, over the years, all too many agents die on the job. Most of them have died in car accidents, like my friend Pat Lebarge, who was killed along with three other agents in a crash in California. They were assigned to a detail protecting the queen of England on her 1982 visit to the West Coast. They had worked a midnight shift and were tired, and their car went off a mountain road. Six Secret Service personnel were killed in the Oklahoma City bombing. One of them was Don Leonard, who was with me on the Rockefeller detail. No agent on a protective detail has ever died in the line of fire—although many have been shot—and several have been killed doing investigative work. In 1973, Cliff's death was the first I'd encountered in the service, and it brought back traumatic memories of Vietnam.

He'd been reassigned to the president's detail. Nixon was in the Bahamas with his friend Charles "Bebe" Rebozo, and Cliff was on the midnight shift with six other agents, being helicoptered out from Key Biscayne, Florida. The pilot came up short on his landing and went into the sea. When helicopter rotors hit water, the helicopter usually flips over and sinks upside down. The guys inside managed to open a window, and six of the agents got out. Cliff was disoriented and never made it. I heard about it shortly after it happened. One of the agents who got out was named Steve Petro. We weren't related, but friends of mine who saw the name thought it was me.

As a direct result of Cliff's death, the Secret Service devised a helicopter survival training course. At first we worked with the

Dilbert Dunker, which is what the navy uses for its pilots. It's a cockpit that slides down a track, hits the water, flips over, and sinks. You have to get out of your harness, climb out, and swim to the surface. It's a *very* stressful experience. Being upside down in water and in the dark quickly disorients you, and you may think you're going up when you're actually going deeper. You have to learn to follow your bubbles, because they always go up. After a time, the Secret Service got a larger helicopter simulator and required all agents who flew in helicopters to go through that training. In the end, Cliff's death may someday save other lives.

By the fall of 1973, with the war in Vietnam still lingering, and war in the Middle East a real possibility, President Nixon promoted Dr. Henry Kissinger from national security advisor to secretary of state, and the Secret Service was ordered to protect him. Normally, State Department Security—known then as SY—provides protection for the secretary, but for some reason Kissinger wanted the Secret Service to do it, and as far as I know, that's the only time we've ever protected the secretary of state. I was assigned as a temporary agent to that detail. What I remember most about Henry Kissinger is how good he was to the agents. The shift leader, Dick Jagen, and I would spend nights sitting on the couch in the den of Kissinger's town house on Waterside Drive, watching Yankee games with him, while he sat at his desk in his pajamas eating sandwiches and drinking coffee. It wasn't buddy-buddy, but it was the sort of situation that can be uncomfortable for agents. However, our presence didn't bother him. He was easy enough to be around, and because we maintained our professional distance, it worked fine. Most of the time I was with Kissinger, he was either at the State Department until late at night or at the White House. Ordinarily, agents didn't go in the building with him. They'd take him to the door and leave him there, but Jagen—who had a reputation in the Secret Service as a tough guy—decided we had to know where our protectee was and ordered us to stay with him. It was my first day on the job with

Kissinger and my first time inside the White House.

I followed the secretary of state through the entrance at the lower level of the West Wing and into the reception area called F-1. He went into the Situation Room, which is just past a desk where a uniformed division officer checks everyone's passes. There was a couch next to the desk, and because I didn't know what else to do, I sat down. It couldn't have been five minutes later when someone stormed up to me, demanding to know who I was and what I was doing there. In those days people working in the White House didn't wear ID cards around their necks, and agents working PPD didn't wear pins in their lapels. But I had my pin in my lapel, so this fellow knew who I was. And I knew that he was the assistant agent in charge of presidential protection. He had a big job, and I was just a new agent, but many agents on Nixon's PPD were prima donnas and never hesitated to remind everyone else that they were the elite. He barked, "Who are you?"

Slowly standing up, I thought to myself, You can see that I am an agent. I answered his question with one of my own. "Who are you?"

He said, "I'm from PPD."

I said, "How do you do. I'm from Philadelphia."

"What are you doing here? You're not supposed to be inside the White House."

"I'm here with Dr. Kissinger. My protectee is here, and I'm going to stay here in case he needs me."

He pointed to the door. "You need to go outside."

There was no way I was going to let him throw me out of the White House, certainly not on my first day inside, so I told him, "If you want me to leave, you'll have to walk outside and explain that to Dick Jagen, my shift leader, who's waiting in the car."

I can only presume that the fellow knew of Jagen's reputation, because he marched off. He was, of course, merely reflecting the bellicose culture of the Nixon White House. Over the next twenty years, I

walked past that couch several thousand times, and always remembered how rude the supervisor from Nixon's PPD had been. When I
became a senior agent, I decided that, because young agents didn't
know how the White House functioned, we needed to take them under our wings and show them what the White House was all about instead of ordering them out. That necessity was driven home to me one
day while I was walking through the West Wing with Dr. Kissinger. I
didn't know where I was, which says a lot about our training, so when
we turned into a hallway and he moved toward a door, I thought we
were about to leave and instinctively opened that door. It was a closet.
Even Kissinger laughed.

Later that fall, sitting again on the couch at F-1, I couldn't help
but notice there was a lot more activity than usual. Just after I arrived
with the secretary of state, all the other cabinet secretaries showed
up. Clearly, there was some sort of crisis, as the entire government
was gathering. I worried that we were going to war. The moment another agent came in to relieve me, I hurried outside to the car and
turned on the radio to hear that Vice President Agnew had just resigned. I sat there thinking to myself, I was ten feet away from where
it was happening.

When my time with Kissinger ended, I returned to Philadelphia. Six months later, I was permanently transferred back to Washington. I did three weeks' training with the Protective Support
Division, in preparation for an assignment to either the president's
or the vice president's detail. Who's to say which one is better? The
PPD means that you're with the president of the United States. The
VPPD is smaller, and therefore seemingly less important, but you
get a lot more direct hands-on time with the protectee, and you do a
lot more advance work. I was assigned to Vice President Gerald
Ford.

There was no official vice president's residence at the time, so
Ford lived with his family in their own split-level ranch house in
Alexandria, Virginia. We turned the garage, which was right under

his bedroom, into our command post. What I didn't know when I joined the detail was that new agents had to suffer a kind of hazing. Toward the end of my first night on the job, the shift leader told me to "do the follow-up," which meant I had to make certain the follow-up car was ready to go. It was just before six AM when I got in, switched on the ignition, and all hell broke loose. The radio was as loud as it could go, the red lights went, the sirens blasted, the air conditioner was on, everything was turned to maximum. I should have cut off the ignition, but in a moment like that you don't necessarily do what's best; you tend to do what's obvious, which is to turn off everything individually. I know that I woke the vice president—and probably half the neighborhood, too. Rumor had it that, whenever this happened, Ford turned over to his wife Betty and said, "Another new agent."

On August 8, 1974, at about 7:30 in the evening, I was standing post in front of the vice president's office on the second floor of the Executive Office Building. It had been announced that President Nixon would make a speech to the nation that night, and it was expected that he would resign. When the time came for Ford to leave, Bob DeProspero, who was the shift leader, and I stepped into the elevator with the vice president. Before the door closed, Ford turned to me and said, "You're new on the detail, aren't you?" I told him I was and introduced myself. He extended his hand and said, "I'm Jerry Ford." As we shook hands, I thought to myself, this man is two hours away from becoming the president of the United States and he has the presence of mind to introduce himself to me.

To drive him home that night, instead of using just the limousine and a follow-up car, we added a lead car, a tail car, and a police escort. As we made the turn onto his block, there were thousands of people lining the street. Agents working out of the command post in the garage had cordoned off the area as best they could and placed the media across the street. But there were cameras everywhere, and the excitement was incredible. We got him into the house and watched Nixon's resignation speech from the command post.

The next day, with Ford getting ready to be sworn in, the old Nixon PPD showed up to take over. That strained what civility existed between the two details. Some of us stayed with Ford for a few days, which wasn't easy, because the PPD guys had no respect for us. On a few occasions, "discussions" with them came close to fistfights. They finally got rid of us, and because there now was no vice president, we had no place to go. After a while, I was sent to the detail protecting Carl Albert, who was Speaker of the House, and therefore next in line to succeed Ford.

A week or so later, when the Fords moved into the White House, the first reception he hosted as president of the United States was for his Vice Presidential Protection Detail and their wives. To say that the PPD guys were seriously annoyed about this is an understatement. They worked while we sipped cocktails with the president. Then, to show what a truly nice man Ford was, he took us all upstairs to the second floor and gave us a guided tour of the residence. The highlight was the Lincoln Bedroom, where Nixon had burnt holes in the carpet with ashes from his pipe.

Gerald Ford was not only the first man to be appointed vice president under the Twenty-fifth Amendment to the Constitution, but also the nation's first unelected president. Now required to appoint someone to serve as his vice president, Ford turned to an old Republican stalwart, Nelson Rockefeller.

Rockefeller was born in 1908, and the silver spoon in his mouth had been inherited from his grandfather, the legendary "robber baron" John D. Rockefeller, founder of the Standard Oil Company. Nelson Rockefeller was a unique mix of entrepreneur, art collector, benefactor, and public servant. Known to everyone as Rocky, he was appointed to office in 1940 when President Franklin Roosevelt made him assistant secretary of state. In 1950, President Harry Truman named him chairman of the International Development Advisory Board. Three years later, President Dwight Eisenhower selected him to chair his Advisory Committee on Government Organization. In 1958, Rockefeller was elected to the first of four terms as governor of New York State. Two years after establishing himself in Albany, he tried to win the Republican nomination for president but was defeated by Richard Nixon. He tried again in 1964 and was defeated by Arizona Senator Barry Goldwater.

Rocky's first wife was Mary Todhunter Clark, known as "Tod," with whom he had five children. After thirty-two years of marriage, they divorced in 1962, and he very quickly married Margaretta Fitler Murphy, known as "Happy." A tall blonde who had, until then, been married to someone else, she was eighteen years his junior. Their marriage produced two sons. During his second attempt to run for president, it was said that a divorced man could never reach the White House, and it was not until Ronald Reagan's election in 1980 that the old adage was cast aside. Rockefeller's third and final shot at the presidency was foiled in 1968 when Nixon again became the Republican nominee. He resigned as governor in December 1973 to organize a conservative think tank, and eight months later was chosen to be vice president.

During his confirmation hearings, there was great interest in his financial resources. One senator wanted to know, "How much are you worth?"

Rocky's answer was "I don't know," and he probably didn't. The figures being bandied about ranged from $30 million to $1 billion.

Logically assuming that he didn't need a government paycheck, another senator asked, "Are you going to take a salary as vice president?"

Rocky inquired, "By the way, how much is it?" When he was told, sixty thousand dollars a year, he made a face, nodded several times, and said, "Sure, why not?"

When we began protecting him, some agents were concerned that he and his family would be troublesome. He had two young sons—Nelson Jr. was about twelve, and Mark was about nine—and we feared they would expect to be waited on. Our misgivings were absolutely unfounded. There was nothing spoiled or haughty about them. The family was unbelievably down-to-earth, and at no time did any of them ever treat us with anything but the greatest respect. I can say, unequivocally, that Nelson Jr. and Mark were terrific kids, that Happy was a genuinely lovely lady, and that Nelson Rockefeller was the consummate gentleman.

While the president flew on a 707, the vice president's plane was a DC-9. It was comfortable; there was an open area up front set aside for him, his guests, and his staff and room enough for us, some staff, and some press in the back. But Rocky had his own Gulfstream. Not being an air force plane, its call sign was Executive Two. Needless to say, it was a very comfortable plane, which meant that, in the beginning, he didn't bother with our DC-9. He thought he was saving the government money by using his Gulfstream, but we couldn't get enough agents onto Exec Two to keep the detail stocked. Whatever money he was saving us, we spent on flying the agents back and forth commercially. It was only after Jimmy Taylor, the head of the detail, explained the situation that Rocky agreed to use the DC-9.

He was constantly commuting back and forth from New York to Washington, spending as little time as possible in the capital. During his confirmation hearings, for example, he would fly down to Washington in the morning and fly back to New York at night. He was sworn in on December 19, 1974, and for the next two years, we didn't spend a single weekend in Washington. We would leave town with him on Thursday night and not come back until Monday.

My daughter, Michelle, was born in 1973, and from the time she was two until she was six, I didn't see as much of her as I wanted. I missed birthdays and school plays and have regretted every lost minute. It's a common lament of agents working details. We all suffer through the same feelings of guilt. When Michelle was very small, she and her mother would drop me off for a plane to somewhere and days later would pick me up on my return. When people asked Michelle where her dad worked, she would answer, "The airport."

The Rockefellers had a huge apartment in New York on Fifth Avenue, a wonderful house on Foxhall Road in Washington, a large summer home in Seal Harbor, Maine, an eighty-thousand-acre ranch in Texas, a ranch in Venezuela, and a magnificent five-thousand-acre estate overlooking the Hudson River in the Pocantico Hills near Tarrytown, New York, about forty-five minutes north of Manhattan, called Kykuit. Rocky took up residence there in 1960, and along with him came a good part of his art collection. Our office was in the basement, next to the kitchen, facing the storage area for his surplus art. More than one agent commented on the fact that any one of the paintings outside our cramped little office was probably worth more than our combined salaries. When Rocky saw our setup and realized how much time we spent down there, he moved his collection of priceless Picassos and tapestries aside and in their place installed a pool table and a Ping-Pong table for us.

Mark and Nelson Jr. had discovered some long disused garbage dumps on the estate that had been covered up sometime in the nineteenth century. They would dig through them looking for old bottles, and sometimes their father would join them. That's how, one day, we lost the vice president.

Rocky had a Jeep he loved to drive, with his sons bouncing around on the seats, and we'd follow behind in our own cars. That particular day, we were waiting for him on one side of the house and, since it was a very big house, we didn't spot him when he drove away on the other side. He didn't know we weren't with him, and we didn't know he had left. After a while we wondered what was taking him so long and someone went around to the front and noticed that the Jeep was gone. Having no idea where he was, we mobilized all of our cars and headed out en masse at full speed to find him. We checked the places where the boys normally dug for bottles. When we didn't find them there we began searching Tarrytown, stopping at every gas station, desperate to locate the vice president of the United States and his sons. There were a lot of very nervous supervisors trying to second-guess where they'd gone. I don't know when we would have pushed the panic button, but half an hour after he vanished, Rocky and the boys pulled up to the house as if nothing had happened. They'd been at one of the old bottle sites. Jimmy Taylor, the agent in charge, was understandably upset, and, needless to say, that never happened again.

The thing is, there's no procedure for what to do if you lose a protectee. You're just not supposed to do that. Later, when I was agent in charge of the vice president's detail, I would wake up in the middle of the night in a cold sweat, dreaming that I couldn't find him, that he was gone, that the vice president of the United States was somewhere and that I was somewhere else and didn't know where he was. It is every agent's worst nightmare.

Our first big trip with Rockefeller occurred just after he was sworn in, when he took his sons hunting on his ranch near Port Mansfield, Texas. He had stocked the property with antelope and melji, which is an Indian water buffalo. The campsite was out in the middle of the range, and because this was going to be one of those rugged, father-son bonding trips, everyone slept in sleeping bags in tents. The writer F. Scott Fitzgerald was right when he said the rich are different from you and me. Hunting with the Rockefellers wasn't quite like hunting with most people. To begin with, they hunted off the back of the Jeep. No trekking for them. Rocky would spot an animal, tell the driver to stop, stand up, and shoot. Then dinner at the campsite was prepared and served by nine chefs and waiters. Everything was laid out on tables covered with white linen tablecloths and graced with candelabras. It might have been a terrific father-son bonding experience, but it wasn't exactly rustic.

In March 1975, my father, Joseph A. Petro, died from an unexpected heart attack while attending a sporting event in Allentown.

He was only fifty-seven. He had been an All-American football player at St. Joseph's College and remained involved in sports for his entire life. At the time, my youngest brother, Andy, was a freshman at Notre Dame while my middle brother, Tom, had just been married and was soon to move to Philadelphia to begin his own career in the Secret Service. I was in Washington. My mother never got over losing her life's partner at so young an age.

Three months later, I accompanied the vice president and Mrs. Rockefeller to Britain, where they were the guests of Lord Louis Mountbatten at his estate Broadlands, in Romsey, Hampshire. Agents were posted all around the house, and inside it, too, working in tandem with the Special Branch officers who protected Lord Mountbatten. I was working a four-to-twelve shift when, just before midnight, all the alarms started going off. None of us knew what it was about, but judging from the noise, it was a major crisis. Everything was ringing and clanging, lights were coming on all over the estate, and we mobilized to full alert with weapons drawn. That's when someone looked up and saw Mrs. Rockefeller leaning out of her bedroom window. She liked to sleep with the windows open and had no idea that every window in the place was alarmed. Rocky ended the evening by shouting up to his wife in his familiar raspy voice, "Way to go, Happy."

When we got back to the States, the head of Happy's detail was due for some time off, and he asked me if I'd take his place as supervisor in August, when Mrs. Rockefeller and her sons went to Seal Harbor. The Rockefeller compound sat right on the point, overlooking the sea, and was as luxurious as all their other places. Rocky told us he bought the property in the 1930s and paid $35,000 for it, then a pricey sum. There was an old farmhouse on the land, and before he ripped it down, he walked through it and decided there were a few things he wanted to keep. He had a great eye for art, saw something he liked about a vase, and when he built the new house, put it on a mantel. He said he never thought much about it again, for the next twenty-five or thirty years, until sometime in the late 1950s. He needed an insurance evaluation of the property, and the appraisers valued the vase at $50,000.

For the first three weeks of August, it was just Mrs. Rockefeller, the boys, one of their friends, and the detail at the estate. Rocky only came up for the last ten days of the month. I took Mrs. Rockefeller sailing on a small boat in the mornings and accompanied her every afternoon on a long walk through woods. I'd always start off behind her, but eventually she'd ask me to walk with her because she wanted someone to talk with. I never assumed that it would happen, but every day throughout that month, a few minutes into her walk, she'd motion, come walk with me. During one of our conversations I mentioned that my daughter was also in town. After that, every few days, Mrs. Rockefeller would hand me some of her children's old books to give to Michelle, each inscribed to Nelson or Mark.

In the middle of Gerald Ford's vice presidency, Congress voted to fund a residence for the vice president. The house they chose was the former home of the chief of naval operations at the Naval Observatory, which is at the end of Embassy Row on Massachusetts Avenue in northwest Washington. Built originally for the superintendent of the observatory in 1893, it's a wonderful three-story Victorian house with a turret and pointed roof at one corner. There's a big entry hall with a fireplace, and off that are a dining room, living room, and library, all with fireplaces and twelve-foot ceilings. There's a terrific staircase leading up to the main bedrooms, and smaller bedrooms on the top floor. Before the Fords could move in, however, he became president. So the Rockefellers would have been the first vice presidential occupants, except that they did not spend a single night there. They preferred instead to live at their twenty-seven-acre estate on Foxhall Road.

In any case, we still set up protection around the residence. Since it was a naval base, the area was gated. So we established a command post across the street from the house, which sat on a big circle off the main road through the base, and set up posts around the house, including one at the front door and one at the rear door. What Rockefeller did, which I thought was magnanimous and patriotic, was to furnish the house and leave it that way for future vice presidents. He bought the huge eagle sculpture that had been used at Dwight Eisenhower's inaugural in 1953 and installed it in the middle of the driveway circle in front of the house. Rockefeller thought it looked majestic there. So did many of us. Later, when Jimmy Carter was elected president, Vice President Walter "Fritz" Mondale decided it looked too militaristic, had it taken down and put in storage, and replaced it with a modern sculpture. Rockefeller, now out of public life, was incensed. He found out where the eagle was stored and got it back.

Rocky could be generous to a fault, and there were times when money simply didn't matter. He once ordered his Gulfstream back to Maine after it had landed in New York because they had forgotten to bring his sons' bicycles. What could that trip have cost, compared to buying two new bikes? Yet there were other times when he bragged about how parsimonious he could be. We were at Foxhall Road one night, waiting by the cars to take him to a formal dinner, when he came out in his tuxedo and seemed especially pleased with himself. He pointed to his dinner jacket, "Boys, what do you think?" We didn't know what to say, but he didn't give us a chance. "Nineteen fifty-two. I haven't worn this suit since 1952."

Then, too, for a man as sophisticated as he, there were times when Rocky had trouble coping with the real world. I was working at Foxhall Road along with Jim Huse, one of the smartest and most articulate agents I've ever known, when the phone rang. It was the vice president, sounding befuddled. "Boys, I've been trying to call the White House and get hold of the president, and the White House won't let me through."

I think it was Jim who asked, "How are you calling?"

He answered, "I'm dialing 456-1212," which meant he was using an ordinary landline and dialing the main switchboard. "I looked up the number in the phone book."

I couldn't believe it. There was a Signal phone in the house—what we call a "drop line"—so all he had to do was pick it up. No dialing was necessary.

Rocky couldn't understand why he wasn't getting through. "Every time I tell the operator that I'm the vice president, she hangs up on me."

We promised him that if he used the Signal phone, which was just next to the one he'd been calling on, the White House operator would let him speak to the president. He thanked us and never phoned back, so I suppose he got through.

Being as wealthy and as worldly as he was, Rocky definitely knew how to travel. When he married Tod in 1930, their honeymoon was a one-year, around-the-world trip. I traveled with the vice president extensively, and his trips were among the most leisurely I did with any protectee. He knew the best places to stay and built in the best rest stops. One of these trips was a state visit to Iran.

Since oil was first discovered in the Persian Gulf, the region has had strategic importance to the United States. In the sixties and seventies, our best friend in the Gulf was the Shah of Iran, Mohammed Reza Pahlavi. His father, Reza, an army sergeant, had staged a coup in 1921 and named himself emperor four years later. At the outbreak of World War II, fearing that the emperor might align oil-rich Iran with the Nazis, Britain and Russia moved in and forced him to resign in favor of his son. The new shah enjoyed power until 1953, when he was overthrown, but was quickly reinstated through the direct intervention of the Central Intelligence Agency. He remained a staunch ally—sometimes referred to as "our policeman in the Gulf"—up to the oil embargo and ensuing crises of 1973–1974, when his tone hardened noticeably in favor of the oil-producing nations. By modernizing Iran, he provoked conservative Muslims, and soon found that the only way he could retain power was with what-ever brutal oppression he could exert through his secret police, the dreaded SAVAK. By 1979, fundamentalist forces drove him into ex-ile. A radical regime led by the equally brutal Ayatollah Khomeini filled the void, establishing an Islamic republic and bringing about decades of upheaval throughout the Gulf. The shah fled to Latin America, took ill, was treated in the United States, but was refused permanent residence by President Carter, and died in Egypt in July 1980 at the age of sixty.

Rockefeller's visit to the shah in March 1976 came at a time when the United States desperately needed him on our side to assure that another oil crisis would not cripple the West. I was on the ad-vance team that arrived in Iran a few days before the vice president, and from the moment we got there it was clear that the shah's regime was doomed.

One of our first meetings was at the U.S. embassy with a CIA agent who would only speak to us in "the bubble room." That was a place, deep inside the embassy, totally encased in plastic so that no one outside using a microwave eavesdropper could hear what we were say-ing. He warned us that there were going to be big anti-shah demon-strations and suggested we return to our hotel. We followed his advice, and within a matter of minutes, I looked out my window and saw tens of thousands of agitated Iranians lining the streets for as far as I could see. They were chanting and shouting and marching down the block toward the hotel. The locked door of my room would never be enough to withstand them, and I knew that if they stormed the place, we would all be dead. Luckily, this time, the crowd went on past the hotel. In November 1979, the same kind of crowd stormed the em-bassy in Teheran and held fifty-two American hostages for 444 days.

Next day, one of our agents went to Shiraz, one stayed in Tehran, and I flew out to Kish Island, in the middle of the Persian Gulf, where Rockefeller was going to spend three days. Today the island has been developed, but then it was a tiny, private preserve owned by the shah.

We landed in a USAF Beachcraft, because there was no real airport, and were greeted by the landing strip caretaker, who was one of the few people on the island.

It is a stunningly beautiful place, off-limits to ordinary Iranians. The shah had built a palace for himself there and small villas for his guests. Rockefeller was going to stay in the prime minister's villa, which sat right on a white beach with water lapping quietly on the sand and sharks swimming a hundred yards offshore. Besides the shah's palace and guest houses, there was a tanker that had run aground at one end and lay rusting on its side, a handful of fisherman who lived in nearby huts, and one of the world's great French restaurants.

Down the island's single road, past the guest villas, there was a modern one-story building where the shah had imported chefs and everything they needed to create fantastic meals. Because money was no object, and because he couldn't take his guests to Paris, he simply brought Paris to his guests. It was the most gorgeous restaurant I've ever seen. The French chefs, and the French waiters in tuxedos, were in residence when the shah and his guests were in residence, and that's where everyone ate all their meals. That first evening, I wandered down there not knowing what to expect, and was greeted with a full menu. The food was absolutely fantastic, and perhaps best of all, there was no bill at the end of the meal. The next morning, there wasn't much to do in terms of advance work, because there was only that one road in from the tiny airstrip, so I drove around for a while, until I was suddenly stopped by a Jeep blocking the road. At that point, twelve men riding on horses came down the road, led by the shah.

When the vice president arrived, I briefed the agents about the island and the French restaurant. I assured them that as far as their meals were concerned, I'd personally made all the proper arrangements and magnanimously told them to order anything they wanted on the menu. For our entire stay there, all of us—the whole entourage, including Rockefeller and the shah—ate breakfast, lunch, and dinner there.

On our final evening, the shah threw a party for all of us. Somewhere along the way, Rocky had bought himself a tiny 35mm camera—they were new and cutting-edge in those days—and as the evening wore on, he started taking pictures. Here he was, one of the wealthiest and perhaps most sophisticated men in the world, not to mention vice president of the United States, and he was lining everybody up for a group photo like someone's father at a wedding, barking out orders, "Hey, shah, move to your right. No, shah, get closer. Yeah, shah, stand there."

The opulence of the shah's lifestyle on Kish Island was incredible. The caretaker told me he was there fewer than thirty days a year. History is filled with the tales of similar monarchs and their lifestyles—and their demise.

Throughout my Secret Service career I carried a .357 Magnum revolver. I worried about keeping a gun in the house with a young child, and so did the Secret Service. In training session after training session, we discussed the dangers of having weapons at home. Training modules built around safety issues—designed purposely to scare the hell out of us—included videos of kids playing with guns and getting killed. When Michelle was old enough to know about the gun, I explained to her how dangerous it was, showed it to her, warned her that she must never touch it, and insisted that she must never allow anyone else to touch it. I never left it around when I wasn't there, and I kept it locked in a briefcase in my closet where she couldn't reach it when I was. I wasn't so much concerned that she would go near it, but I didn't want any of her friends to discover it and take it out.

Some agents wear a weapon when they're off duty. I did when I was in Philadelphia, running criminal investigations, just in case I bumped into a perpetrator who wasn't happy to bump into me. But

I didn't bother wearing it off duty in Washington because I didn't think it was necessary. Anyway, I'm not fond of guns. The only gun I owned was the weapon I was issued. I never fired it in anger, and, as far as I'm aware, only two protective agents in the Secret Service have ever fired shots in anger. That was in 1950, when Puerto Rican nationalists tried to assassinate President Truman. But once, with Rockefeller, I came very, very close to being the third.

It was June 21, 1976. We were in a motorcade, driving through small towns in New Jersey, on our way back to Newark Airport from an event. People lined the route because a presidential or vice presidential motorcade—with all the outriders and police cars and limousines and cars following the limousines—is a special sight. We were going about thirty-five mph through one of those towns, and Rocky had his window down halfway waving to people. I was on the right rear seat of the follow-up car, with an Uzi submachine gun on my lap. My window was wide open, and I was doing what I was supposed to do, which was to look at the crowd ahead of the vice president's limousine.

Suddenly, to my horror, at the front of the crowd I spotted a young boy go into a combat stance and raise his arms. He was holding a weapon and pointing it straight out into the street.

I screamed, "Gun," and other agents noticed, it too. Instinctively, I raised the Uzi, aiming it right at this kid. There was absolutely no time to think about this; it all came down to training. With my weapon pointing directly at him, I was a fraction of a second away from pulling the trigger—a fraction of a second away from killing this kid because when we shoot we don't miss—when something didn't look right. The gun he was holding was red. I was now only fifteen feet away from him—this was all happening very fast, as the motorcade was speeding away—and my finger was tensing to squeeze the trigger when I realized that he was holding a water pistol.

Agents were already out of their cars as we speed by. They tackled the kid, and by then we were gone. My heart was racing, and I broke out into a cold sweat as I moved my finger away from the trigger and brought the Uzi back inside the window to my lap. He was fifteen years old, and had come within a millisecond of getting killed. He was looking straight ahead, almost in an hypnotic state. His head was cocked a funny way, and he was in a combat position. The nightmare haunted me for years. It was the red gun that made me stop.

If the water pistol had been black, I would have pulled the trigger.

★ ★ ★ ★

CHAPTER SEVEN

MOVING UP IN THE WORLD

Nelson Rockefeller chose not to run for vice president, and Gerald Ford lost in 1976, giving way to a peanut farmer from Plains, Georgia, named James Earl Carter.

When Gerald Ford announced that he would seek a second term in 1976, he asked Nelson Rockefeller to be his running mate. But by then Rocky was ready to call it quits. That didn't mean, however, that he wasn't going to keep his hand in the game. There were a lot of political battles going on—particularly with Ronald Reagan making a run against Ford for the Republican nomination—and we took Rocky to the party's convention that summer in Kansas City. He spent much of his time on the floor with the New York delegation supporting Ford. They were right next to the Utah delegation, which was supporting Reagan. In politics things can get heated, and when one of the New Yorkers yanked a Reagan sign away from one of the Utah delegates, someone from Utah ripped out the New Yorkers' phone. A scuffle started, and Rockefeller, who was still the vice president, was in the middle of it. Agents jumped in immediately and extracted him from the melee. The following morning at the hotel, I was in the elevator with the vice president and some other agents when he turned to us and said with gleeful expectation, "Well, boys, what are we going to do tonight?"

The agent in charge, Jimmy Taylor, joked back. "Mr. Vice President, you get into a fight tonight and you're on your own."

With only a few months left in Rocky's vice presidency, it was announced that Mrs. Rockefeller would make an official trip to Moscow. So in October 1976, I flew there as lead advance agent with another agent, Roy Wilson. Our Secret Service counterparts in the USSR were a pair of lieutenant colonels in the KGB, Igor Sinitzin and Alexander Turnovsky. The four of us were joined by a young, good-looking, well-dressed woman who spoke perfect English and was introduced to me as the representative of Intourist, the Soviet agency that handled foreigners' visits. During the cold war, you couldn't travel anywhere in the USSR without Intourist overseeing your trip. She was meant to be a temptation, but of course, she, too, was a KGB officer, as were most Intourist officials.

We checked into the National Hotel on Red Square, and at some point while looking around my room, I happened to notice the phone next to my bed. There was nothing particularly distinctive about it. I looked at it simply because it was there. I then left the room to start advancing Mrs. Rockefeller's visit. It was later, when I got back to my room, that I noticed my phone again and realized it wasn't the one I'd seen earlier. I followed the wire to the wall and had to laugh because there was residual plaster on the floor where someone had drilled a new hole for the bug.

We traveled through Moscow looking at the sites Mrs. Rockefeller was going to visit. The two KGB officers led the way, with the nicely dressed lady and me in tow. What fascinated me was that I never saw either of these guys show any credentials. During the cold war, Russia was famous for having huge lines everywhere. People had to line up no matter where they went. At the GUM department store on Red Square, customers actually had to wait on three separate lines.

They stood on the first line to pick out what they wanted to buy, then stood on the second line to pay for it, then stood on the third line with their paid receipt to pick up the item they'd just bought. If you went to a restaurant, you waited in line to get a table. Then, if there were only six people eating in the restaurant, which meant there were nineteen empty tables, the maître d' would seat you at the same table with the other people, leaving the nineteen tables empty. The rules applied to everybody, except some people, like my new KGB pals. These two would march us right up to the front of every line, say something to the guard, and we would be whisked in. The line at Lenin's Tomb was a mile long. But not for us. And no one standing in the line behind us ever complained.

Red Square was filled with old ladies in babushkas sweeping the streets, and in the hotel, on every floor, there was a woman sitting at a desk where you left your key. The whole country was overstaffed and underefficient. I didn't have anything in my room to worry about, and I don't think Mrs. Rockefeller had anything either, although during her stay we stationed an agent at her door to make certain nobody got in. When the maids came to clean, the agent went in with them.

The day before her arrival, I was part of a small group attending a meeting in the Kremlin with the head of the KGB's Ninth Directorate protection service. I'd been asked by the CIA station chief at our embassy to make a list of the Russians attending this meeting. Arriving at the Kremlin, we were escorted into a beautiful office and introduced to a man who looked as if he'd stepped straight out of Hollywood casting. Maj. Gen. Mikhail Dokuchayev was a bulky fellow, then in his fifties, with a well-worn round face. He also had a barrel-chest full of medals, including the Hero of the Soviet Union—the equivalent of our Congressional Medal of Honor—which he'd won as a seventeen-year-old during the battle of Stalingrad. This was also a man who had plenty of skeletons in his closet, because that's how you get to be a KGB general.

Another thing that struck me was his huge desk and the table next to it overflowing with telephones. He must have had fifteen of them. I'd never seen so many phones in anyone's office and was fascinated as to why he needed them. It turned out that the Russians had not yet been able to build multiline phones, so that every line worked off a separate instrument. They were clever enough, however, to put a little light on each phone so that when one rang, the general wouldn't have to pick up all fifteen to take a call. I remember thinking that the Soviets have nuclear weapons and intercontinental ballistic missiles, yet they can't create a more sophisticated telephone.

Our discussions went well, which didn't surprise me, because the Secret Service and the KGB have always had very good relations. This in spite of the fact that they were a military organization with a dark past and we are strictly a law enforcement agency with a very noble and proud past. Yet the KGB was the agency that protected the Soviet leaders, and in that regard, we had similar problems, similar methods, and a similar outlook. We understood each other.

The interpreter who'd come with us from the embassy was very nervous in Dokuchayev's presence—the KGB had that effect on most Russians—and while I began speaking to him in English, she repeated to him what I'd just said—in English. He listened to her and answered in Russian, which she then translated into English for me. I said something else in English, which she repeated to him in English, and he answered in Russian. It went on that way for three or four questions and answers before any of us realized that he understood English perfectly.

At the end of the meeting, I wrote down Dokuchayev's name phonetically to take back to the CIA station chief. But the U.S. regional security officer saw me doing that, worried that I might not have written it correctly, and asked Dokuchayev, "Can you please spell your name for us?"

Dokuchayev was annoyed by the question, stood up, announced

in English, "The American embassy knows very well how to spell my name," and walked out. Years later, I reminded him of the meeting. I said, "I'm not sure that the embassy did know how to spell your name."

The KGB facilitated everything and couldn't have been more helpful, except that they did it in their own inimitable style. Toward the end of the visit, Mrs. Rockefeller hinted to someone on her staff that she really wanted to attend an opera at the Bolshoi Theatre. We weren't sure it would be possible to add that to the schedule, especially since tickets took the average Russian years to get, but when we spoke to our KGB hosts about it, they responded, "No problem." On the appointed night, about an hour before the performance, I accompanied one of my KGB counterparts to the theater where, once inside, he pointed to the various boxes. "Which do you think she would like best?"

I shrugged, "Which one's available?"

He picked one close to the side of the stage and proclaimed, "We will take that one."

By now, people were arriving for the opera, including the people in the seats he'd chosen. He walked into the box and simply asked them to leave. I was aghast. Who knew how long those people had waited for tickets and planned for that evening? I knew that if Mrs. Rockefeller ever found out, she'd be furious. I also knew that if the press ever found out, it would be extremely embarrassing. If the situation was reversed, if the Secret Service had ever dared to pull such a stunt at the Kennedy Center simply to appease a Russian dignitary, we'd have a war on our hands. This was the KGB, however, and the people in the box left quietly. I never mentioned it to Mrs. Rockefeller.

I spent the evening sitting in the hallway, in front of the door leading into the box, in a whispered political discussion with my two KGB friends. Both of them wanted to know, "Why is it that we can get along so well, and our countries cannot?" Here it was 1976.

America and Russia were both armed to the teeth, capable of destroying the entire planet, and neither of these Russians agents could understand why we were supposed to hate each other. Then again, neither could I. They were my age, they looked like me, we all had kids, and we all had the same issues. We also shared the same fears. I'm afraid their questions went unanswered.

Russia under the Soviets was a society in which so many questions didn't get answered, mainly because there were no answers. It was a society overflowing with illogical contradictions. At the end of Mrs. Rockefeller's visit, after she had left Russia, the two KGB officers produced a bottle of vodka. Along with the Intourist woman and a few people from our side, we went up to my room, and there they poured full glasses and we drank to peace and friendship. After that, they drove Roy Wilson and me to the airport, where a second bottle of vodka appeared and was emptied to more toasts. They then delivered us to the edge of the customs area, where they said goodbye. Roy and I turned in all our rubles—because a large sign right there said we could be arrested if we tried to smuggle rubles out of the country—went through customs, and checked in for an Aeroflot flight to Copenhagen. The woman behind the counter now announced that our bags were overweight and insisted that we owed the Soviet airline $250. I got out a government travel request to pay her, but she stated, "No GTR, only rubles." So I reached for some traveler's checks but she wouldn't accept them either. "Rubles, only," she demanded.

But the law explicitly prohibited us from having any because we'd come across the customs barrier, so I tried to reason with her. "How did you expect us to pay with rubles when we've already been through customs, which means we've already gotten rid of our rubles?"

She pointed to the Bureau de Change on the other side of the Customs and Immigration barrier, which was a low rope with a sign that warned, "Do Not Cross." She said, "Go there." But that meant going back into Russia without passing through Customs and Immigration and then coming back to her counter, again bypassing Customs and Immigration. I objected but she persisted, "Just climb over the rope." Convinced that I would be thrown into some Gulag, I stepped over the rope, bought some rubles, nervously stepped back over the rope, and paid her. Nobody said a word. That's how things worked in the USSR. That's why the rope was low enough for people to climb over.

There was a stark difference in style between Nelson Rockefeller and Walter Mondale. The new vice president couldn't wait to move into the official residence at the Observatory. He and his family would be the first to live there and to enjoy the beautiful Rockefeller furniture. I was now a shift leader on his detail, heading up the transportation section, which was my first supervisory job.

I won't say I disliked Mondale, but he was slow to warm to and didn't necessarily try very hard to warm to us. Maybe it had something to do with how the new administration didn't much care about the ways of Washington. During the transition—those nine weeks after the election and before the swearing in—we spent time with Mondale at the Carter farm in Plains, Georgia. There was a guest house out by a lake on the property, which is where Mondale stayed. It was very rustic. Jimmy Carter might have liked that, but I'm not sure Walter Mondale did. I got up one morning and went over there early, only to discover the vice president–elect and his staff were eating beans for breakfast, because there was nothing else to eat.

Right from the start, the Carter White House was terribly cost conscious. For example, we would fly cars to events around the country. They told us to save money by trucking them. That ended up being even more expensive, because the cars often arrived damaged. Carter was known for his micromanagement of everything, and one of the stories that circulated around the White House was that he personally had to sign off on anyone using the White House tennis court. The cost-saving decision that affected us the most was his decision not to use the standard presidential limousines, insisting instead on riding in a Lincoln Town Car. I can appreciate the fact that he didn't want to look extravagant, but what he didn't know was that to armor the Lincoln Town Cars cost more than our armored stretch Cadillacs.

Carter used to jog either on the towpath at Georgetown University or around the south grounds of the White House. That was fine with the Secret Service, as most agents can hold their own when it comes to running with a protectee. But the deputy agent in charge of PPD, Steve Garmon, once found himself with a jogged-out president and no cars. Steve and a couple of other agents were running with him that day in Georgetown. The cars were waiting at the appointed place when the president turned to Steve and said, "I'm going to run a little farther today." So Steve got on the radio and told the drivers to meet them at the next pickup point. About halfway there, Carter decided, "Let's go back to the original pickup point." This time when Steve got on the radio to call the drivers, he couldn't reach them. This wouldn't happen today with cell phones, but there were dead spots for the radios, and they were in one.

Steve had no luck getting in touch with them all the time that he and the President were running back to the starting point. When they got there, Steve saw a phone booth. He knew if he called the White House, they'd contact the cars, but he was in jogging shorts and didn't have any money. So he dialed zero and got the Bell operator on the line, introduced himself, and asked for the White House. The operator said sure, and hung up. Shades of Rocky getting the same response. Of course, he eventually got through, and the cars arrived immediately. Later, someone gave him a plaque with a quarter in the middle of it.

The Mondale family was not particularly athletic, although they enjoyed skiing vacations. We had a lot of skiing experience with

Jerry Ford, and there were several agents who handled themselves expertly on the slopes. Because the vice president was always covered with a hat, goggles, and ski gear, he wasn't an easily recognizable target, so the main worry when skiing with him was injury. Still, we practiced "attacks on the principal" on ski slopes, just as we practiced AOPs wherever we'd go.

I left the Mondale detail after about a year for one of the most fascinating areas of the Secret Service. The Intelligence Division was an outgrowth of the Warren Commission's investigation into the assassination of John F. Kennedy. The Secret Service realized it needed to do a better job of distilling intelligence information and maintaining liaison with the intelligence services and the FBI. Intelligence has become very sophisticated over the years and is today an essential part of protecting the president and others.

Inside the division, there is the Domestic Intelligence Branch, and the Foreign Intelligence Branch. Both are staffed with agents who work alongside civilian research specialists tracking cases and sharing information with the CIA, the Defense Department, the FBI, and dozens of other sources. They analyze information, distill it, and distribute it to the people who need to know. Shared information is a hot topic today in the wake of 9/11, but the Secret Service has been sharing information for a long time. There is reason to believe that the FBI had information in Dallas in 1963 that it did not pass along to us. The selective exchange of intelligence was not an isolated incident at that time.

John Hinckley had come to the FBI's attention prior to his attempt to kill Ronald Reagan. Granted, it was marginal information, and there is an argument to be made that it was too marginal to pass along. Yet, the FBI did have a file on him, and there is also an argument that goes, if they had passed the information along, we might have interviewed him, and he might not have bothered to show up that afternoon in front of the Hilton Hotel. Then, too, the FBI had information on a lot of people like John Hinckley, and it's easy to criticize with hindsight. In that sense, it's no different than the intelligence that was not shared before 9/11. Some of the intelligence was too vague and some of it didn't make any sense until after the fact. That said, it's very difficult to look at a single piece of intelligence swimming around in a whole sea of intelligence and pick something out as being significant. It's much easier to look back and see what was missed. Unfortunately, we only know for sure what we missed when it's too late.

The Intelligence Division Duty Desk is manned twenty-four hours a day by three agents and one supervisor who take calls referred from the White House. It's here that we deal with all the people who demand to speak to the president. On good days, we get three or four nuisance calls. On bad days, usually around the full moon, we get twice as many. The rest of the time, we coordinate information between various people and field offices within the Secret Service and operate as a kind of command post. If somebody wants to get hold of the director on a Saturday night at ten o'clock, they know that the Duty Desk is always manned, and that the phones there will always be answered.

Whenever an oddball called the White House, our routine was simple. We'd listen to what he or she had to say and would try to get as much information as possible. If the information was disconcerting, we'd run a trace on the line and, if need be, send out the cavalry. One night while I was there, a caller started making very specific threats. The system worked perfectly, and police officers in Illinois arrested him in a phone booth, still on the line with us. Most of the disturbing calls we take are either from people in mental institutions or from very disturbed people who ought to be. My guess is that such calls account for about 95 percent of the threats against the president and vice president.

The problem is the remaining 5 percent. The Secret Service needs to find out who those people are and to determine whether they have the capacity, the means, and the opportunity to carry out their threat. Every sinister call, and every sinister letter and every sinister fax and every sinister e-mail, is looked at and evaluated. Information is forwarded to regional offices where agents open files on these people and begin to investigate them. The same applies when someone is referred to us. Almost everyone who comes to our attention is interviewed. Agents need to determine several things. One is to find out with whom we're dealing. Once we establish a person's identity, we run a very thorough background check. We want to know where that person went to school, whether that person has ever been arrested, who his friends are, and, in essence, find out everything we can about that person. We then do the most important thing of all, and it is, decidedly, also the most difficult thing of all: We determine whether or not this person qualifies as a dangerous subject.

If the answer is yes, the person is put on a watch list. These people are then interviewed routinely, sometimes as often as every thirty days. Most of them are in mental hospitals, and the interview serves to confirm that they're still there. If the president is due in town, we need to be sure that the person won't be out on a day pass. If he is, we find him. It's a certainty, for example, that John Hinckley is on a watch list. Just because his attempt on the president happened a long time ago, and just because someone somewhere proclaims him mentally stable enough to be out on weekends, that doesn't mean the Secret Service has forgotten him, or ever will.

We also want to know how certain people are feeling. In cases where people on the watch list are being treated for mental problems, agents may talk to their doctors. Though the patient-doctor confidentiality is an issue, it can be helpful to get the doctor's opinion about a person's proclivity for violence. We find that most doctors take our discussions seriously. If, after all that, a person poses some sort of danger, even if he or she hasn't actually committed a crime, it's not unheard of for us to impress upon the person's family that their relative needs further psychiatric help. If that doesn't work, or the family refuses, we have the right to go court to ask that someone be committed.

Intelligence agents are sent into the field for every presidential visit. They work with the local field office and local police intelligence to identify potential problems. I always looked for what we called "unusual direction of interest." There are letter writers, for example, who send mail by the ton to the president. They may not be outwardly dangerous, but by sending so many letters, they are demonstrating obsessive behavior. We interview and reinterview those sorts of people because we need to get a sense of what's going on in their head. In many cases, the best way to do that is to go to their homes and see what's on their walls, see if any guns are visible. You can get a really good idea of whom you're dealing with when you can see how they live.

There is an intelligence agent riding in the president's motorcade, and there are intelligence agents at every event, in the crowds, looking for faces they recognize. Often you hear intelligence agents complain that a lot of their work is routine, and that some of the work seems like a waste of time. But it's very difficult to judge how dangerous a person might be. There's no doubt that the Intelligence Division is underappreciated because there is no way to quantify their successes. It's their failures that make the papers. The classic example of that was the interview of Sara Jane Moore the night before she fired a shot at President Ford. The agent who interviewed her, the late Gary Yauger, was hauled up before Congress. In his testimony, he discussed how we do this sort of thing and how he came to determine that Moore was not dangerous. Ultimately, Congress concluded that, based on what Yauger knew that night and, given the circumstances, he made the best assessment he could at the time. Obviously, it's a judgment call, but it weighs heavily on intelligence agents.

Intelligence is an imprecise science, at best. We have never been able to use intelligence in predicting an assassination attempt. But it can help to establish a deterrence. Once you've identified someone who might be thinking about violence, the single act of interviewing that person can be significant. When an agent shows up at someone's door, the person might conclude, They know who I am, I can't get away with it, so I'd better not do anything. Again, there's no way to accurately measure the success rate of deterrence, and it's impossible to know the number of attempts that have been stopped this way. But there must be some. Suppose that, of the bulk of the people who make nuisance calls or write threatening letters, 95 percent don't have the means or the capability or the opportunity to do something. Then suppose that, of the remaining 5 percent, there is some percentage—minuscule, perhaps 0.001 percent—who do have the means or the capability or the opportunity to do something. The fact that they don't then carry out their threats suggests that the Secret Service agent who interviewed them had an effect.

From Intelligence, in 1979, I was promoted to a very substantial position at the Treasury Department as special assistant to the secretary (SATS). I was in the service just ten years, and I was already working directly for the secretary. I served two: Michael Blumenthal and G. William Miller. I reported to the assistant secretary for enforcement and operations, Richard Davis, who'd been an assistant to Watergate prosecutor Leon Jaworski. Davis was a smart guy who oversaw Customs, the Bureau of Alcohol, Tobacco, and Firearms (ATF), and the Office of Foreign Asset Control (OFAC).

My office was small, looking out to Fifteenth Street and the south grounds of the White House, but it was directly above the secretary's office. He and I shared a private elevator. Well, to be more precise, his private elevator came up into my office. When Stu Knight, then director of the Secret Service, took me to my office on my first day, he said to me, "Your most important job is to keep this office." It afforded the Secret Service a unique position within the Treasury Department, and he didn't want to lose it. We, of all the agencies inside Treasury, had the most direct access to the secretary.

"Keep the office," he said over and over again. And I did, for two years.

Like the Intelligence Division, the SATS job had been created by the Warren Commission, which felt that Treasury wasn't well enough aware, on a day-to-day basis, of what the Secret Service was doing. In the fall of 1979, when Fidel Castro arrived to address the United Nations, I took Richard Davis to New York so that he could see firsthand what we do.

The Secret Service had set up a command post on the second floor of a building directly across the street from the Cuban mission, which is on Lexington Avenue at Thirty-eighth Street. The visit was coordinated with the New York Police Department, which had set up barricades everywhere. Now, Castro routinely does things at very odd hours, like landing at Kennedy at 3:00 AM and flying back to Havana at 3:45 AM. It gave me a chance to show Davis how we could cope with anything at any hour. There were thousands of police lined up, literally shoulder to shoulder, from the Cuban mission to the United Nations. We rode in the motorcade, in the backseat of the spare limousine. I told Davis that if he wanted to get the full Secret Service experience, we'd put a beard on him and he could be the decoy.

Castro gave his speech, then came straight back to Thirty-eighth Street, where he spent most of his time. The night of his departure, we pulled both limousines into the mission's two-car garage and shut the doors so that he could get into the car safely and so that nobody would know which car he was in. The way the cars were lined up, the spare limousine was closest to the mission's back door. For some reason Davis and I were alone in the garage with the two drivers, standing near the spare limousine, when the door flew open and Fidel was there, standing in front of us. I knew he was big, but I never realized that he was so tall and so imposing. He looked at us and started to get into the backseat of the spare limousine, until I put up my hand to stop him, and motioned, "It's that car." He was surprised, but turned and went to his limousine, and by then the detail guys were there, too.

During those years that I was the SATS, civil war broke out inside the Secret Service. A political struggle began between two factions, and it would have severe repercussions for many years to come. It was a sad time. Although I served the secretary of the treasury, I was also, as a practical matter, the staff assistant to the director of the Secret Service. I'd walk back and forth from Treasury to headquarters every day, sometimes more than once. The director, Stu Knight, was a man I respected enormously. A Canadian by birth, Knight had served in the U.S. military during World War II and had won the Silver Star for bravery in the Pacific. He was dignified and impressive both physically and in his manner. He had been a very good agent and, as director, skillfully balanced the protective and the investigative functions. His deputy, Mike Weinstein, had been my first boss in Philadelphia. Weinstein was the smartest and best manager in the Secret Service. A man of unquestioned integrity, he should have succeeded Stu Knight in the director's office, and that he never became director was an enormous loss to the Secret Service.

At the time, the agent in charge of Los Angeles was Bob Powis. He was a powerful figure in the service because Los Angeles was a big and important field office. Some people jokingly referred to him as "the West Coast director." He was a dynamic guy who commanded a staunch loyalty—field agents worshipped him—over the years. A whole faction of Powis guys permeated the service. Knight saw the challenge coming from Powis and did what I thought was a clever thing. Instead of leaving Powis on the West Coast, where he had great independence, Knight brought Powis back to Washington as assistant director of protective operations. It was all about adhering to the old adage, Keep your friends close and your enemies closer. Knight wanted to keep an eye on Powis, and perhaps neutralize him, by removing Powis from the investigative side of the Secret Service where he'd earned his potent reputation. Unfortunately, it backfired. Factions quickly formed as Powis put his old Los Angeles guys in various senior protective positions.

There are, I suppose, four categories of agents in the Secret Service. There are those who really like investigation work and don't want to do anything else. There are those who want to do protective work, perhaps because they love the glamour of being at the White House and don't want to do anything else. Then there are agents who go back and forth, making a point of doing both throughout their career. And finally, there are agents who choose training or technology and prefer to manage their careers that way. But there are very strong forces on all sides, pulling in all directions, and, as a result, ill feelings have developed between the investigative and protective factions. Some agents refer to other agents as the "protection pukes" or "investigation pukes," and those tags can stay with you for your whole career. The lines became very distinct during the Knight-Powis battle and contributed to a lot of the problems that the Secret Service had at that time.

A showdown was coming, and I knew that if Powis won, I'd be viewed as a Knight guy and would fall victim to it. That's when a lucky opportunity arose. I was selected to go to Princeton University as a fellow at the Woodrow Wilson School of Public and International Affairs. I was the first agent to go there since 1966, when Stu Knight attended. So, in the fall of 1980, I started graduate school.

The Reagan election in November 1980 tipped the scales toward Powis, who'd known the new president during his years as California's governor. Powis soon became deputy assistant secretary of the treasury, working for the assistant secretary of enforcement and operations, to whom the director of the Secret Service reported. An alliance quickly formed between Powis and John Simpson, who'd been agent in charge of the Reagan detail during the 1976 Republican nomination campaign. As Powis moved up, so did Simpson. They squeezed Knight and Weinstein from both sides, and before long my friends were gone and John Simpson was director.

I returned from Princeton in 1981 to a routine job in Internal Affairs, and, with Powis and Simpson now running things, I did not feel encouraged. When Powis moved on, Simpson shifted his own guys—most of them refugees from the Spiro Agnew vice presidential detail—into positions of authority, replacing the old Powis team. The Knight-Powis battle now became a Knight-Powis-Simpson struggle. But then, for some reason, John Simpson promoted me to deputy assistant director for public affairs, making me an official spokesperson for the Secret Service. I never knew why he did it, except that I might have been the token Knight guy they needed to keep around in order to make the civil war look more civil. I didn't like the way Simpson ended up where he was, or what he did to Knight.

Public affairs was new territory for me, and I wasn't always at ease dealing with the press. However, one of my predecessors was a really sharp character named Jack Warner, and he'd once been interviewed on a midnight radio show in Washington hosted by Larry King. Jack was with him for a couple of hours, and no one ever gave a better interview about the Secret Service. When I took the job, I got a tape of that interview and listened to it every now and then, because it was a master class in public affairs. It was Jack on that show who best summed up November 22, 1963: "The Secret Service failed." He told Larry King to forget the circumstances surrounding that day and to forget the excuses and to put everything else into this one single context: "We lost the president." Jack Warner was the best, and I listened to his interview with Larry King because I wanted to be that good.

Dealing with the media is a risky business and I learned quickly that I could never win. I would do an hour-long interview with a reporter, and when the story ran, invariably something would be misquoted, or exaggerated, or embellished, or it wouldn't come out the way I intended. Jack was famous for saying that every time he gave an interview, the next day the director would want to know, How could you say what you said in this second paragraph? Jack's customary response would be, "I don't know how I said that, but look at paragraph eight, that's pretty good."

I could never convince someone that I didn't say what I'd been quoted as saying because the journalists were always in control. Part of the problem was the fact that I was a Secret Service agent, not a journalist. The rest of the problem was that the Service didn't approach public affairs the way I thought it should. We needed to be out there telling our story. Instead, we were holding back, emphasizing the word "secret" in Secret Service. We needed to have a professional do this job, not an agent. We wouldn't allow a journalist to protect the president, so why did we have agents fuctioning as journalists?

After almost two years in public affairs, John Simpson promoted me to assistant special agent in charge of Ronald Reagan's protective detail. And so began four amazing years.

★ ★ ★ ★

CHAPTER EIGHT

WORKING FOR THE
PRESIDENT

*As hard as we try to plan for every possible problem, each trip creates
new problems.*

I met Ronald Reagan on Easter Monday, April 3, 1983. It was my
first day on the detail. I was ushered into the Oval Office just before
he went outside to the south grounds for the traditional Easter Egg
Roll. Bob DeProspero introduced us and asked me to escort the
president. He was very gracious, but it was a perfunctory meeting,
and after shaking hands with me, all he said was, "Welcome and
good luck." There was nothing historical about it, except that it was
the beginning of our four-year relationship.

This was the third time I'd worked for Bob, and I'm sure he had
some influence over the director's decision to bring me to PPD.
He'd been my shift leader briefly on the Ford vice presidential detail
and my supervisor on the Rockefeller detail. He'd been deputy agent
in charge of the PPD when the president was shot, and was given
the top job when Jerry Parr was appointed assistant director of the
Secret Service.

Bob was a short, good-looking fellow, serious and dignified, from

West Virginia who was only a few years older than me. He'd been a wrestler in high school and at the University of West Virginia. A strictly-by-the-book kind of guy who rarely smiled, he joined the Secret Service right after college and was as good a protection agent as the Secret Service has ever had. I learned a lot from him and found that on those occasions when we disagreed, Bob usually ended up being right. This was a man who set such high standards for himself that even those agents who felt intimidated by him worked doubly hard.

Bob took over the PPD at a time when everyone was determined that there simply could not be another attempt on the president's life. He was the perfect guy at the perfect time to do that job. A mutual friend, Tom Quinn, who is one of the most thoughtful and innovative agents I've ever known—and who looks strikingly like Clint Eastwood—always referred to PPD as "the tip of the javelin." It's the sharp end of the Secret Service and performs the single most important task that we do. Bob innately understood that and had a well-defined, unalterable, and well-respected philosophy about how to protect the president. He knew what was necessary to achieve what he wanted and very quickly instituted a lot of new procedures and policies. For example, he determined that everyone who could get a view of the president should be put through metal detectors. It was a political issue, a budget issue, a logistical issue, and a civil liberties issue, but he maneuvered through and got what he wanted. Today, screening everybody in every crowd is standard operating procedure. He also invented "the hospital agent." Whenever the president was moving, Bob stationed an agent at the primary trauma hospital just in case we had to go there. That decision was controversial because a lot of guys on the investigative side thought that it was unnecessary. Yet Bob was not going to leave any stone unturned and the more he tightened procedures, the more he was criticized by investigative agents in the field for overdoing it.

I'd like to think that one of the reasons the director and Bob brought me in was to help him create a better relationship with the presidential staff. Unbeknownst to me at the time, Bob used to tell people that I was his "ambassador to the staff." There's no question that the immediate relationship we share with the president is important, but our effectiveness depends to a large extent on our relationship with the people closest to the president. There are negotiations that go on every day, for every event and every trip, and that's done with the staff. Bill Henkel had only just come to the White House the year before I did. Even though he sometimes strutted around with the air of "the best political advance guy ever," he discovered in Kansas City that I was on his side, that I would help him get what he wanted, and that he couldn't intimidate me. In turn, I quickly came to see that underneath the arrogance, he was the best political advance guy ever.

Mike Deaver was another one with whom we needed to establish common ground. He knew what he wanted and how to get it and didn't much care what any of us thought. If we agreed with him, that was fine; if we didn't, that wasn't going to get in his way. He had flawless political instincts and the president's confidence. Deaver's genius was in knowing how to emphasize the president's strengths and how to build an image for him by creating situations that highlighted those strengths. Years later, in a documentary about the Reagan era, Deaver explained to PBS, "All you wanted to do is fix the camera on his head and let him talk. You didn't need him to walk around the desk or sit on the corner and do all of those things that people have to do to make politicians interesting."

I saw Deaver up close for the first time on a survey trip to La Paz, on Mexico's Baja Peninsula. It was a fairly simple trip, only one city, but it gave me the opportunity to study Deaver and begin to figure out what motivated him. I needed to know how he viewed the Secret Service. I watched closely to see how he introduced me, to see where he wanted me to sit, to see if he asked me questions, to see if he gave everyone on the other side of the table the impression that the Secret

Service was important. And he did all those things. Security was significant, and he considered my views important. The complex trips that followed were made so much easier by having established this common ground.

During those first few weeks at the White House, I worked hard to form relationships with the staff that would carry us through the next four years. I came to see that I was dealing with two very impressive guys and that the Deaver-Henkel combination was unbeatable. On that trip to Japan, where I had my run-in with Mr. Motoishi, the Reagans visited Prime Minister Nakasone and his wife at their country home. Marine One landed on a school playground where the greeting committee was a school full of adorable children, dressed in their best school uniforms, carrying flowers. The photo op was foolproof, except that when the president, Mrs. Reagan, the prime minister, and Mrs. Nakasone went over to meet the children, the Japanese police moved in to separate them from the White House entourage. The cops weren't going to allow anyone to get too close, and they crowded out the White House photographer, Pete Souza.

Never one to let anything get in the way of what he wanted to accomplish, Deaver tried to hurry the photographer through the crowd. But the police weren't having it. They grabbed Souza and threw him out of the group. Deaver pushed him straight back into the melee, and again, the cops shoved him away. I worried because the Japanese police were getting too physical with Pete. I couldn't get over there to help, but Henkel, who was always very quick and could probably read Deaver's mind, saw his opportunity. As Deaver continued trying to get Pete past the police, and with the Reagans and the Nakasones now walking away from the kids, Henkel grabbed a little boy and a little girl, maneuvered himself in front of the Reagans and plunked the two children down right there. The president and first lady greeted the kids with huge smiles while Souza did an end run to a spot where he could get his photographs. Those pictures ran in newspapers around the world.

On that same trip, Deaver, Henkel, and I, along with several others, did not fly home with the president. Instead, we went on to China to do the survey for a scheduled Reagan visit five months down the line. None of us knew what to expect, other than that we'd need to be flexible, which turned out to be the case. It was all right for us to fly into Beijing on our own plane, but the Chinese decided that our plane had to stay in Beijing. They would fly us anywhere we wanted to go. We courteously accepted their offer, because we had no other choice, and wound up touring the country on a vintage Russian-built, Chinese Air Force turboprop. We were all seasoned fliers and knew enough to be extremely nervous from takeoff to landing.

We scouted several cities and wound up at Xian, where the ancient terra-cotta figures are displayed. It's a grim place. We stayed at a Russian-built hotel and were presented with unappetizing meals. In central China, they do not eat the Chinese food we know in America. Every night, dinner would be presented on a lazy Susan overflowing with food that none of us recognized. The foreign ministry people were wining and dining us the best way they knew how, but the food worried us as much as their airplane. At the risk of insulting them, I made this rule for myself, and it became a kind of dictum for the rest of the group: If you can't tell us in English what it is, we won't eat it. If someone said, that's duck, that was fine. But when they answered, I'm not sure how to say that in English, that wasn't fine. Although sea slug and camel tendon soup translate easily into English, I kept hoping for mu shu pork.

Deaver had read an article in the *Washington Post Sunday Magazine* about the gorges on the Yangtze River. Sadly, many of them have disappeared under water now. But there was a possibility that we might take the president there, so we flew to Bagong—in the middle of nowhere—and got on a cruise boat that took us through the gorges. This was so remote that some of the people who came out to the locks to watch us had never seen Westerners. The gorges were absolutely spectacular. The walkways alongside the river had been carved into the rock. It must have taken these people hundreds of years to build the footpaths, which was the way they got coal down from the hills to the barges on the river. The food on the boat was better than it had been in Xian, although the Chinese sometimes made spelling mistakes on the menu. One night the menu read that we were having "crap soup" and "shrimp with crap."

Realizing that the facilities outside Beijing were not up to American standards, Deaver decided the president would stay in the capital and in Shanghai, but that Xian would be a day trip. There were some obligatory things for the president to do in Beijing, like reviewing the troops in Tiananmen Square and the big banquet dinner in the Great Hall. That was fine. But our Secret Service radios apparently were not so fine. The Chinese didn't understand why we were bringing our own cars, so we explained why. And they were slightly nervous about all the weapons we were bringing. We explained about those, too. But the radios really annoyed them. We tried to make them understand why we needed to be in constant communication, but they were adamant that we should not use our own radios. It turned out that the frequency we were using was the same frequency used by local taxicabs. So we changed our frequencies.

It was agreed that in Beijing the president would stay at the official guest compound where Richard Nixon had stayed when he first visited in 1971. The Chinese appreciated the symbolism. A whole series of buildings and cottages, the compound provided enough comfort that it would be acceptable. But just before the president arrived, I got pulled aside by one of the Technical Security Division (TSD) guys.

Made up of agents and technicians, the TSD is an elite hi-tech group that, among other things, maintains the integrity of the president's communications. It's a critical job that they do behind the scenes, running audio countermeasure operations. Because "the other side" has top-of-the-line equipment—mini-minicameras and state-of-the-art microwave receivers, and, who knows, goldfish that are also listening devices—the TSD is always trying to outdo those people by working with the spy agencies to develop their own equipment. They are constantly taking precautions, regardless of where the president is—including the White House—to assure that no one can eavesdrop on his conversations. Now, the word from the TSD agent in China was that they had found a bug in the nightstand between the twin beds in the President's bedroom. In line with procedure, they had left it in place.

This discovery was nothing new, neither startling nor particularly dangerous. Listening devices get found regularly throughout the political world, and throughout the corporate world, too. People in positions of power come to expect that someone somewhere will try to eavesdrop. Witness the events in 2003 when a bug was found in the Philadelphia mayor's office, and the next year when one was planted in the office of the secretary-general of the United Nations, Kofi Annan. There are even some people who jokingly complain when the other side doesn't consider them important enough to invest in a listening device.

Though listening devices are common, it's rare that video cameras show up in rooms because, generally speaking, governments are more interested in what a president has to say than in his personal habits. And, in the end, foreign governments don't usually bother taping everybody or on every occasion, even though they have the capability to do it. But when the president shows up, the countries where you would expect that he'd be bugged usually give it a try. I wouldn't be surprised to find out that the Chinese still do it, or that the Russians still do it, or that it happens to U.S. diplomats all the time in the Middle East. Who knows, maybe even the French do it. I'd like to think our friends know better than to try it, but even in friendly countries we never take the president's communications for granted.

The trip to Xian turned out to be a logistical nightmare. We needed to get the post standers in place before the president arrived, which meant flying them to Xian the night before. Bob DeProspero stayed with the president and I went on with thirty post standers—including my younger brother, Tom—to Xian. We were escorted to the hotel where the advance team, led by Rob Kasdon—it had been there for ten days—was in misery. A dust storm had come off the Mongolian desert and covered everything, everywhere, with orange soot. It was in the closets, on the beds, in the bathrooms, and very quickly under everyone's fingernails. Next, the food the Chinese provided was inedible. So the guys had to arrange for canned goods to be shipped in from the States—baked beans and tuna and crackers—which was fine the first day, but after ten days of baked beans and tuna and crackers, mealtimes were wearing very thin. The post standers and I arrived at Xian at about eight o'clock at night, and I naively said, Surely there must be something to eat somewhere. The only place, someone answered, is "The Room of Much Happiness." That's where they'd stocked the canned goods. There was a hot plate and there were soft drinks and, granted, the room was filled with food, but lukewarm baked beans in a setting of orange soot wasn't what I'd call a "happiness" experience.

The next day's event went well, although one of the post standers got into a confrontation with some Chinese. He was guarding a door and wouldn't let anybody in—it was a language problem—and we had to extract him from an obstreperous crowd. After we got the president onto his plane for the flight back to Beijing, my plans were to take the post standers on to Shanghai. That's when I was told that the plane the Chinese had provided to get us from Xian to Shanghai had no baggage section. But I had thirty people, and each one had two suitcases.

One of our C-130 car planes was waiting to take the limousines to Shanghai, so I got a couple of guys to help me find two trucks and load up the luggage. I delivered them to the plane and appealed to the pilot. "There's no way to get this stuff from here to there without you, and if we have to leave the bags here, they'll never be seen again." He agreed to take them. That was the easy part. I decided to load the suitcases inside the cars—front seat, back seat, trunks, wherever— figuring we could then just drive the cars onto the plane and that we could stow any remaining bags wherever there was room.

But a mechanic from the Secret Service garage showed up with other ideas. "You can't do that." I asked why? He said, "Because you'll scratch my cars."

I acknowledged that he was responsible for the cars, but asked him to understand that we were dealing with a major problem. I promised we would not scratch his cars. He guaranteed that we would, especially when the bags started shifting around in flight. I had to inform him, "I don't particularly care, because I need to get these bags to Shanghai and this is the only way I can do that."

"No," he said, "you cannot do that. I won't allow it."

I overruled his objection by ordering the agents to keep loading bags into the cars and onto the plane, and that's how the luggage got to Shanghai.

As hard as we try to plan for every possible problem, each trip presents us with plenty of new ones.

In the early hours of October 25, 1983, Ronald Reagan ordered the invasion of the Caribbean island of Grenada. There'd been a bloody and violent Marxist coup d'état directly supported by Cuba, and Reagan believed he needed to act. Among his reasons for invading the island to liberate it from the Marxists and Cubans was that nearly a thousand American students were on Grenada. Six weeks after the rangers, navy SEALS, and marines landed, the students were safe, the American soldiers came home, and a pro-American government established itself on the island.

A few months later, the government invited the president to visit the island and planned to greet him as a conquering hero. But when we did the survey trip, we quickly concluded that this poor Caribbean island simply could not support the logistics of a presidential visit. They didn't have enough police, couldn't build a stage, didn't have enough barricades, and that was only the beginning of a list that went on for several pages. So we had to bring in everything, from wood for the stage to portable toilets for the crowds. The president was going to speak in a big field, and the government was telling us they expected forty thousand people to show up. That's pretty major, considering that there were only about sixty thousand people on the island.

We flew a C-141 full of equipment down there to set up the rally and the parade, including five miles of yellow rope for rope lines. Two days before the president arrived, I flew down to Grenada to check the security arrangements. I was driving through the countryside and spotted tethered animals everywhere. There were cows and horses and goats and sheep, all tied with brand-new, very distinctive yellow rope. It seems that, as we tried to utilize the rope for our purposes, the local farmers had their own ideas on how to utilize it.

As hard as we try to plan for every possible new problem, old problems also arise.

When we took the president back to Japan in 1986, I worried that there could be a fallout from the Motoishi incident. I'd tried to soothe Motoishi's feelings after that first trip by sending him a little gift. I'd been walking through a West Wing hallway where the photo office hangs pictures of recent events and spotted one in which he was standing right next to the president. The deal with the photos was, if you saw one you wanted, you put your name and phone number on the back of it, and if no one senior to you asked for it, you could have it. I'd asked the president to sign it, and I'd mailed it to Mr. Motoishi. Now, seeing him again on the preadvance, he was guarded but friendlier. I decided that was progress. Bizarrely, five years later I was having lunch with an advance team from Japan planning their prime minister's trip to Washington, when one of the officials said to me, "Mr. Petro, you are very famous in Tokyo." Several other officials nodded. I didn't understand until someone explained that these men were police officers who worked for Mr. Motoishi.

This time, though, I didn't have to deal with him. My counterpart was a man named Kanishigi, who seemed pleasant and spoke very good English. I already knew that the Japanese were concerned about our weapons and that they intended to make an issue out of it. I wondered if there was any way I could avoid getting into that argument at the next big meeting of the two advance groups. So over dinner at the ambassador's residence, I quietly mentioned to Mr. Kanishigi that perhaps we could go outside and have a private word. In the courtyard I said, "You and I have something to work out, and I don't want to raise this at the meeting, and I don't think you want to raise it at the meeting either. We have to agree on the weapons." He nodded, and I went on, "I will guarantee that no one will see our weapons, that agents will wear their sidearms under their shirts, and that we will not bring automatic weapons to the sites."

After staring at me for a moment, he nodded again. "This is the way we should do it." We shook hands, and weapons were never mentioned again.

Weapons are often a bone of contention with the British, too, but we've come to an understanding there. Under the agreement with them, we get to have the same number of weapons they do. I won't say what the number is, but it is sufficient to protect the president.

We insist on bringing weapons with us because Congress expects us to be responsible for the president wherever he is. Our rules of engagement are the same overseas as they are in the States. We will take whatever action circumstances require. Firing a weapon on foreign soil would be a big deal politically and legally. Fortunately we've never had to do that. As an agent who has carried weapons on foreign soil, I can honestly say that I never thought about the political or legal ramifications, I only concerned myself with the safety of our protectee. I was prepared to do whatever I had to do, and would deal with the consequences later. We carried black diplomatic passports on foreign trips, which imply diplomatic immunity, but had there been a gun incident in the line of duty, I'm not sure that would have mattered, at least not in the immediate aftermath of the shooting. I believe that, in any reasonable situation, if an agent were to use his weapon overseas, as long as it turned out to be justified, it would not be a problem in most countries. If, on the other hand, an accident occurred and someone was killed, that would indeed be problematic. So we've worked it out with the Japanese, and we've worked it out with the British, and we've worked it out with most other countries, but we still have problems in, of all places, Canada. Our nearest neighbors can be the most obstinate.

In 1985, the president was going to do a two-day trip to Quebec City for a summit hosted by his pal, Prime Minister Brian Mulroney. Deaver, Henkel, and I did the survey with a smaller group than usual because this was, on paper, a very simple trip. We checked into the Château Frontenac and met with a small group of foreign ministry people, Prime Minister Mulroney's people, and the Royal Canadian Mounted Police, who have protective responsibilities. The initial meeting lasted only fifteen minutes before we broke into smaller groups.

I brought with me the advance agent and an agent from our Syracuse field office. Three Mounties sat across from us, led by Deputy Commissioner Bob Roy. He was a big, burly fellow who got straight to the point. "Mr. Petro"—he glared at me as if I were some sort of underling being lectured to—"when the president comes to Quebec City, you may not bring your vehicles, your radios, and your weapons. You will have only one person at each site and two people in the motorcade."

"Really?" I stood up. "Well, then, it doesn't seem like we have much to talk about, does it," and I walked out. I found Deaver and told him what had just happened, ending my description of Roy's pronouncement with "It's an insult."

Deaver went straight to Mulroney's chief of staff and told him what had just happened, finishing his description of the event with "It's not acceptable."

The chief of staff hurried off to find Roy and, a few minutes later, returned to inform Deaver and me, "It's all right, you can go back to the meeting. The problem is solved."

I sat down again with an unhappy Mr. Roy. He asked me what we wanted. I went down the list, which included cars, radios, weapons, post standers, the works. He said nothing about our requirements, and we moved on to discuss the sites. The president and the entourage would stay at the Château Frontenac—we took over the entire hotel—and everything was going to happen within five blocks. We got through the meeting, and even though Roy barely spoke to me, everything seemed to have been settled.

When I returned to Quebec City a few days before the visit, word from the RCMP was "No weapons." I told Deaver, and he phoned the chief of staff, who walked into the prime minister's office and came out with permission for us to bring weapons into Canada. This was from Brian Mulroney himself. I assumed that was the end of that.

We flew up with the president, attended the first night's banquet, and got him back into the hotel by 10:30. Once he was in his room, I came downstairs to check on the cars for the next morning. I walked into the lobby, which was filled with the press corps, and Roy was there. He spotted me, walked up, shoved his finger in my chest, and said in a very loud voice, "You lied to me."

Astonished, I listened to him go into a tirade about agents transmitting over the radio. But no one had ever said we couldn't. Then he warned, "I don't give a shit what the prime minister told you, if I find an agent with a weapon in Canada, I'm going to have him arrested."

Now I took his hand and placed it on top of the holster hidden under my shirt. I said, "If you're willing to accept the consequences of arresting me in the lobby of this hotel, with the president of the United States upstairs, be my guest."

By now, everybody in the lobby was also waiting for me to be arrested.

Roy's face got red, he spun on his heels and stormed off.

The next morning, I was on the president's floor, in front of the suite, when Roy appeared. The RCMP was not excluded from the floor because they also had a responsibility for the president's safety and we operated a joint command post. At the working level, everything in Canada was great, the guys all got along just fine. The problem was the chip on Roy's shoulder. I stared at him as he approached, thinking here we go again. But this time, to his credit, he extended his hand and apologized. We wrote it off to a stressful day. I did tell him, though, that we'd just come back from China and got more professional courtesy from the Red Chinese officials than we get from the Mounties. I reminded him, "We're the same people, you and me. I have no trouble with the Communist Chinese, but I can't get along with the Canadians. Why is that?"

It's a question that is still unanswered.

★ ★ ★ ★

CHAPTER NINE

DOWNTIME

At some point, on every ride, he would remind us, "The best thing for the inside of a man is the outside of a horse."

The president of the United States lives above the shop.

There is no getting around the fact that the White House is a government office building and, therefore, not necessarily the most relaxing place in the world to live. The West Wing is where the president's offices are, and the East Wing contains additional office space, including the first lady's office. The private quarters are on the second floor of the central part of the White House, which is known as the residence.

The rooms are comfortable, Pullman style—in a straight line— but hardly regal and not very large. There is a long hallway running through the middle of the floor. On one side, with the elevator and the entrance, there is a kitchen, a small gym, and the large guest room known as the Queen's Bedroom. On the other is the Lincoln Bedroom—which was not Lincoln's bedroom, but his study, the room in which he signed the Emancipation Proclamation—the Oval Yellow Room where the Reagans held private receptions, and some sitting rooms.

The president's suite is on that side, too, comprising a living room, a dining room, a dressing room, and a bedroom. For the record, according to the White House historian's office, there are 132 rooms in the residence—which is the original six-floor mansion. There are 35 bathrooms, 412 doors, 147 windows, 28 fireplaces, 8 staircases, and 3 elevators. That may sound grand, but there are also, always, lots of people around—stewards, staff, the Secret Service— and their presence becomes very tiring. Most presidents quickly learn that they need to get out of there on weekends. Both Jimmy Carter and Bill Clinton spent weekends at the White House in the beginning, but after a while they started going regularly to Camp David.

Officially called "Naval Support Facility Thurmont," it's a U.S. Navy base protected by U.S. Marines. High in the Catoctin Mountains of Maryland, some seventy miles from the White House— about twenty-five minutes on Marine One—it became the official presidential retreat in 1942 and was named Shangri-La by Franklin Roosevelt. President Eisenhower renamed it after his grandson. The property is made up of several rustic but comfortable cabins in a wonderful wooded setting. The president and first lady would fly up on Friday afternoon and stay until Sunday afternoon. It was a great place for agents, too, because it is so secure we could give them a lot more freedom than anywhere else. The president and Mrs. Reagan would go for long walks and we could safely be a hundred yards behind and not have to worry. As long as we kept them in sight, we felt they were very safe at Camp David.

When I first joined the president's detail, I wanted to see the layout at Camp David. I was given a number to call, and the camp commander's office set up a tour for me the following week. After I hung up, I started going through the mail, and, by sheer coincidence, there was a request for a Secret Service plaque to be given to the commander at Camp David: a certain William A. Waters, who was being rotated out. I stared at the name, told myself, "It can't be," took up the phone again, and telephoned Camp David. I asked to speak to Commander Waters. The clerk wanted to know who was calling, I told him my name and waited until a familiar voice came on the line and said, "Joe?"

I answered, "Bill?"

Commander William A. Waters was Lt.(j.g.) Bill Waters, the fellow I'd shared a hooch with in Vietnam in River Division 512. Reuniting with him was a wonderful treat, and when I went up there with the president and first lady, I stayed in the cabin called Rosebud, directly across the path from the cabin where Bill, his wife, and kids lived.

There was a regular routine when we were there. After dinner on Friday and Saturday night, at precisely eight o'clock, the senior agent, the military aide, the chief pilot of Marine One, assistant press secretary Mark Weinberg, the personal aide, the doctor, and the camp commander would line up at the door of Aspen Lodge— which was the president's—and wait to be ushered in for the evening movie. On Friday nights, the Reagans usually showed an old movie. On Saturday nights, it was a new release. There was a screen that dropped down from the ceiling of their living room and a projector built into the wall at the back. The president and Mrs. Reagan would sit on the sofa. Behind them, on one side, was the aide and chief pilot. I sat behind them on the other side with the camp commander. Everybody had assigned seats, and there were little tables next to each seat. Precisely halfway through the movie, a steward would bring out popcorn and Cokes and put them on everybody's table.

The first night I went to the movies, when the popcorn arrived, I turned to Bill at precisely the same moment that he turned to me, and the two of us smiled broadly, thinking the identical thought. We discussed it later. In our wildest dreams, neither of us could have imagined in 1969, sitting in a hooch eating his mother's popcorn and watching a movie, that one day we would be doing the same thing with the president of the United States.

My vote for the most interesting film we saw at Camp David was *Hellcats of the Navy,* starring Ronald Reagan and an actress who used to call herself Nancy Davis. She played a nurse, and he played a submarine captain. It was the last of her eleven films, made at Columbia in 1956, and the only film in which they appeared together. The two of them sat on the couch, watching it, holding hands, and looking very amused.

Occasionally the Reagans would have guests at Camp David. Prime Minister Margaret Thatcher of Britain visited a few times. And despite the very informal setting, she was always prim, proper. And she always had her purse with her. You could tell that the president and Mrs. Reagan liked her because the three of them never stopped talking and laughing.

On Saturday mornings, we went riding. There were some gorgeous trails through the woods, and occasionally we'd go off-site. Because riding was so much a part of the president's life, and because he was such an accomplished rider, when I joined the detail I went through intensive training, spending two hours every morning at six, for two months, taking advanced riding lessons from the U.S. Park Police.

The president had been given a world-class jumper named Giminish, a big, gorgeous gelding who was a real handful to ride. But the president not only demanded good horses, he could handle them. There was another horse he rode sometimes called Straights and Doubles, a spirited ex-racehorse. When the president wasn't riding Straights, I was. He never rode western, like a cowboy, because he was a lot more than an actor who could ride. He always rode with an English saddle, which is a better way to ride because you're more part of the horse. And he always did the Italian dismount. That truly set him apart. It consists of a fairly elaborate and somewhat athletic move. When the horse came to a stop, he would take both his feet out of the stirrups and throw his right leg up over the head of the horse, then slide down the left side of the horse, landing on the ground, standing at attention holding the reins. He does it in the movie *The Cavalry Charge,* and I never saw him get off a horse any other way. I've tried it a few times, and it's not so easy. It's also dangerous. The president was basically dropping off the horse, as opposed to stepping off the horse, and those horses were huge. We worried that he could lose his footing and fall, or that a horse could be startled and throw him. So without saying anything to him, we always made sure that one of the agents was standing behind the president's horse when he did his dismount. We never had a problem, but an agent was there, just in case.

For the same reason, we spent a lot of time practicing AOPs on horseback. Whatever we did on the ground was coordinated with the HMX helicopters because, if there was an emergency, we'd have to get the president to a hospital. One agent would pretend to be the president, actually riding Giminish, and another agent would pretend to be the first lady, actually riding her horse. We'd go through every variety of emergency. We'd rehearse falls, broken legs, broken arms, and heart attacks, always acting as if it were the real thing. It was especially important to practice with the horses because we couldn't predict how they'd react, especially to gunfire and explosions. Real life is not like a Hollywood picture. The president told us that when he was making those movies, the studio deafened the horses so that they wouldn't react to gunfire. It was the only way to film cowboys shooting off the backs of horses. We discovered that we couldn't shoot more than once before these horses went crazy. In fact, after a while, the horse would spot the gun out of the corner of its eye and get violent because he knew what was coming.

In the beginning, we made a lot of mistakes. Horses create a dynamic that is unique, because they are reactive animals and always tough to handle under such conditions. During one practice session, a horse got so scared that it took off with the rider and literally jumped over a car. But we learned from our mistakes and that AOP training led us to develop scenarios so that, if there was a firefight, we'd be able to get off the horses to return fire. We also learned how to get the horses out of the way so that they wouldn't become part of the problem. We did the same training at the Reagan ranch in California. On a number of occasions, we took the team out there three or four days before the president arrived to work AOPs on those trails. The president was aware of our practice sessions, and I think he would have liked to participate. He never said as much, but I could tell he thought about it.

Mrs. Reagan always came along on the riding excursions because he was so passionate about it, but also because she was nervous about him riding. Certainly after his colon cancer operation, she was constantly trying to get him to stop riding. He was in his midseventies and didn't ride tame stable horses. Nor did he ever ride follow-the-leader, he was always out in front. She rode western, and although I wouldn't categorize her as a great rider, she was definitely competent. I'm not sure how much she enjoyed riding. I think she wanted to be there to make sure that he was safe and perhaps believed that he would ride too fast if she wasn't there keeping track. Letting him gallop off into the distance wasn't going to happen whether she was there or not. Anyway, we never rode very fast. We would canter occasionally, but we trotted most of the time, and walked a lot.

Horseback riding is an inherently dangerous sport, and we paid a lot of attention to safety issues, always making certain that the horses were right and that no unnecessary chances were taken. The president was eventually thrown from a horse when he got older, after he had left office, and suffered some head injuries. And we had a lot of agents who got hurt on horses in training. So safety was always a primary concern for all of us and a legitimate concern on Mrs. Reagan's part.

If you believe Mark Weinberg's version of events, I saved the president's life one day at Camp David. He was in the room and saw it. But Mark was also the assistant press secretary who was always saying,

"If it's not photographed, it's like it never happened," and unfortunately, it wasn't photographed.

We were in the cabin called Laurel, which is where everyone eats dinner and where there's a huge fireplace. It was winter, and the fire was roaring. A photographer was doing a photo session with the Reagans and wanted to shoot some pictures in front of the fireplace. The president and first lady sat down on the hearth. Instinctively, I went over and stood next to the fireplace. The photographer took a whole series of pictures, and when he was done, Mrs. Reagan stood up. Then the president started to stand up, and it was one of those moments when someone stands up too quickly and slightly loses his balance. He took a step forward and then half-fell toward the fireplace. I reached over and braced his back, and he regained his balance. It was nothing more complicated than that, and it happened so fast I didn't think about it. I'm not sure the president even realized what had happened.

But Mark saw it and said, "You just saved the president's life. You saved him from falling into the fire." Of course, I didn't. He wasn't going to fall into the fire, and even if the situation had been worse and he had fallen into the fire, it wasn't going to kill him because there were a dozen people standing around to get him out. But Mark kept saying, "You saved the president's life," and the only answer I could come up with was to throw back to him his own quote, "If it's not photographed, it's like it never happened."

Weekends at Camp David were happy times for the president and Mrs. Reagan. You could see it in their eyes and see it when they walked together. They were always holding hands. But even the best of the days and nights at Camp David couldn't come close to the joy they shared at their ranch.

Appropriately named Rancho del Cielo—Ranch in the Sky—it was 688 acres some thirty miles up the coast from Santa Barbara, on Bald Mountain in the Santa Ynez Valley, with sweeping views of the Pacific. The Reagans bought the place in 1974 for $527,000 when he was governor of California. The ranch was rustic, not at all luxurious, but it was where they both loved to be. You could actually see the physical change in him as we took off in Air Force One for the flight out west. He became buoyant. The next morning, he'd climb up the steps from the ranch house in his boots and breeches and a golf shirt like he was thirty years old.

There was the clay-tiled adobe ranch house, which was not very large. It had two bedrooms, a small kitchen, a small dining room, and a nice-sized living room, decorated in western style with woven Indian blankets, with a large window overlooking the ranch. Behind that was a small guest house with two more bedrooms. Those buildings were surrounded by a wooden fence that he himself built, and beyond that, up a slight incline, was a tall post with a bell. The sign on the gate at the house read, "The Reagans—1600 Penna Ave."

There was a little pond, not more than twenty to thirty yards long and ten to fifteen yards wide, with a dock and a canoe with the hand-painted name TRULUV on the side. There was also a small house where the caretaker lived, and above the pond, a tack room and a four-stall stable. The horses were hardly ever there, as he preferred to let them run off and graze. There were other animals, too, notably a bull and a donkey. And up the hill there was a small area where the animals were buried when they passed on.

The barn was fairly big, and next to it we built three Quonset huts—one to serve as a staff building, one to serve as a residence for the doctor and the military aide, and the other to be our command post. The staff building had a conference room and a couple of meeting rooms, and the WHCA officers worked out of there. Just over the top of the hill, the marines built themselves a landing zone and a hanger for the helicopters and their own command post. We didn't sleep at the ranch. There was always an on-duty working shift, obviously, but when we were off duty, we slept at a hotel in Santa Barbara.

We had uniformed guards at the gate and around the outer

perimeter. Naturally, the entire ranch was fenced in and constantly patrolled. Contrary to press reports, we did not have secret surveillance equipment hidden under plastic boulders. The ranch was actually hard to alarm because the hills were filled with coyote and deer and all sorts of wild animals that would set off the alarms all the time. We used some electronics and a lot of line-of-sight security with night-vision devices. The plastic boulders—which were bought off the shelf at big hardware supercenters—were there to cover some WHCA equipment, not to hide it from trespassers, but so that the president wouldn't have to see dishes and antennas all over the property.

Among ourselves we referred to the ranch as "Camp Dust," because it was very dry and unbelievably dusty. It was also, at times, very foggy up there. I arrived one morning at 7:30 when the fog blanketed the entire mountain and was much too thick for the helicopters to fly, which caused real worries in the case of a medevac emergency. It was so bad that I literally couldn't see a foot in front of myself. It started to lift at about 9:30, and when it did, right there in a field about 150 yards from the house, we spotted a little yellow pup tent. It was inside the property, which, it goes without saying, was much closer than we wanted anybody to be. Immediately, we moved in on the tent and scared the hell out of some poor guy in a sleeping bag who opened his eyes to find himself surrounded by nine heavily armed agents. He was hiking, got lost in the fog, didn't know where he was, and pitched his tent for the night. We took him out of there, interviewed him, ran a background check, decided he was who he said he was, concluded there was no threat to the president, convinced him he'd picked a very bad place to camp, and sent him on his way.

The first time I went to the ranch, several things struck me. I was surprised how remote it was. Although it was only forty minutes by car from Santa Barbara, driving there was sometimes dangerous. Once you got to the base of the mountain, there were seven miles of very windy roads that weren't easy to negotiate. Another thing I noticed was the media's ability to see everything that went on there. There was a mountain about five miles away where the press set up their cameras with lenses that must have been eight feet long. Whenever you saw television pictures of the Reagans riding at the ranch, they were taken from those cameras across the valley. Back at my hotel at night I'd see news footage of us riding on a part of the trail where they had a view. It always amazed me how intent the media was on capturing every moment of this man's life, even ten seconds of him on horseback.

Oddly, I was with him one day in the tack room, just the two of us, when I looked over his shoulder at a print on the wall that depicted three horses drinking out of a trough. What caught my eye was the artist's signature. I said, "That's odd, Mr. President. Do you know the artist who did this print?" It had probably been there for twenty years, and if he ever bothered to look at the signature, he didn't seem to recall it, because when he looked at it now, he was as surprised as I had been. Although he was no relation to me, the artist's name was Joseph Petro.

Life at the ranch was very routine, which is exactly the way the president wanted it. After doing paperwork and reviewing his intelligence files, he would come up to the tack room at the same time every morning, and we would saddle the horses together. Then he'd ring the bell on the tall post, and Mrs. Reagan would come up. We'd walk and trot for an hour and a half to two hours, while he constantly told stories. We'd go by an old hanging tree, and he would explain that, by legend, this was where they used to hang cattle rustlers. Then there was a tree we pass and, every time we did without fail, he'd say, "Nancy, look," and point to it because in the bark he'd carved a big heart with, "NDR RR 8/21/77."

We'd get up high enough to see the islands offshore, and he'd tell stories and go through a repertoire of jokes. He told us about when he was an actor and about being on film sets. He told us about playing football, and also about being a lifeguard one summer at Lowell Park in Dixon, Illinois, when he saved seventy-seven people from drowning. His favorite story was how, in 1934, while he was broadcasting the ninth inning of a Chicago Cubs–St. Louis Cardinals game as a wire reader for radio station WHO in Des Moines, Iowa, the wire suddenly went dead. But he continued broadcasting the game, play by play, for six entire minutes, until the wire came back on, and the listeners never knew that "Dutch" Reagan had simply made up an entire inning. And then he'd re-create the play by play for us.

When he was finished with that, he'd start reciting "The Shooting of Dan McGrew" by Robert Service.

> *A bunch of the boys were whooping it up in the Malamute saloon;*
> *The kid that handles the music-box was hitting a jag-time tune;*
> *Back of the bar, in a solo game, sat Dangerous Dan McGrew,*
> *And watching his luck was his light-o'-love, the lady*
> *that's known as Lou.*

He could recite all ten stanzas. In fact, his memory was so remarkable that he once told me about a speech he'd given in 1953 and, just like that, slipped into five minutes of it.

By 12:30 or so, we'd be back. The Reagans would have lunch and at two o'clock he would spend the afternoon clearing trails. He had someone who ran the ranch, and the two of them would get chain saws and ride off with us in tow, to clear brush. Reagan had an old red Jeep at the ranch that he used to drive himself. That was the only time we let him drive. When he did, I'd climb into the right front seat next to him. And as soon as we were off, he'd start telling more stories, nonstop.

We were always there with him when he worked, but never joined in doing any of the work. We weren't there to help, just to protect him. That was always awkward because we felt like we really should be pitching in. He never asked, and we had to resist volunteering, because, to tell the truth, it looked like fun. Although letting the president of the United States loose with a chain saw wasn't exactly ideal. He had plenty of them in the barn, but his favorite was one given to him by a chain saw company with the proviso that they could photograph him using it. He agreed. A photographer showed up one day to take an hour's worth of pictures of him cutting down some brush. On the way back to the ranch, I asked the photographer, "What do you think?"

He said, "It's been a great afternoon, but I can't use any of the pictures because the president violates every safety rule there is."

In truth, he wasn't overtly careless with the chain saw. He just did the kinds of things we all do—like using it over his head and not always wearing safety glasses. Only once was there a problem, and it was minor. The chain saw nicked his thigh and there was a little blood. The doctor got there right away, and in order for him to take a look, the president of the United States found himself standing out in the middle of the woods with his jeans down around his ankles. I can only wonder what the television crews across the valley would have done to get that footage.

So he'd spend the afternoon cutting wood on trails, and then, the next morning, we'd ride those trails so he could proudly ask his wife, "What do you think, Nancy?" He was his own person at the ranch. He was active and robust, an outdoors guy who never pretended to be anything else. He was just like any guy who worked on his property and wanted to show his wife what he had done. And at some point, on every ride, he'd remind us, "The best thing for the inside of a man is the outside of a horse."

Evenings were usually just the two of them. They'd occasionally have guests, but they didn't have many, and seemed to cherish their time alone. Queen Elizabeth and Prince Philip went to the ranch on one occasion. It was pouring rain that day, and part of the road up the mountain was nearly washed out. As I recall, she only stayed a couple of hours, for lunch. Mikhail Gorbachev visited there, too. Someone gave him a cowboy hat which, to the glee of the media, he wore backward. But for the most part, it was just us. Some staff people would come up every morning for his national security briefing, but they didn't stay long. The Reagans had a housekeeper who cooked and cleaned and two ranch hands. But that was it. They were always very private at the ranch, almost certainly because privacy was something they couldn't always get at the White House.

Being there alone with him made us all the more aware of the fact that the Secret Service was part of a very small clique with incredible access to the president. Only a few cabinet secretaries and some staff had that, and we had to be particularly careful about how we used it. If the director needed to get some information to him about a problem, we would talk to him. Otherwise, we tended to do everything else through normal channels.

Except once, on April 1, two days before Easter 1986. I was nervous about this, but I was determined to go ahead with it, having discussed it the night before with a couple of agents. The president came up that morning, as usual, to tack the horses. I would have my horse tacked, and he would tack his horse by himself, and then I would help him tack the big western saddle on Mrs. Reagan's horse. There were a lot of straps so I would get on one side and he'd stand on the other and I'd pass the straps to him.

Standing a foot away from him that morning, I said, "Mr. President, by the way, I need to speak to you about something."

He said, "What's the problem, Joe?"

"I got a call last night from headquarters asking me to cut costs out here at the ranch."

At this point he stopped tacking the horse and was very concerned. "Oh . . . well . . . what can we do? What are you planning?"

I said, "I spoke to some of the fellas"—that's what he called us—"and we came up with a solution." I pointed to the tack barn just as the two agents, who happened to be the best riders in the Secret Service, Barbara Riggs and Karen Toll, rode by on the same horse.

The president looked at them, then looked at me, and I said, "April fool." And he burst out laughing. That was his kind of joke.

When Mrs. Reagan came up, the first thing he told her was, "Honey, you're not going to believe what the fellas pulled on me today." He told her the story and started laughing all over again.

If it's true, as I believe it is, that PPD reflects the president, then that sort of joking around might have been possible to some extent with Clinton and both the Bushes. But I'm sure it never happened with Nixon, and I don't know how much PPD could joke around with Carter. I'm proud that we could do it with President Reagan.

I saw him get angry only a couple of times. He was angry in Tokyo with Mitterand. And he was angry once at the ranch when he made a joke and the world took it wrong. But on that occasion, August 11, 1984, I think he was most angry at himself.

The president would come up to the Quonset hut staff room once a week to deliver his Saturday morning live radio broadcast. A WHCA team would set up the equipment, and he would do a microphone check. Reagan usually said something funny, but on that particular morning his mike check included the ad-lib, "We will commence bombing Russia in five minutes!"

Everyone knew he was joking, and everyone laughed. The president did the broadcast, and from there we went to saddle the horses. We were still in the tack room when someone came in to say that his mike check had accidentally gone out live and the media was having a field day with it.

He said to me, "I can't believe that people would make such a big deal out of that." He'd been around radio long enough to know the old adage, there is no such thing as a dead mike, and was irritated with himself for making such a silly mistake. But he was also disappointed that the press was jumping on this the way they were.

He felt perhaps that they owed him the benefit of the doubt, and that out of common sense and common courtesy, they should have just forgotten about it.

From that weekend on, mike checks were limited to "One, two, three, testing, one, two, three."

The Reagans would spend three weeks at the ranch every August, then come out two or three other times throughout the year, for a week or so, as at Easter and Thanksgiving. Once they got to the ranch it was unusual that they would leave. Although the same Easter weekend that we played the April fool's joke, the president told me that he and the first lady would like to go to services on Sunday. The closest church was down in the valley, and I asked him if anybody there knew about this. He said no, that they'd only just decided. I sent an advance agent to scout the church and began working out the logistics of how to do this safely. Because we didn't have time to advance the trip properly, I had to warn the president that if word got out, we couldn't go. He understood. The only people whom we told about this was a small press pool, and they were sworn to secrecy.

The next morning we helicoptered the Reagans to a ranch in the valley about a mile from church, which happened to be the place where we stabled our horses. The cars were there and we loaded everybody up, but had to wait a few minutes until the advance agent at the church radioed back that it was okay to proceed. We were sitting in the limousine when Mrs. Reagan caught my eye and pointed to her chest. I nodded and said, "Mr. President, would you please come with me. I'm afraid it's vest time."

We'd secured a room at this ranch in case we needed a place to go, so I took him there. He took off his jacket and I put it on a chair. Then he took off his shirt and I put the vest on him. He put his shirt back on, and I reached for his jacket, which was suddenly covered in cat hair from the chair. I tried to get as much of it off as I could, but when we got back into the car, Mrs. Reagan saw his jacket and she said, "Ronnie, where did you get all this cat hair?" And she rode all the way to the church brushing his jacket.

I think there were two reasons why they didn't leave the ranch often. The first was because they were so happy there. The second was that he knew it was a major production every time he went somewhere and was uncomfortable with causing so much disruption. The parishioners at that Easter service were both surprised and excited to see the Reagans, but their presence changed the character of the service, and the president realized that. He also recognized that it took a lot of people to go through a lot of hoops to make this sort of thing happen.

He was a man who thought about things like that.

The only regular commitment they made each summer to leave the ranch was for an annual barbecue near Santa Barbara, hosted by the president's old friend Fess Parker. He was an actor famous in the 1950s for playing Davy Crockett on television. He was an old-school gentleman, just like the president. In 1985, President Reagan sent Parker to Australia as his official representative for some event, and when he returned, there was talk that he might be appointed U.S. ambassador to Australia. It didn't happen, and that was Australia's loss.

It was ostensibly a press party, but Parker always invited the Secret Service agents and their families. My daughter had a little autograph book that she used to carry around, and of course both the president and Mrs. Reagan happily signed it. At her first barbecue, I told Michelle she should ask Fess for his autograph, too. She didn't know who he was, but I loved the idea of her having Davy Crockett's autograph. I introduced them, and stood by, a really proud father, as Davy Crockett hugged my little girl. She asked if he would sign her book, and he said, "Sure, but I need to do something first." With that, he took her autograph book and walked off.

I thought Michelle was going to burst into tears. Her eyes got huge as she watched him walk away. I knew he wasn't going to keep it or lose it, but eleven-year-old girls don't know that. She kept saying, "What if he leaves it somewhere?" I promised it would be all right, and about five minutes later, Fess came back and handed the book to her. He'd gone off somewhere to sit down and take the time to pen a very long, very lovely message to her. Caring about an eleven-year-old was exactly the kind of thing that Ronald Reagan would do—and did. That those two should have been lifelong friends should surprise no one. Warm and friendly to a fault, Fess Parker was himself, and Ronald Reagan was himself, and you just can't fake that.

When the summer ended, the president was visibly sad to leave the ranch. Mrs. Reagan might have preferred more time in Los Angeles, but the ranch was where he was happiest, and obviously that was fine with her.

The routine was that from the ranch they would go to Los Angeles and stay at the Century Plaza for a couple of days to decompress, before heading back to Washington. They'd see their Hollywood pals, and he'd ease himself into the business of being the president. The staff was there, and he'd start having meetings. And yet, with all that entailed, with all the power and all the fame and all the glory that came along with being the president, somewhere in his mind, I know, he really wanted to be on the outside of a horse, or chainsawing brush on a trail.

★ ★ ★ ★

CHAPTER TEN

HEALING SOME OLD WOUNDS

The shadow of World War II still loomed large in the 1980s. Ronald Reagan joined the other Allied leaders to commemorate the Normandy landings in June 1984, and ten months later, fell victim to an honest mistake when he agreed to commemorate Axis war dead at a cemetery in Bitburg, Germany.

The president's ancestral home was Ballyporeen, Ireland, and when he showed up there, Ireland went mad for Reagan.

I'd flown to Ballyporeen two hours before him, landed in a field under a pouring rain, and was met by the advance agent, Barbara Riggs. She was drenched to the skin, and I pointed that out to her. She mumbled, "Just wait," It didn't take long before I was also soaked. But a strange thing happened. Call it the luck of the Irish. As the two of us stood there, looking like drowned rats, Ronald Reagan's helicopter landed, and the moment the president stepped out of Marine One, just like that, the rain stopped and the sun broke through the clouds.

They loved him in Ballyporeen, and he loved Ballyporeen. But then, there has never been anybody in the White House who could work an event the way he could. We'd planned a stop at a local pub which had honored him by changing its name to "The Ronald Reagan." The president strolled in, proud to be the first president ever to have a pub named after him, and ordered a beer. He chatted with the folks gathered around the bar as if he belonged there, as if this were his local hangout. The White House photographer took photos, and a few minutes later we left. One of the photos turned up years later, framed, on the wall of a restaurant I go to in New York.

From Ireland, the president went to London for a brief stay, while I went to Bayeux, France, to advance the Normandy trip. I'd been warned that there were problems, but I never expected that French arrogance would put the president's life at risk. During the survey, some months before, and the preadvance, in May, everything had been agreed. Now, with two days to go, the French decided they weren't going to play by the rules.

Seven national leaders were attending this fortieth anniversary of the D-day landings, including the president, the queen of England, and the prime minister of Canada. So the logistics were not easy. Still, the French seemed to ignore the fact that the president, who was by far the most popular of all the guests, was also the highest-risk target. And when I sat down with the French security people in Bayeux, I reminded them of that. The man directly across the table from me was Jacques Lejeune, head of the VO—the Voyage Officiel—the French equivalent of our Dignitary Protective Division. He was about my age, and spoke very good English. I knew he understood what I was saying, but instead, he chose to pretend that he did not.

A huge ceremony was to take place at the landing site on Utah Beach, and it had already been agreed that we would have three agents with the president on the beach. Lejeune was now saying only one. I explained why that wasn't acceptable. The reviewing stand was about a hundred yards from the limousines and twenty thousand people were expected to be there. I reminded him, "This is not a small event. Leaving the president exposed like that so far from cover is a nonstarter."

However, Lejeune dug in his heels. "The queen of England will have one security agent, President Mitterand of France will have one, and President Reagan of the United States will have one." I refused to back down, and, in pique, Lejeune declared, "There will be no Americans on Utah Beach."

He'd crossed the line, and I was furious. "You didn't say that in 1944, and you're not going to say it tomorrow. This is nonnegotiable. I am not asking your permission, and I am not looking for an answer. Whether you like it or not, we will have three agents on Utah Beach. One will be at the stage, and two will walk with the president." It was not what he expected, and sensibly he did not force the issue. In reality, he and I both knew that he didn't have any choice.

The events of June 6, 1984, began for us at Pointe du Hoc.

The president and Mrs. Reagan arrived from London by helicopter, and were both outwardly moved at the majesty of the sheer hundred-foot rock face that 225 American Rangers had scaled in the first hours of D-day to gain a foothold on French soil. The day before, some current Rangers had reenacted the climb up the cliff and took with them two of the original guys, who did it again. Now, with his back to the sea at the Ranger's "Dagger" monument, the president stood on that windswept point and addressed a small group of sixty-two survivors of Pointe du Hoc.

He told them, "Forty summers have passed since the battle that you fought here. You were young the day you took these cliffs; some of you were hardly more than boys, with the deepest joys of life before you. Yet you risked everything here. Why? Why did you do it? What impelled you to put aside the instinct for self-preservation and risk your lives to take these cliffs? What inspired all the men of the armies that met here? We look at you, and somehow we know the answer. It was faith, and belief; it was loyalty and love."

After the speech, he saluted them, then shook their hands and spoke with each of them. He later wrote of that morning: "With gray hair and faces weathered by age and life's experiences, they might have been elderly businessmen, and I suppose some of them were; but these were the boys, some of them just starting to shave at the time, who had given so much, had been so brave at the dawn of the assault."

We took the president and first lady through the concrete pillbox that still stands there from that morning, the place where German soldiers first spotted the invasion fleet. We then helicoptered to Utah Beach and the formal ceremony with the other heads of state. People lined the sand dunes as far as you could see, looking down at the beach. The heads of state assembled near the VIP tent, and then the president, Bob DeProspero, and I walked out onto the beach. As soon as the crowds saw him, they started shouting, "Ron-nie . . . Ron-nie . . . Ron-nie . . ."

François Mitterand was clearly unhappy about this and tried to pretend it wasn't happening. Canadian Prime Minister Pierre Elliot Trudeau reached over my shoulder to tap President Reagan on his shoulder and say, "Ron, they're calling you." The president's eyes opened wide, and he gave that familiar sound of surprise, "Oh," and as he turned around to look, and then to wave, the entire beach erupted into applause.

From Utah Beach, we went to the huge American cemetery overlooking Omaha Beach, where one of the most memorable moments of the Reagan presidency took place.

Michael Deaver was looking for a clean picture of the Reagans in the cemetery, but that was never going to be easy because there were so many people involved with this visit. There was the White House staff, the press, the host committee, the cemetery people, the many guests who'd come along, and, of course, a lot of Secret Service agents. However, by now our relationship with the White House staff was so solid that when Deaver or Henkel told us what they wanted, we could always find a way to make it happen. We placed agents at certain points around the cemetery and indicated to the president and Mrs. Reagan where to walk. It sounds somewhat callous that it had been arranged, but it needed to be planned so that the photo op could be done safely. It's the best example I can recall of what I'd said when I first met Deaver and Henkel, "Tell me what you want, and we'll help to make it happen."

The photograph of the Reagans leaning down to place a rose on a grave, in the midst of all those other graves, is arguably one of the greatest photos of his presidency.

From there, the president and first lady joined President Mitterand at the Omaha Beach memorial, where Ronald Reagan delivered one of the most moving speeches I've ever heard.

"Someday, Lis, I'll go back," he read from a letter that had been sent to him at the White House by a woman named Lisa Zanatta Henn. It quoted a letter she'd received from her father, Pfc. Peter Zannata, who'd been in the first assault wave to hit Omaha Beach with the 37th Engineer Combat Battalion. "I'll go back, and I'll see it all again. I'll see the beach, the barricades, and the graves."

As he went on reading Mrs. Henn's words, a stillness settled over everyone there, and eyes began to redden. "He made me feel the fear of being on the boat waiting to land. I can smell the ocean and feel the seasickness. I can see the looks on his fellow soldiers' faces—the fear, the anguish, the uncertainty of what lay ahead. And when they landed, I can feel the strength and courage of the men who took those first steps through the tide to what must have surely looked like instant death."

Mrs. Henn's letter explained, "I don't know how or why I can feel this emptiness, this fear, or this determination, but I do. Maybe it's the bond I had with my father. All I know is that it brings tears to my eyes to think about my father as a twenty-year-old boy having to face that beach."

The president spoke for a few minutes about what had happened there forty years ago, and then, looking straight at the woman who'd written to him about a letter from her father, his voice began to waver. "Lisa Zannata Henn began her story by quoting her father, who promised that he would return to Normandy. She ended with a promise to her father, who died eight years ago of cancer: 'I'm going there, Dad, and I'll see the beaches and the barricades and the monuments. I'll see the graves, and I'll put flowers there just like you wanted to do. I'll never forget what you went through, Dad, nor will I let any one else forget. And, Dad, I'll always be proud.'"

I was standing off stage on the left, not far from Mrs. Reagan. There were tears in her eyes, and in my eyes, and when I looked, there were tears in the president's eyes. By the time he finished and turned to walk toward his wife, tears were running down his face.

Normandy was a triumph for the president, but the following year's trip to Bitburg, Germany, turned out to be quite the opposite.

An economic summit had been called for mid-April in the West German capital, Bonn. The chancellor, Helmut Kohl, was in political trouble and had asked the president if he'd consider making a stop in his home district. There was some debate among the president's staff as to whether he should visit a concentration camp on this trip, and for whatever reason, the staff decided he should not. Instead, with the photo of the Reagans at Normandy so fresh in everyone's mind, the idea came up that he might lay a wreath at a German war cemetery, symbolically putting an end to World War II.

The Germans suggested Kolmeshohe Cemetery at Bitburg, which was perfect because there was a big U.S. Air Force base nearby, and the cemetery was also in Kohl's home district.

In February, I was part of the survey team, along with Deaver and Henkel, who visited the cemetery. The original idea was that the president would fly in to the base, meet Kohl at the cemetery, lay a wreath, go back to the plane, and fly on to Strasbourg. The president demonstrating America's respect for the German military men who died in the war seemed like a simple thing.

When we visited the cemetery, we were struck by how drastically different it was from an American war cemetery. Instead of a field of crosses and stars in lines, the tombstones in German war cemeteries are flush to the ground with iron crosses scattered among the graves. The place had the right security ingredients for us and the right atmospherics for the political part of the visit. We left thinking we'd found the right place. But it was February, and we hadn't seen many of the tombstones because they'd been covered with snow. When it melted, someone discovered that there were SS graves here. Word got out, stirring up a lot of passion, understandably, within the American Jewish community. It didn't help to explain that there isn't a World War II German military cemetery anywhere in that country that doesn't have some SS graves.

Later, when the snow had melted and the gravestones were clearly visible, I walked around that cemetery looking for the SS graves. I'm not sure exactly how many there are. Some reports say around sixty; the White House eventually said forty-eight. This, in a cemetery that holds more than two thousand war dead. The stones marking the graves that I saw had the soldier's name, rank, date of birth, and date of death. And I didn't see a single SS grave of anybody over nineteen years old. Many were even younger. These were kids who'd been conscripted into the Waffen SS to fight in the Battle of the Bulge. All of them died in that battle. These were not hard-core SS. These were not camp guards. Still, the fact that these soldiers were there created all sorts of dilemmas. There was no way that the White House could get out of the visit to Bitburg without creating a huge political issue for Kohl. So in an effort to minimize the political downside of Bitburg, Deaver, Henkel, myself, and a few other people returned to Germany to find an additional historical site.

The U.S. ambassador to Germany was Lt. Gen. Vernon Walters,

U.S. Army, Retired, one of the most distinguished men of his time. A linguist who spoke seven languages, he had served seven presidents in various capacities, beginning with Harry Truman, helping to shape the Marshall Plan. He had been deputy director of the Central Intelligence Agency, a member of the NATO Standing Group, ambassador at large, and ambassador to the United Nations. He had his staff prepare sites for us. At the top of the list were some very old synagogues and several concentration camps. But when we got to Bergen-Belsen, the camp where Anne Frank died, all of us were so moved that we knew the president needed to go there.

Originally built in 1940 as a prisoner-of-war camp, within three years the Nazis were using it as a concentration camp, cramming tens of thousands of human beings into this place and holding them there under the most appalling conditions. Although the camp had no gas chambers, more than fifty thousand people died there of Nazi brutality, starvation, and disease. Liberated in 1945, Bergen-Belsen became one of the most harrowing symbols of the Holocaust as British army films of trenches filled with bodies were shown around the world.

Today, there are no buildings left at the camp. There are just huge mounds surrounded by stone walls with plaques that note the number of people buried beneath them.

Deaver scheduled the stop at Bergen-Belsen for the morning event and Bitburg for the afternoon event.

That settled, Deaver, Henkel, General Walters, and I had dinner at a small restaurant where Gen. George Patton and his staff had once stayed. According to General Walters, the woman who ran the restaurant—who was then in her seventies—had also been Patton's girlfriend while he was in residence. She never confirmed the rumor, but she did dance on the table at the end of the evening. Sometime between the story of her fling with Patton and her cabaret act, Deaver mentioned a call he'd received at the White House just after the story broke that there were SS graves in the cemetery in Bitburg.

The voice on the other end of the phone said, "Mr. Deaver, this is General Ridgeway. My president is in trouble. I will lay the wreath at Bitburg."

Matthew Ridgeway, who was ninety at the time, had succeeded Gen. Omar Bradley as commander the 82nd Airborne Division in 1942 and had jumped with his troops into France during the D-Day invasion. He'd also led the XVIII Airborne Corps in the Battle of the Bulge, commanded the 8th Army in Korea, and had succeeded Gen. Douglas MacArthur as supreme commander of the United Nations and United States forces in the Far East. He'd served as supreme allied commander-Europe and, after that, had become chief of staff of the United States Army.

So here was a genuine American hero still wanting to serve his country and to protect his president. You didn't have to be a political animal of Michael Deaver's intellect to see the value of Ridgeway's offer. But it took Deaver to realize that Ridgeway couldn't lay the wreath all by himself, that he had to do it with a German general. Ambassador Walters was assigned the task of finding one. He eventually came up with Lt. Gen. Johannes Steinhoff, a Luftwaffe ace who'd spent almost the entire war flying on the eastern front against the Russians. After the war, he'd joined the West German air force and had served there for a time as chief of staff.

Deaver's plan was to bring General Ridgeway together with General Steinhoff at Kolmeshohe; together, they would lay the wreath in the cemetery. The media would not be told about this part of the ceremony until the last minute. So Ridgeway was flown secretly to Germany, where he spent a few days resting at the base in Bitburg. At the same time they brought General Steinhoff into the area.

At around eight o'clock on the morning of the visit, just before leaving for Bergen-Belsen with the president, I got a call from the advance agent at the cemetery, who said, "You're not going to believe what happened. Somebody got in here last night and placed fresh flowers on each of the SS graves."

The flowers were removed immediately. I can't draw any conclusions from the flowers, other than the obvious. It made me feel very uneasy.

The visit to Bergen-Belsen was very emotional. There is no way to describe what it's like to be at a concentration camp. Anyone who has ever visited one knows that words fail while you are there, and there isn't much to say when you leave. The president and first lady were deeply moved by what they saw. Later he would say about Bergen-Belsen that the horror of the Holocaust had been forever burned into his memory there.

Once we were in the air, heading for Bitburg, the White House released the news that two combatants who'd never met, Gen. Matthew Ridgeway and Gen. Johannes Steinhoff, would lay the wreath at the cemetery. By doing that together, in the presence of the president of the United States and the chancellor of West Germany, the American people and the German people would finally be putting World War II behind them. To me, the symbolism was staggering.

We arrived at the cemetery. The president and the chancellor walked in together and stood next to each other. Then the two old generals walked in separately, and stood on the outside flanks. The moment came when they turned and faced each other, paused, and then they shook hands.

By design, the president never touched the wreath, which was unusual. The two old men laid the wreath, then walked with the president and the chancellor to the rear of the cemetery, where Deaver sprung his next surprise. Waiting for the official party were relatives of the July 1944 conspirators' coup against Hitler. He'd assembled members of Von Stauffenberg's family and members of Rommel's family, and members of the families of the famous generals who were executed for plotting against the Führer.

A report later noted that we were at the cemetery for only eight minutes. We returned immediately to Bitburg Air Force Base, where

President Reagan spoke about the day. In his speech he mentioned that not everyone was happy that he'd come to Germany. "This visit has stirred many emotions in the American and German people, too. I've received many letters since first deciding to come to Bitburg cemetery, some supportive, others deeply concerned and questioning, and others opposed. Some old wounds have been reopened, and this I regret very much, because this should be a time of healing."

Here we were, forty years after the end of the war, and for the first time—and for the final time—two generals on opposite sides shook hands and laid a wreath. Then, together with the president of the United States and the chancellor of West Germany, they greeted the families of the men who had plotted to assassinate Hitler. But the media missed Deaver's point. The message he had been hoping to send didn't get home. The news back in the States that day was all about the SS graves.

★ ★ ★ ★

THREE WORDS IN GENEVA

For the first time in United States–Soviet cold war relations, both countries had strong, healthy, and politically determined leaders. For a time it seemed as if they were on a collision course. Then they met face to face.

Some historians have written that the cold war began to thaw when Ronald Reagan and Mikhail Gorbachev sat down together at a dining-room table in a small house just outside Reykjavik, Iceland, in October 1986.

The topic on the agenda at that meeting was the Strategic Defense Initiative (SDI)—the project that came to be known as Star Wars. President Reagan seemed determined to develop this antimissile satellite system against the express wishes of the Soviets. To ease the strain, the president had even offered to share Star Wars with the Soviets. However, Gorbachev wasn't having it. "Excuse me, Mr. President, but I do not take your idea of sharing SDI seriously."

The president responded, "If I thought that SDI could not be shared, I would have rejected it myself."

The meeting in Iceland ended without an agreement, although it led to further talks, and the following year Gorbachev and Reagan signed a pact to destroy intermediate-range nuclear missiles.

But I would argue that the thaw in the cold war began one year before the Reykjavik summit, when the two leaders first met each other in Geneva, Switzerland, in November 1985.

There, in a cabana overlooking Lake Geneva, these two men had a private conversation that began with three words, and accordingly set the stage for their relationship. And I was one of only three other people who heard them.

The centerpiece of Ronald Reagan's rise to the presidency and his first term in office might well have been his description of the Soviet Union as "the evil empire." It was in a speech before the British House of Commons on June 8, 1982, that he first associated the Soviet Union with the word "evil." "Must civilization perish in a hail of fiery atoms? Must freedom wither in a quiet, deadening accommodation with totalitarian evil?"

Nine months later, in a speech in Florida, the president inexorably linked the two by referring to "the aggressive impulses of an evil empire . . . "

For the first four years of his presidency, Reagan had no one to deal with in Moscow. Leonid Brezhnev had been general secretary since taking power from Nikita Khrushchev in 1964. When Brezhnev died in 1982, the former head of the KGB, Yuri Andropov, moved into the Kremlin. He lasted two years before he died and was succeeded by Konstantin Chernenko, another old man and the third of the three leaders whose career and political philosophy could be traced back to Joseph Stalin. But when Chernenko died in 1985, a new style of Soviet leader emerged.

Mikhail Gorbachev was younger, more astute, and openly less autocratic. He'd inherited a near-bankrupt economy, eastern bloc allies who had grown weary of Soviet rule, a political system that was simply not working, and a relationship with the West that was going nowhere. He recognized that there were radical changes happening in the world, among them the earliest stirrings of globalization, and somehow understood that if he did not force change, his country

STANDING NEXT TO HISTORY

would be left so far behind that it could not survive. He shocked his own Communist Party, shocked the Russian people, and shocked the rest of the world, too, by putting two new words into the English vernacular—"glasnost," which means "openness," and "perestroika," which means "reform." Ronald Reagan finally had someone in Moscow that he could do business with.

We began planning the president's meeting with Gorbachev in Geneva nearly five months before the event. On the survey trip, in mid-July 1985, I discovered that my Russian counterpart was KGB general Mikhail Dokuchayev, whom I'd first met in 1976 with Mrs. Rockefeller.

Ever observant, Bill Henkel—who was leading the US delegation—was intrigued by the way the Russians positioned their officials around the conference table. At our initial meeting in the Soviet mission in Geneva, with huge pictures of Lenin glaring down at us, Dokuchayev sat to the right of the foreign ministry man leading the Soviet delegation. After every question, the foreign ministry man would lean over to Dokuchayev to get a whispered response. As long as the KGB was pulling most of the strings, Bill therefore sat me next to him, directly opposite Dokuchayev. Not all advance people would have been astute enough to do that. It wasn't a question of pampering my ego, it was Bill's way of telling the Russians that security was at the top of our concerns.

At the end of that first meeting, we broke up into smaller groups. Dokuchayev and I went off on our own with an interpreter and quickly agreed that the best way to deal with our Swiss hosts was to show a united front. The Swiss were going to make the final decision on a whole host of activities and prerogatives, from the arrival ceremonies, to the makeup of the motorcades, to the size of our security requirements, to the many complexities of protocol, and to the actual venue for the summit. If the Russians and the Americans asked the Swiss for different things, they would stall; if we both asked for the same thing, they would cooperate.

It had been decided by the Swiss that they would orchestrate the arrival ceremonies at the airports and the formal opening ceremony at a beautiful estate with gorgeous grounds called Le Reposoir. The two sides would then alternate as hosts, starting with the Americans. I believe that was decided with the toss of a coin.

Bill determined that we needed two venues, one where the president would stay, another where we would host meetings. The main reason for that was to give the president some privacy. At the same time, Bill was particularly concerned with putting the president in the best psychological position, both personally and in the eyes of the world. So the decision was made to bring the Reagans over a day or two early. That would allow the president to get accustomed to the time change. Gorbachev was only a few time zones from Moscow after an easy daytime flight. But the president would be six time zones from Washington at the end of an overnight flight.

Because Bill was always thinking of the photo ops to demonstrate the youthfulness and the vigor of the president, he suggested that the day before the summit the president could go riding. I located a fabulous stable just outside the city, almost on the French border. Run by the Rey family, they had fifty-five quality horses, including some Irish thoroughbreds. On a subsequent trip, I returned with riding gear to find a horse for the president and to check out the trails we'd ride. Meandering through beautiful forests, a few trails crossed into France, which created a diplomatic complication, in as much as the president of the United States would be riding a horse in France, in the company of armed Secret Service agents without the French having granted permission or, for that matter, necessarily knowing about it.

In the meantime, we scouted more than a dozen venues. We drove around all day for several days in minivans. What a tiresome chore that was. In the end we wound up accepting an invitation from the Aga Khan to let the president and Mrs. Reagan borrow his magnificent eighteenth-century estate, La Maison de Saussure, bordering Lake Geneva in the small village of Creux-de-Genthod.

For the meeting venue, we selected the twenty-room Fleur d'Eau, a sensational villa also overlooking the lake. The main house was perfect for our purposes, but I'm sure what sold it to Bill was the stone cabana with a fireplace at the bottom of the grounds, alongside the lake.

The Russians elected to receive us at their mission in Geneva, a Soviet-style office building that had a substantially different atmosphere.

The next few trips narrowed down the options: what would happen at the airport; where we would hold press conferences; who would attend the various dinners each night; and the specific time frame throughout the entire visit into which everything had to fit. On each trip, I made it a habit of having lunch and dinner every day with Dokuchayev. Little by little, our relationship grew more personal. When he happened to mention over one meal how he loved walking hand in hand with his six-year-old granddaughter through a park, I thought to myself, what a paradox. Here was a senior KGB officer, who obviously must have done some pretty nasty things in his life, and yet his private joy was walking with his granddaughter through a park. On the last trip, we exchanged gifts. He gave me two books. The first was one he'd written about his World War II experiences. It was in Russian. The second was called *World War II: Decisive Battles of the Soviet Army.* This one was in English, written by a couple of Soviet generals from their perspective. I then gave him two gifts. The first was a copy of David Eisenhower's account of his grandfather's experiences, called *Eisenhower at War.* The second was a bottle of Old Grand Dad whiskey. I handed that to him with the words, "This is in honor of your granddaughter."

Among the many problems we had to work out was the motorcade. The Swiss would have to approve it, to avoid having one country show up with a hundred cars and the other with a mere twenty-six. Dokuchayev and I agreed that the best thing to do would be to go to the Swiss with identical motorcades, so we each took a piece of paper and I lined up my motorcade while he lined up his motorcade. And all the time I kept thinking to myself that there would be plenty of differences. I was wrong. We lined up, almost identically, car for car.

From there we talked about how many agents would be in each building and who would go into which rooms. The meeting rooms at Fleur d'Eau and the Russian consulate weren't huge, and if we each brought eight agents, they would fill up fast. So we choreographed the president's arrival at the consulate and Gorbachev's arrival at Fleur d'Eau. We made it very clear who would come inside with the president and with the general secretary; who would stay inside; and where the agents who didn't come into the room could wait. After all, we didn't want them standing outside in the cold. The question of guns did not come up because we all had guns.

There was some concern, though, about the motorcade and where the cars would stage. This was important because we each had twenty-six cars, and the Swiss might have nearly as many. Obviously we couldn't park seventy to seventy-five vehicles at the front door. Both the general and I wanted to be certain that our vehicles weren't blocked, that we both had access to our own control car and our own communications car, and all those things had to be taken into consideration. So now we went through each site and choreographed where the motorcades would arrive and where the motorcades would stage. It was a tedious but very necessary process. It was never a simple process, but it could have been a lot simpler had the State Department not made it more complicated.

Unlike Soviet Foreign Minister Eduard Shevardnadze, who was protected by the KGB, Secretary of State George Shultz was protected by State Department Security (SY) and although they did their own advances, they weren't party to these meetings. Whatever deals Dokuchayev made with us applied as well to Shevardnadze. But in the eyes of some SY agents, whatever deals the Secret Service made with the Soviets did not necessarily apply to them. Technically, they were wrong. Many years before, the Secret Service had signed a memorandum of understanding with the State Department that gave the Secret Service operational control over combined events. State Department Security could be part of the planning process, but we were in charge.

At Fleur d'Eau, for instance, it was our call who would be allowed into the meeting room with the president and general secretary. We decided there would only be one Secret Service agent and one KGB agent. There would not be an SY agent because if he was coming in, then Shevardnadze would want a second KGB guy, and there simply wasn't enough room. Those were the arrangements, and we felt very strongly that everyone had to abide by them. But SY decided to move the goalposts.

A few days before the actual visit, I returned to Geneva for the fifth time to meet Dokuchayev and to iron out last-minute difficulties. As soon as I arrived, our lead advance agent there, Ed Russell, informed me that the State Department had unilaterally decided they weren't bound by our agreements with the Soviets, and that the head of the secretary's detail intended to be in the meeting room. I said he couldn't come in, because that would mean, at the very first event, we'd already broken our agreement with the Soviets.

I went to speak with the SY agent in charge of the secretary's detail, but his stance was that nothing the Secret Service decided with the Soviets applied to him. Technically, it did, so I needed to warn Dokucheyev that this fellow's misinformed ego risked creating some diplomatic embarrassment.

The night before the summit, the Swiss put everyone through a full dress rehearsal. They wanted to go over every minute detail of the various ceremonies. At one point, the U.S. and Soviet motorcades were lined up side by side, which gave me a chance to explain my "State Department problem" to the general. I told him that State

Department Security was refusing to honor our agreement by insisting on his right to go into the room.

Dokuchayev thought about that for a moment, looked up at me
and said, "Solution." He crushed his right fist into his left palm. "Secret Service should do this to State Department."

I said, "General, we can't do that. You could, but I can't." It
was an interesting insight into him and what he thought the relationship should be. If the Secret Service was supposed to be in
charge, either we got what we wanted immediately, or we crushed
whoever defied us and then got what we wanted. "The last thing I
want tomorrow morning is a fight with a State Department agent at
the door."

He understood the position I'd been put into, and quite ele-
gantly solved the problem. "I will make sure that Shevardnadze's
person is not in the room."

Later that evening, Dokucheyev caught me staring at the large
suitcase his aide was carrying. It had a phone cradled on the top.
The general very proudly announced, "Joe, I can call my wife on
that phone in Moscow."

This was a long time before cell phones, so I said, "You're kidding."

"Yes, I can." He turned to his aide and ordered him to dial
Moscow. A moment passed, the aide handed the phone to Dokuchayev, who started speaking to someone on the other end in Russian, then handed the phone to me and said, "Say hello to my wife."

There was a lot of noise on the line, and I had no idea who I was
talking to, so I said Hello, how are you, I'm here with the general,
it's very nice to speak with you, and gave the phone back to
Dokuchayev. When he hung up, I said, "That's really great," and he
nodded several times to show me how proud he was of Russian technology. "But I can talk to my wife, too," I told him, and went over to
the president's limousine. I opened the door and said to the driver,

"Get Signal on the phone and ask them to dial my wife on my drop line." As a branch of the Army Signal Corps, WHCA provided most senior people at the White House with these special, direct-line, no-dial phones at home. It was the one phone that everybody always answered.

A minute or two went by and the driver nodded to me that my wife was on the line. I reached through the open window, grabbed the phone, said hello to my wife, just as the Swiss called for the motorcade. The limousine started moving. I walked alongside the car trying to motion to Dokuchayev to take the phone, but Dokuchayev wouldn't budge. I kept motioning to him, "My wife is on this phone," as the car picked up a little speed. Now I started running to keep up, "It's my wife on the line," but Dokuchayev stood still, and I had to hang up. I came back to where he was standing and said, "That was my wife on the phone in America, and you could have spoken to her from Geneva all the way to America. That's American technology."

He shook his head. "I don't know that. I don't know who was on the phone. Maybe it was your wife, maybe it wasn't." And then he added, "Soviets win first test."

President and Mrs. Reagan arrived in Geneva three days before the conference, on Saturday night, November 16, and we installed them in Aga Khan's villa. But that November was the coldest to date in Swiss history—it was bitterly and brutally cold—and despite the fact that everything was set up and ready to go at the stables, there was just no way the president could go riding.

The Aga Khan and his British-born former-model wife, Sally Croker-Poole, escorted the Reagans around the estate. Then, before leaving, she handed the president a note from one of her young sons. The boy asked the president if he would be so kind, while he was staying there, as to please remember to feed his goldfish.

When the president read that, he assured the Aga Khan and his

wife, "Absolutely." He said he would be honored to do it and promised that he would do it himself. So one of the first things he did the
next morning was feed the goldfish. And he did it every morning
that they were there.

On Monday morning, at Bill Henkel's insistence, the president
did a "rehearsal." Although it was still bitter cold, and Mrs. Reagan
wasn't happy about him being exposed to this weather, Bill walked
the president through Fleur d'Eau and down to the cabana so that he
would be totally familiar with the setting. Just like an actor getting familiar with the set, Henkel knew how important it was for the president to "understand the surroundings" and be at ease within them.

The following morning, Tuesday, November 19—the first
morning of the summit—tragedy struck. The president went into
the boy's bedroom to sprinkle fish food into the bowl and one of the
goldfish was belly up. Obviously it wasn't the president's fault, but
he felt terrible about it and was genuinely upset. After all, he'd given
his word that he would take care of the little boy's goldfish, and now
one of them was dead on his watch.

He kept telling us how he felt responsible, which didn't surprise
any of us, because that's the way he was. So he summoned a few
people on his staff and told them that he needed to replace the goldfish. He sent a staffer to find a replacement goldfish, but it had to be
one that looked just like the dead one. Later, he penned a handwritten note to the little boy, apologizing for what had happened, and
put it in the boy's room, himself. With all the other things he had on
his mind, he was forever an old-school gentleman.

We delivered the president to Fleur d'Eau with plenty of time to
spare, and while we waited for the general secretary to arrive, Bill
Henkel had a discussion with the president about what he should
wear when he walked out the door to meet Gorbachev's car. The
president wanted to know what Gorbachev had been wearing the
night before when he arrived in Geneva. Henkel told him, a heavy
top coat, scarf, and hat. The president asked Bill what he thought

Gorbachev would be wearing this morning. Bill answered, "Probably the same thing." The president would only be outside a few minutes, and it was still freezing cold, yet he decided not to wear his top coat. That decision showed his innate sense of public image. He couldn't be sure what Gorbachev would be wearing but realized that if he walked out that door in his coat and Gorbachev was only wearing a suit, he'd look like an old man, and certainly much older than Gorbachev. That's not an image he ever wanted to project. He wanted to be seen as vigorous and healthy, so he stepped out of the door and into the cold morning in a beautiful blue suit with a white shirt, all pumped up, looking fifteen years younger than he was.

The big Zil pulled up and Gorbachev stepped out wearing a huge topcoat, a hat, and a scarf. The two men greeted each other warmly, but by the expression on Gorbachev's face, it was obvious what he was thinking—why didn't somebody tell me that Reagan was dressed this way so I could have taken off my overcoat? Gorbachev even made a smiling gesture toward his coat, as if to say, you're dressed like that and I've got this. The president gave him one of those friendly shrugs, but the message was clear.

In his memoirs, President Reagan mentioned that moment. "There was something likable about Gorbachev. There was warmth in his face and his style, not the coldness bordering on hatred I'd seen in most senior Soviet officials I'd met until then."

The two leaders, along with the secretary of state and the foreign minister, went into the room, followed by one Secret Service agent, one KGB agent, and the fellow from SY. The principals sat down around a large table while the rest of us stood off to the side. The conversation stayed in broad, general terms about what everyone hoped to accomplish. After about twenty minutes or so, once the opening session formalities were over, Henkel and Reagan made their move. The president turned to the general secretary and invited him to take a walk down to the lake.

I have no idea whether Shultz or Shevardnadze knew about this, but I could see that neither wanted this to happen, because both of them were excluded. It's human nature, I suppose, that they both wanted to be involved in all the discussions, and I suspect that if Shultz could have stopped it, he would have. It was obvious that he wasn't happy about it. Of course, I knew it was going to happen because it was all planned. I even had my coat with me because I would be standing outside the cabana for however long the president and Gorbachev would be inside.

The entourage, which was the two of them, an interpreter, the two military aides with the nuclear codes—ours was the "the football," and because we didn't know what the Russians called theirs, we dubbed it "the soccer ball"—and three agents from both sides, left the main house for the walk down the path toward the lake.

The cabana was ready for them, with a blazing fire in the hearth, two large comfortable leather chairs facing each other, a small table in between them, and a seat just behind that for the interpreter. A steward was standing at the open door with a tray of coffee. The president and the general secretary took their coffee, walked into the room, and sat down in the large leather armchairs, and then the interpreter sat down facing them. I was standing inside with the KGB guy, waiting for him to leave, while everyone else was outside. But the KGB guy didn't step out, and as long as he was there, I wasn't going to leave. For all I knew, he was thinking the same thing, that if the American doesn't leave, I'm not leaving either. All of a sudden, the doors closed behind us and we were in the room, with no place to go. The president wasn't bothered, and neither was Gorbachev.

Some years later I read that before coming to Geneva, he'd phoned two of his closest political allies—Margaret Thatcher in London and Brian Mulroney in Ottawa—both of whom assured him that he would like Gorbachev. He'd also been briefed that Gorbachev was an intelligent man with a good sense of humor, but that he was not the sort of man who would feel immediately comfortable being on a first-name basis with the president.

So when the president took a brown manila envelope out of his pocket—it contained a letter that he'd handwritten—he leaned over to Gorbachev, handed it to him, and then, in that wonderfully warm and friendly voice of his, said, "Mr. General Secretary"— Gorbachev looked straight at the president, who smiled one of those Reagan smiles—"I'd like you to read this."

That was the moment, right there. The amiable tone of the president's voice, those three words—"Mr. General Secretary"—and the way he smiled when he handed the envelope to him. That's what set the stage for what they discussed in the cabana that morning in Geneva. And that's what put these two men on the same track to end to the cold war.

Gorbachev opened the envelope and read the letter. And then they began to talk. The president, as he himself reported later, pointed out that the two of them had been born into humble families in a rural part of their country. Now, as the leaders of their countries, these two men from the same background could, if they chose, start World War III. Or they could bring about a lasting peace. Gorbachev agreed that they had a lot of things in common, including a desire for peace. They spoke about the development of nuclear weapons in the years just after World War II, and about the Strategic Defense Initiative. After half an hour, they decided to go back to the main house.

On the walk to the house, the president stopped Gorbachev to speak with him privately. He invited the Soviet leader to come to Washington. Gorbachev accepted immediately, and invited the president to visit Moscow. The Reagan memoirs noted, "Not once during our summit did he [Gorbachev] express support for the old Marxist-Leninist goal of a one-world Communist state or the Brezhnev doctrine of Soviet expansionism. He was the first Soviet leader I knew of who hadn't done that."

Elsewhere it's been written that the secretary general arrived in Geneva with a defensive attitude. That he didn't trust the Americans. That he assumed the U.S. military-industrial complex had total control over the political system. Also, he was dealing with a former movie star and couldn't be sure that the president wasn't anything more than a front man for those military-industrial interests. That was the way things worked in his own country. There's no doubt that he had a lot on his mind. He must have believed, as so many people did, that President Reagan and the pope were conspiring to topple Communism in Poland. If that happened, if the Solidarity movement could hold on, then political change throughout the eastern bloc was inevitable. He had to know that the tide was turning. He'd foreseen the headlines, and they made him nervous. It's easy to believe that, in Gorbachev's mind, he and his colleagues were fighting for their lives.

But from the moment when Gorbachev got out of his car and throughout their meetings there was a rapport between the president and the Soviet leader and that clearly affected whatever conceptions Gorbachev brought to Geneva. I'm convinced that the president totally disarmed Gorbachev with his one-on-one charm, because as I stood in that cabana and watched his body language, it was clear to me that Mikhail Gorbachev liked Ronald Reagan.

I've thought about that meeting in the cabana over the years, and about how Bill Henkel created the environment for it to happen. I've wondered, too, how the world might be different if that first encounter had taken place at the dour Soviet mission. The president was not someone who liked what the USSR stood for. He had been consistently very negative about the Soviets, and Gorbachev knew that. If that first meeting had been at the Soviet mission, and if Gorbachev had gone there expecting more of the same from President Reagan, perhaps he would have gotten it as part of some self-fulfilling prophesy. But the ambience of Fleur d'Eau's stone cabana, Reagan's warmth, and Gorbachev's receptiveness made a difference.

Once Gorbachev accepted the president's invitation to Washington, the meeting in Geneva was only about going through the motions. And about Raisa Gorbachev. Until then, the wives of Soviet leaders were either not seen, or they looked drab. The contrast between Mrs. Khrushchev in a babushka and Jackie Kennedy in Dior was startling. The contrast between Mrs. Reagan in designer clothes and Mrs. Gorbachev in designer clothes made the world understand that Raisa Gorbachev's husband was not like the others. She was the first Soviet leader's wife with a public persona, and he was smart enough to bring her onto the world stage with him.

Seeing the leaders and their wives together confirmed everyone's excitement that these were new times. After one of the dinners at the Soviet mission, the Gorbachevs walked the Reagans to the door, and what I saw were not two world leaders and their spouses, but four friends saying good night to each other after a pleasant dinner. Both Reagans kissed Raisa goodnight and both Gorbachevs kissed Nancy good night, and as the Reagans walked out the door, all four of them were laughing about something because the president always ended everything with a laugh.

I wasn't in the room for the second meeting at Fleur d'Eau. Instead, I stayed in the joint command post we'd set up with the Russians. It was the first time anything like that ever happened. The Soviet military aide was sitting there with his "soccer ball" right next to Casey Bower, our military aide with "the football." Looking at them, I realized that the codes in this room could blow up the entire planet several times over. For the first, and possibly the only time, the American nuclear codes were within a foot of the Soviet nuclear codes. I stared at them for the longest time, then asked both military-aides out loud, "What if we all have to leave in a hurry and you two guys grab the wrong suitcases?"

Casey gave me a disapproving stare, which made me understand I'd said the wrong thing. Both men believed that the safety of the free world depended on each of them maintaining control over his suitcase. The retaliatory strike could only begin with that bag. The president couldn't order a strike without the football, and Gorbachev couldn't order a strike without his soccer ball.

When we left Geneva, I made a point of saying a warm goodbye to Dokuchayev. I wanted him to know that I thought he was a special man. We'd spent a lot of time together and had spoken candidly about our hopes and our concerns, and how it didn't make sense for us to be enemies. Just as the Secret Service reflects the man in the Oval Office, Dokuchayev was where he was because he reflected the new man in the Kremlin. Gorbachev understood that they needed to open up and deal on a different level with the United States. In a very real sense, Gen. Mikhail Dokuchayev of the KGB managed that quite well.

★ ★ ★ ★

CHAPTER TWELVE

LEAVING THE PRESIDENT

Every agent pays a very high price for the honor of being with the president. Time is never your own.

There were two occasions when I saw Ronald Reagan very down. One was political. One was a national tragedy.

At the start of the 1984 presidential campaign, in a debate with Walter Mondale, he hadn't done particularly well, and that depressed him. It was clear that the election was his to lose. But Mike Deaver knew what it took to get him back to being himself. He set up an old-fashioned whistle-stop tour through Ohio. He pulled "The Magellan" out of mothballs—that's the armored train that presidents Roosevelt and Truman had used for their campaigns, the same one featured in the famous photo of Truman holding up the *Chicago Daily Tribune* with the headline, "Dewey Defeats Truman."

The president stopped at fifteen cities, giving speeches off the back of the train, and as the crowds got bigger and more enthusiastic, a change came over him. Deaver reinvigorated the president with the tour, and the president reinvigorated his campaign by ending every speech with the famous line from his film *Knute Rockne: All*

American, in which he played George Gipp. He'd look at the crowd and urge them, "Win one more for the Gipper."

The tragic occasion that deeply affected the President occurred in January 1986.

On the twenty-eighth of that month, at 11:38 in the morning, NASA flight 51-L took off from Cape Canaveral, Florida. It was the twenty-fifth launch of a space shuttle and the tenth time that the *Challenger* was used. Seventy-two seconds after liftoff, the *Challenger* exploded and all seven crew members were killed. The nation was plunged into mourning. Even the State of the Union address, which had been scheduled for that week, was postponed.

Within a few days, NASA had organized a memorial service at the space center in Houston. It was planned that the families of the seven astronauts would attend, along with the president and the first lady. The event was pulled together very quickly, and the advance team that went to Texas had only twenty-four hours on the ground to put everything in place. NASA invited nearly ten thousand people, and when we considered the size of the crowd, plus the short lead time that we had, I wasn't totally convinced that the security arrangements were as complete as they could be. Not that corners were cut or that things weren't being done properly. We were able to do everything we normally did, but it was all put together too fast, and I was concerned about that. So on the flight down to Houston I made the decision that the president should wear the armored vest. It had been a horrible week for the country and a particularly emotional week for the president and the first lady, and I just wasn't sure when to tell him.

About fifteen minutes before landing, as the plane began its final approach, I went into his suite and almost apologized for having to do this. I said, "Mr. President, I am about to make a very tough afternoon even worse."

He looked at me with an expression that did not hide the emotions he was feeling for the *Challenger* families. "You mean that I have to wear the armor?"

I said, "I'd like you to." He nodded okay, stood up, took off his shirt, and put on the vest.

We arrived at the Space Center and met privately with the seven *Challenger* families. They were standing quietly in clusters. The president and first lady went to every one of them, spoke to them, hugged them, and held their hands. Both of the Reagans could be so wonderfully warm and compassionate, and somehow, in moments like this, they always knew what to say. I stood next to him, trying not to cry. I told him later, "I don't know how you can do that, you know, how you can maintain your composure." He gave me one of those slow Reagan shrugs and just shook his head. After half an hour with the seven families, we went outside for the service.

My younger brother Andy works for NASA, and I'd phoned him the night before to say that I'd arranged for him to sit up front. But he said no, that he wanted to be with his coworkers, which, of course, was the right decision.

During the service I sat behind the president. On his left was Jane Smith, the wife of the *Challenger* pilot, Commander Michael Smith, USN. Their two young children were sitting with her, and for the longest time Mrs. Smith sat there stoically, the perfect navy wife. At one point, Mrs. Smith handed the president an index card that her husband had left for her. On it he'd written some words by H. G. Wells: "For man, there is no rest and no ending. He must go on, conquest beyond conquest. This little planet and its winds and ways, and all the laws of mind and matter that restrain him. Then the planets about him and, at last, out across the immensity to the stars. And when he has conquered all the depths of space and all the mysteries of time—still he will be but beginning."

The president was openly touched by her gift. Later, after making a copy, he returned the card to her because it was just too personal and he didn't feel right about keeping it. In his memoirs he wrote, "I'll never forget her generosity in offering me that part of her husband's final days."

While the president spoke, I watched Mrs. Smith. She stayed composed throughout the entire ceremony, that is, until the flyover. Navy planes came over low and slow—in the missing wingman formation—and when that lone plane headed straight up into the sky as the rest of the formation continued without the missing man, that's when she lost it. But then, that's when we all lost it—the president, Mrs. Reagan, and ten thousand other people, too.

It's impossible for anyone not to react at a moment like that, and yet one of the things that no one teaches you about being an agent is composure. In theory, you always try to be as composed as the president. But we're human, too, and holding back tears, or at times holding back laughter, is not always easy. I remember sitting behind the president during one of those big televised galas at Ford's Theater. The irony of protecting the president within a few feet of the box in which President Lincoln was assassinated was not lost on me. The cameras occasionally cut to the Reagans so the audience could see how they were reacting, and every time they did that, I appeared on camera with them. One act was a juggler, who was absolutely hysterical. The president was halfway bent over with laughter, and I sat there trying to maintain a professional composure. I kept telling myself that laughing wouldn't look professional, and yet, because everybody else was laughing, I'd look out of place if I wasn't. Every agent has to decide for himself whether or not to show those emotions. But there are times when you can't control them, like that night at Ford's Theatre, or that morning in Normandy when the president read the letter from a D-day hero to his daughter, or that afternoon in Houston. Even now, I can't tell the *Challenger* story without becoming emotional.

After the ceremony, the president and first lady got into the car for the ride to the airfield. It was a very quiet car. I don't think either one of them said a single word. And if the flight down to Texas was somber, the flight home to Washington—leaving those seven families to grieve in Houston—was silent.

There were two major changes at the White House after the 1984 election. Mike Deaver left, and so did Bob DeProspero.

Described in the papers at the time as the Reagans' "virtual surrogate son," there was some speculation that Deaver had been pushed out by Nancy Reagan. She was apparently quoted years later as suggesting that Deaver had come down with a case of "Potomac fever," meaning that he'd reached the point where he felt he could cash in on his White House experiences and make some money as a lobbyist. But I don't think any of that is true. Deaver had indicated on various trips that he intended to leave, so it really wasn't a surprise to those of us who worked with him. There was also some speculation that he'd been eased out because of an alcohol problem. I never saw any signs of that either.

What I did see was what Deaver did for the president, and that cannot be overstated. He understood better than anyone else the sheer power of Ronald Reagan's charisma. The president used to say that if you liked someone on the screen, chances are you would like him in person. Because Deaver knew how likable the president was, he translated that to the small screen. Bill Henkel admirably followed in Deaver's shoes, which were, without a doubt, very big shoes.

Around the same time, Bob DeProspero decided he had to move on. Being agent in charge of PPD is one of those jobs you simply can't do for more than three or four years. It's too stressful, too demanding, and, in the end, too draining. The pressure is constant, and the travel is relentless. Every agent pays a very high price for the honor of being with the president. Time is never your own. You can't plan weekends or family events because something always comes up. Most agents who have that job are ready to leave when the time comes. Bob was promoted to assistant director for training.

One of the straightest, most incorruptible men I have ever known, Bob was, first and foremost, true to himself. Not even the president could tempt him to lower his own high standards. It was Bob's birthday and we were on Air Force One, going somewhere, when President Reagan came back to our compartment with two glasses of champagne. Bob politely refused to drink it because he was on duty. Under the same circumstances, I probably would have taken a sip, if for no other reason than to be congenial. But Bob never faltered. What's more, the press was sitting behind us and they could see us. Who knows what they might have made out of the agent in charge sipping champagne on Air Force One. Bob always knew what he was doing.

Throughout the Secret Service today, you can still find remnants of the "DeProspero model." It may not be called that by agents who never knew him, but the values he instilled in those of us who worked for him were passed down to the next generation of agents, and from them to agents on the job these days. He used to tell us, "If you want something and can't get it and it feels as if you're hitting your head against the wall, you may be hitting a stud, so move a little bit to the left or the right and keep hitting the wall until you find a soft spot, and then you'll get through it."

An important part of being a leader is to take what you learn and teach that to the people who follow. There was a period of about fifteen years when almost every assistant director of the Secret Service, plus the director and the deputy director, came out of Bob DeProspero's PPD. He assembled an extraordinary group of men and women whose success in the Secret Service was no accident, and the success of the Secret Service under their leadership remains a testament to the DeProspero model.

Bob was also a very sensitive man. He understood human nature, which is why, before he left PPD, he sat down with me alone to explain why someone else would be taking over PPD. As assistant agent in charge, I'd had fleeting thoughts about becoming agent in charge. But Bob said that, whereas I could be the agent in charge—and should be—I wasn't going to get the job. "You don't have enough gray hair." His point was that I wasn't salty enough. I'd only been in the Secret Service fourteen years.

Instead, the man taking over was Ray Shaddick. He was the shift leader with the president on the day he was shot—when Jerry Parr shoved the president into the limousine, Ray was right there with him—and therefore looked on by the president as part of the team that had saved his life. It was an easy decision for me to accept. I liked Ray, respected him, and knew that he was the right man for the job. He'd left PPD shortly after the assassination attempt to become agent in charge in Honolulu. I'd gotten to know him on all those survey and preadvance trips to Asia because we went through Hawaii so often.

A tall, good-looking California guy with a mustache—and a more than competent racquetball player—he was totally devoid of ego, one of the things that made him such an outstanding supervisor. This was a man with no pretensions, very low-key, who delegated extraordinarily well. Because he had no overwhelming desire always to be in the picture, he shared his responsibilities with me, for which I will always be grateful. Frankly, I'm not sure I would have been as gracious if I had been agent in charge. We were soon alternating trips, so that I'd go out of town with the president while he stayed in Washington, and vice versa. Not every agent in charge operates that way. Then again, not every agent in charge is as superb a manager as Ray. He left PPD right after the 1988 election to work for a few years as assistant director for investigations. He then decided he wanted to leave Washington and took a downgrade to become agent in charge in Atlanta. This was a man who stepped away from being assistant director to become an agent who reports to the assistant director. Ray Shaddick was a unique man. He retired out of Atlanta and is today head of security for CNN.

Both Bob and Ray served the president well and were able to

institute changes for the better. For instance, agents coming onto PPD were subjected to a two-week trial period so that we could see them and evaluate them. It was important that they be compatible, that they fit in, that they fit the model Bob and Ray were looking for. And not everyone was. Getting onto PPD was difficult enough, and while many agents volunteered, and many others were recommended, there were never enough spots for all applicants. This gave us the opportunity to become even more selective.

Bob's philosophy of always stationing an agent at the primary trauma hospital whenever the president traveled soon manifested itself in "hospital agents" on overseas trips. The White House medical unit traveled with us on preadvance trips to see hospitals and make suitable arrangements. Throughout the West, hospitals are generally well equipped to handle any type of emergency, though that might mean, in some cases, entrusting the life of the president to a foreign surgeon. That might not be a problem in the United Kingdom, France, Germany, Canada, or Australia, but arguably it could easily become a problem in the third world. In such circumstances, the medical office arranges for a U.S. Navy ship having full trauma capabilities to be stationed offshore.

In medical matters, privacy and the presidency are often mutually exclusive terms, and there are times when the lack of privacy really means no privacy at all. When President Reagan was diagnosed with colon cancer in the mid-1980s, he was operated on at Bethesda Naval Hospital. A suite of rooms is set aside at the hospital for VIPs, and it is at the president's disposal, if and when he needs it. There's a meeting room and there's a sitting room, but the room where he sleeps is a hospital room. After his operation, he recuperated for a little while at the White House, then went out to the ranch. Once he was back at work, he had routinely scheduled colonoscopies. As we have a requirement that, regardless of where the president is, an agent must always be with him, I was in the room with him twice while the doctors did the procedure. I was never terribly comfortable being there, but I must say that the president never seemed ill at ease.

In addition to instituting the hospital agent and developing a new attitude toward medical facilities on foreign trips, DeProspero and Shaddick fought for and obtained control over the Uniformed Division at the White House, and changed it.

When I was there, the UD officers reported to the assistant director for protective operations. The PPD, the agents with the president, also reported to the assistant director for protective operations, but along a separate chain of command. It was always an issue that we, the agents, had no operational control over the UD officers at the White House. In practice it wasn't necessarily that restrictive, but in theory it could have been, and that created some tensions. If we were in the State Dining Room and there was a UD officer there and I wanted him moved, I could say, Please move, and generally he would do that. But he didn't have to, because, technically, he didn't report to us. It was the same thing at the Naval Observatory when I was running the vice president's detail. It had the potential to be a problem, and occasionally it did become one. Today, the chief of the UD at the White House reports to the PPD special agent in charge.

We increased our emphasis on running AOPs, going through an ever widening range of scenarios, which included airport arrivals and departures. Granted that not much can happen on a plane, except a medical emergency, and we've got the doctor right there with some medical facilities on board. But we worked AOPs in those situations, and the rarer ones, too, like those on horseback. Increased training of the agents on PPD was emphasized with an eye toward finding out what to expect, finding out where the choke points were. We even thought about running some AOPs at the White House, but it's a working office, and the press is there at all times. After looking at the various options, we worried that if people saw us running around with guns drawn and with helicopters overhead, they might not understand that it was a practice drill. So we decided it really wouldn't be practical to do that. Since my day, I understand, the Secret Service has built a replica of the White House façade at Beltsville.

DeProspero and Shaddick also recognized that the nature of threats was beginning to change, and began adjusting accordingly. Back in the days of John Kennedy, the principal threat to the president was an assassin. For the next two decades—and this was reinforced by the assassination attempt on Ronald Reagan—the Secret Service believed that it needed to prevent another Oswald or another Hinckley trying to shoot the president with a handgun or rifle in the traditional way. But as we moved through the 1980s, and the world began to change, the threat began to change, too. We've seen it more dramatically since the late 1990s, and in its most startling form on September 11, 2001.

The potential of the lone assassin still exists, and you have to protect the president from him, but it's no longer the only scenario. The threat has become much more sophisticated. There are suicide bombers and car bombs, rockets, mortars, and mines, and chemical weapons. Since 9/11, the threats have multiplied. It's a very different world. So the Secret Service has had to make those adjustments and create circumstances and procedures that counteract them all. And anyone who traces the history of the changes the Secret Service has made in the face of that changing threat can go straight back to Bob DeProspero and Ray Shaddick and the way they ran PPD.

One event that is now standard operating procedure for the president and vice president in a motorcade is called "an impromptu." It's when they drop by somewhere unannounced to say hello and stay just long for the press to get some pictures. Skillfully handled, it is the impromptu that often turns up on the evening news. But they are never as impromptu as they look. The stops have to be planned in advance, and measures have to be taken to make certain they're safe.

Knowing that impromptus are part of the package, staffers and advance agents study motorcade routes and pick out two or three places where an impromptu might happen. They choose diners, bowling alleys—Dan Quayle could hardly pass a Dairy Queen without wanting to stop because, as he always pointed out, "We have the same initials"—coffee shops, sometimes even bars and restaurants, any place where Middle America might feel a kinship with the president or vice president.

The place where we would stop would be decided at the last moment, and once it was, a few minutes before the motorcade would arrive, we'd send an agent in. He'd order a cup of coffee, look around, and decide whether or not it was safe. He'd check out the best way in and the best way out. If there was a big sign saying "Welcome Mr. President," we'd drive by. We'd also call it off if the agent reported back that the place was rowdy or too crowded.

In theory, impromptus were generally considered safe. The chances that someone with a weapon would be waiting in a diner or a bowling alley for the president to show up on an unannounced visit were pretty remote. That is, as long as no one knew we were coming. A minute before the stop, the agent inside the venue would report back to the limousine that it was or wasn't okay to stop. Only that agent, the immediate staff, and those of us in the limousine would know. The police with the motorcade probably could have guessed where we'd stop, but they weren't told until the very last minute. The motorcade would pull up unannounced, then we'd do the impromptu and leave as fast as we could. Five minutes was about as long as we could stay without starting to draw a crowd. After all, anyone driving by would see limousines and police cars and motorcycles parked out front and wonder, What's going on?

When I was a young agent, impromptus were rarely done, but we live in the age of the media, and they've become part of the politician's repertoire. President Reagan liked diners. He would walk in, say hello to everybody, order something—but not drink it or eat it—and stick around just long enough for a local news crew to get some tape of him there. Then he'd say good-bye and we'd be gone. Almost every motorcade we did with him had at least one impromptu.

I recall being with him once in Pittsburgh on our way to the airport when we did an impromptu at a bar that was filled with people drinking beer. In walked Ronald Reagan. Even if the people there hadn't voted for him, they were still awed by the sight of the president of the United States standing right there. People called out, "Hey, Ronnie, can I buy you a beer?" No one could do an impromptu like him, with the possible exception of Bill Clinton. And every now and then I stumble across some place where there's been an impromptu, and sure enough, there's a prominently displayed picture of President Reagan and the cup or glass he used.

Once, with Dan Quayle in Phoenix, Arizona, we were driving by a high school and he spotted a football practice going on. It was right there by the road, so we pulled in. He got out and walked around the field with all the players. It was perfectly safe, not at all disruptive for the school, and five minutes later we were back in the car. It made for some terrific photographs.

The inauguration of the president of the United States is a military event run by the Military District of Washington. The Secret Service handles all the security arrangements, but the U.S. Army has traditional charge of the event and all the protocol.

At his inaugural in 1977, Jimmy Carter walked for several blocks from the Capitol to the White House. But it was planned that he would only walk certain blocks and ride the limousine for the rest. Pennsylvania Avenue is lined with buildings, and they have thousands of windows, so we sent people into the buildings to make sure every window stayed shut. Each side of the street had countersnipers watching with binoculars, making sure no one opened a window. Had there been even one, President Carter's walk would have ended abruptly, with agents escorting him quickly into the limousine.

For all sorts of reasons, not the least of which were weather and the fact that President Reagan was considerably older in January 1981 than Carter was at the time of his inauguration—it was decided that the Reagans would not walk. Instead, he would use an open car for the trip down Pennsylvania Avenue. In those days there was a hole in the bubble top, where the president and first lady could stand up and wave. They were exposed from the waist up. The assassination attempt a few months later meant that 1981 was the last time an open car was ever used at any president's inauguration.

Four years later, I was scheduled to take President Reagan from the Capitol down to the White House in the inaugural parade. This is something every agent wants to do once in a lifetime. But it was so bitterly cold that the parade had to be canceled. And as far as I know, it was one of the few times in our history that's ever happened. The president took his oath of office inside the Capitol under the rotunda.

That night, the president and first lady made the rounds of all the usual parties, which might have been fun for the people attending them, but wasn't necessarily fun for the Reagans or the agents with them. All too often, for the president, the first lady, and the working shift, parties are a real chore. For the agents the worst of these are, ironically, the most glamorous for the guests—state dinners. These are highly programmed black-tie evenings, filled with protocol. I attended dozens of them, but after the first few they lost their glitter and became routine.

They begin with the president and first lady greeting the visiting head of state on the North Portico. The visitor either stays at the Blair House—which is the official guest house across the street from the White House—or at his embassy or at a hotel, and timing is critical. Military officers are lined up on the north grounds, and the cars are scheduled to arrive at specific times. The president steps off the North Portico to greet the visiting head of state and spouse and escorts them upstairs into the Oval Yellow Room of the residence for a private reception. The movie *The American President* is a realistic version of how it works.

At a certain point, the other guests at this private reception come downstairs while the president, first lady, guest of honor, and spouse go out the side door and down the grand staircase, during which "Ruffles and Flourishes" is played. The four of them then go into the East Room to stand in a receiving line. After that, everyone goes into the State Dining Room at the other end of the building for dinner. The dining room is usually set up to accommodate a dozen round tables of ten people each. The president sits in front of the Lincoln fireplace, facing the room, and the first lady sits at the other end of the room facing him. There's then a whole protocol list of who sits where. The head of state sits with the first lady and the spouse sits with the president. The Secret Service supervisor sits on a chair placed behind and to the left of the president, right next to the fireplace. Another agent sits behind the first lady.

The chair behind and to the left of the president is actually closer to the table where the secretary of state sits. In my day that was George Shultz. I don't know if this was ever publicized, and I don't think it was contrived, but at every state dinner there were actresses, especially with the Reagans, and it always seemed that the prettiest women—I'm thinking of Brooke Shields, Christie Brinkley, and Cindy Crawford—always ended up sitting next to Shultz.

During dinner, certain things happen at certain times. The president gives the toast, and the visiting head of state responds with a toast. Then, at a precise moment, the string section of a military band comes in and wanders through the room. After dinner, cordials and coffee are served in three rooms—the Blue, Red, and Green—

where everyone mingles until the president, the first lady, and the guests of honor move into the East Room for the entertainment. In my day that could be anyone from Andy Williams to Itzhak Perlman. Everyone had assigned seats. The president would sit in the front row with the first lady and the guests of honor. After the entertainment, which lasted half an hour, the president, first lady, and the guests of honor would move into the main foyer, where a military dance band would be playing. The Reagans would normally dance once, say good night to everyone, and leave.

By then it would be close to eleven o'clock. The agents were always anxious for the president and first lady to go upstairs, because we'd been working all day, and the sooner they left, the sooner we could leave. The rest of the crowd usually stayed much later, and there were times the dancing went on well past midnight. That's the way state dinners are still done today. If a Secret Service agent says that he or she enjoys these evenings, you can bet they're new to the job.

In the United States, wherever Air Force One flies, air traffic control clears the airspace so that the president's plane is alone. Many countries are pretty competent at doing the same thing, but some occasionally try to show the president that he's welcome and thereby upset a lot of people in the offering. Every now and then some country will scramble fighter jets to accompany Air Force One on its approach to the landing field. No one on board appreciates that, especially the air force pilots, who do whatever they can to get those fighters away from their plane. Other nations have odd requirements. The Soviets, for instance, used to require that one of their own pilots be on the plane whenever Air Force One flew into Soviet airspace.

Each president has his own habits and needs. George H.W. Bush, for example, usually went out to Andrews Air Force Base several hours before he was scheduled to leave on a long overnight flight. He'd get on board at, say, eleven o'clock and promptly go to sleep. The plane would then leave at whatever time it needed to, often several hours later, which gave Bush the benefit of a full night's sleep. It wasn't easy on the agents, who needed to be there with him, but it was convenient for him. I find it difficult to imagine how he could sleep through takeoff. President Reagan's little habit was to slip out of his trousers and get into gray sweatpants, which he wore with his white shirt and tie.

For the most part, the president stayed in his stateroom throughout the flight and worked on his upcoming events, although on the big international trips he would sometimes wander through the plane—in his sweatpants—and often go talk to the press. The depiction of what happens on that plane in the film *Air Force One* was suspenseful, but not at all realistic. The idea that terrorists could somehow take over the president's plane is completely far-fetched. It simply could not happen. Everyone going on board Air Force One is put through a metal detector, except the agents and the president. All luggage is X-rayed and specially tagged for each trip. When you arrive in a city, you don't carry your bags, the air force and the Secret Service secure the luggage and it gets delivered to each room. That was one of the nicest perks of being on the detail. You'd put your bag outside your room before you went to bed, and when you got to the next city, your luggage would magically appear in your room again.

There were no flight announcements by the pilot on Air Force One, at least not in those days. Also, unlike regular commercial flights, once the plane landed and taxied off the active runway, you could stand up, and most people did. Agents didn't normally wear weapons when we flew—so they'd stow them in a carry-on bag. It was while the plane was taxiing that the shift would be getting ready to leave the plane, putting on their weapons and their jackets and heading for the back door. I always moved up front so that I could get off the plane right behind the president.

The working shift and the supervisor flew with the president. The rest of the Secret Service detail was either on the car plane or the press plane. For foreign trips, the press plane was a 747, which meant we could get more than three hundred people on it. Some agents also flew on the backup plane. It's not generally known that wherever the president goes there are two planes for him in case there is a problem with one. Provisions also have to be made for the U.S. Air Force's flying command post. We didn't see much of it, but it was always somewhere nearby in case it was needed. Everybody knows about its existence, and it has appeared in films like *The Sum of All Fears,* but the plane and its operations are classified. I will say, however, that the size of the president's entourage, and the equipment needed to support his trips, sometimes astounded people in the host nations. When we went to China with President Reagan, the Chinese were very surprised at the number of people we were bringing with us. It was during the survey trip, with Bill Henkel and Mike Deaver, when we sat down with our Chinese counterparts, that one of them produced a big map of the airport where the president was going to land. He pointed to a spot off to the side and proudly showed it to us: This is where we will put your president's airplane. He couldn't understand that there would be nine hundred people and that we'd have nineteen planes.

President Reagan traveled more on Air Force One than the three previous presidents combined. According to White House records, the Boeing 707 with the tail number 27000 flew 566,386 miles with presidents Nixon, Ford, and Carter, and 631,640 with President Reagan. Today, 27000 is a permanent exhibit at the Ronald Reagan Presidential Library in California.

If the president flew that much, staff members racked up at least three times as many miles for the survey, preadvance, and advance trips that had to be made before the trip with him. I certainly got more than my share of them, and in all the miles I flew as part of

PPD, only twice did I ever experience anything approaching a problem. The first time was on the advance to China, flying in the backup 707, tail number 26000.

At certain times of the year, Midway Island is inundated by huge albatrosses, affectionately known as gooney birds. Some of them stand nearly four feet tall. Landing there to refuel, we were all amazed at the literally thousands of gooney birds that covered the airfield. The navy had to run trucks up and down the runway all day long to clear away the birds. The usual survey-preadvance gang was sitting in the staff area, all of us very accustomed to flying in this particular airplane. But this time, as we pulled off the ground, the plane lurched almost straight up in the air and began to shudder. Bells now went off in the cockpit. We were suddenly losing lift and shaking so badly that I realized the plane had stalled and was about to crash. The crisis lasted fifteen seconds, then the bells stopped, and we leveled off and flew away. A few minutes later, the air force advance officer—who had come along to check runaways and approaches for Air Force One—walked out of the cockpit white with fear. He explained that as we took off, a flight of gooney birds took off in front of us. If we had hit them, they'd have gotten into the engines, and we would have gone into the water. So the pilot pulled back to avoid the birds, and that set off the stall alarms. He said we were at the absolute edge of the envelope, within seconds of dropping tail first into the water.

Neither the president nor the press corps was on the plane, so it never made the papers. Although the second, and only other, time something happened in flight, the president was aboard, and so was the press corps. It didn't make the papers either, probably because none of the reporters knew how close we had come to crashing.

It was snowing badly that morning as Air Force One made its approach to a certain midwestern city. I had trouble seeing anything out the window because of the weather. Then, all of a sudden, the plane made a hard right turn, and now, out my window, I could see buildings right there. They were very close. We landed a few seconds later. It looked to me as if we'd missed the approach to the runway and nearly smashed into one of those buildings. None of the crew ever mentioned it. No one else ever spoke about it either.

After four years on PPD it was time to leave, but I left filled with regrets. Although I was being promoted to agent in charge of the Dignitary Protective Division (DPD)—a very good job with a lot less travel—I felt as if I were leaving my second family, not just the agents and the staff, but the Reagans as well. We were well into Reagan's second term, the political pressure was off, and it was a more relaxed time. The Iran-Contra scandal hadn't been exposed yet, and speculation about the president's health was only just starting to make the news. I can honestly say that from the first day I walked into the Oval Office, until September 28, 1986, when I left, I never noticed any change in his memory or his comportment.

The last trip I took with him was to Omaha, Nebraska, on September 24, 1986. We went through a whole series of events, and I kept thinking to myself, This is my last motorcade with him, the last speech with him, the last rope line with him. When we got on the plane to fly home—my last flight on Air Force One with him—the president came back to spend a few minutes with me, to say thank you.

It was traditional that when you left PPD, you and your family would be escorted into the Oval Office for a photo with the president. So a few days later, Barbara and Michelle came with me to the White House. The president was his usual self, warm and friendly and funny. Michelle was now fourteen, and when he spoke with her and gave her some gifts, she kept saying to the president, Thank you, thank you, thank you. She was very cute, and he seemed delighted.

What I was only beginning to realize was the toll the Secret Service in general, and the PPD in particular, had taken on me. Being assigned to the president, especially as a supervisor, means you can never get your job out of your head. You're always worrying about something, not just some visit, but about doing the right thing under stress, about being ready when something wrong happens, about all of the agents under your supervision. And you're always thinking about time—how time is never your own. It affects so many of the things that are important in your own life.

CHAPTER THIRTEEN

SHEPHERD ONE

On May 13, 1981, Pope John Paul II was shot while riding in an
open convertible in St. Peter's Square. For the second time in my life,
I would be protecting someone who had barely survived an assassina-
tion attempt.

The ruler of Samoa loved roller coasters. He loved amusement
parks, and he loved California, too, where there are a whole lot of
amusement parks, particularly ones with roller coasters. As agent in
charge of the Dignitary Protective Division (DPD), I asked my old
friend Earl Devaney to look after him whenever he came for a visit.
But the ruler of Samoa was a heavyset gentleman, and Earl wasn't a
small guy either, which didn't leave a lot of room inside the roller
coaster cars. So Earl recruited a younger, slimmer agent who rode in
roller coasters all over California with the ruler of Samoa. We used
to call such requirements "Other duties as assigned." Although Earl
usually preferred the more sarcastic label "Just another opportunity
to serve."

During any given month, DPD might have fifteen to twenty
heads of state on visits somewhere in the United States. While I was
running DPD, we looked after individuals such as the prime minister of Japan, King Hussein of Jordan, Margaret Thatcher, and her

successor, John Major. In many cases, heads of state brought their children along, and it never came as a surprise that somewhere on the itinerary was Disneyland or Disney World. Because most of those visiting dignitaries are otherwise unknown to the American public—how many people in Florida would recognize the prime minister of Belgium?—escorting them around was easy. There are issues such as, Do we stand in line? but those things are easily expedited, and a lot of Secret Service agents in Florida know the ins and outs of Disney World.

We also looked after Mikhail Gorbachev, who made two trips to the States. On his second trip, in December 1988, I met his plane at Kennedy Airport. When Dokuchayev came down the steps, he spotted me on the tarmac, hurried over to throw his arms around me, and said loudly in English, "My good American friend." For the head of the KGB detail to embrace an American in front of the press like that was a very public statement. Sadly, it was the last time I saw him. Fourteen years later, in June 2002, I found myself in Moscow and asked about him. I was told that he'd retired. I tried to find out where he was. No one seemed to know.

By now, Gorbachev was considerably more media savvy than he'd been in Geneva. On a motorcade trip through Manhattan, he ordered his driver to stop so that he could say hello to some American people. I was in the lead car with the chief of patrol of the New York Police Department when I heard on the radio that Gorbachev was stopping. By the time we were out of our car, Gorbachev was on the sidewalk trying to shake hands with a crowd of a hundred startled New Yorkers. Minimizing the risk to him meant minimizing the time he was exposed like that, but he wasn't on the street very long because he didn't need to be. The whole thing lasted about four minutes. As soon as the press got photos and video footage of him, he was back in his car and the motorcade was moving again. The NYPD chief was very upset about the impromptu. Fundamentally, I didn't disagree with him, because having Gorbachev on the street when we weren't expecting such a stunt wasn't a good thing. However, if we'd told Gorbachev he couldn't do an impromptu in New York, what would he say when the president went to Moscow and, in a similar way, wanted to greet people in Red Square?

It was the same reason why we allowed the Russians to bring their own Zil limousines on that trip, the first time that had ever happened. It's called reciprocity, and it underlined one of the key areas of my job at DPD. We never wanted them to tell us we couldn't bring our cars to Russia.

In fact, reciprocity became such a concern of mine at DPD that I told our Canadian RCMP counterparts, When you come to the States you're welcome to bring weapons. To show them how sincere I was, I even offered to issue guns to them for every visit. They always refused. I did the same thing with the British, who also refused. However, the point was made: They could do in our country what we needed to do in their country.

Reciprocity notwithstanding, I was told that the main reason I was moved to DPD was to handle the pope's visit, scheduled for September 1987. He would travel to nine cities in ten days and participate in over a hundred events. This would be the longest trip the pope would ever make to the United States, and it required the single largest protective effort in the history of the United States Secret Service. It would also be the most stressful ten days of my life.

The man coordinating the visit was Bob Lynch, general secretary of the National Conference of Catholic Bishops (NCCB). An intelligent, articulate, and personable man, he'd been serving as a parish priest in Miami in 1979 when he was called on to help with the pope's first trip to the States that year. Only a few cities were included—New York, Boston, Chicago, and Washington—but Lynch so impressed the NCCB and the Vatican staff that they moved him to Washington. Now in his midforties, he and I met for the first time in January 1987. During that meeting, he said that for the pope's visit in 1979, the Secret Service had disguised an agent as a priest and he wondered if we would do that again. I said no. Besides the fact that there was no operational advantage, it was deceptive and inappropriate. I told Bob, "We are who we are." He then explained that he wanted to visit the cities on the pope's agenda three times before the pope did. It would be the typical survey, preadvance, and advance routines. For the advance, we would be joined by some senior staff from the Vatican, including Father Roberto Tucci, the man in charge of papal visits.

Lynch said that, in each city, the pope would stay at the bishop's or archbishop's official residence, and that I would stay there with the pope. At first glance, protecting the pontiff under those conditions was very straightforward. The bishops and archbishops were also proposing venues and events. That worried me because their choices would be based on a religious agenda without an intensive input of the security considerations. Some stops were obligatory. The pope had to visit local cathedrals. Others seemed nonnegotiable from the start, such as the absolutely gigantic outdoor masses. So the survey trip became all about sitting down with the bishops and archbishops, listening to what they wanted the pope to do and where they wanted the pope to go, then seeing the sites for ourselves. It would be my only opportunity to make my views known if a venue or event was unacceptable. Because I didn't know Lynch very well, I could only hope that when I said something was unacceptable, he would be my advocate.

I underestimated my new friend. Throughout the survey trip, we discussed every site, every parade route, and every event, and he made a real effort to understand the intricacies of protecting the pope. Then, at the risk of infuriating those bishops and archbishops, when he knew I was right, Lynch stood shoulder to shoulder with me.

Getting decisions set in stone, however, was not always easy. In New Orleans, for example, the pope was going to hold a special event for ninety-six thousand children at the Superdome. When I saw where Archbishop Philip M. Hannan intended to build the stage, I disapproved. Hannan was a high-powered, determined man who had assisted in serving the funeral mass for John F. Kennedy in 1963. He and I stood on the fifty-yard line while I indicated, No one can sit in the seats from this section to that section because we don't want people sitting behind the pope. My no-go zone took thousands of seats away from him, and he refused to understand why that mattered. I reminded him we'd do the same thing with the president of the United States, but he never accepted the argument. However, to the archbishop's chagrin, those seats stayed empty.

While we were on that trip, my mother, Dorothy, had a hip replacement operation. She was in Florida and a bit frail. I was in Phoenix and couldn't get to her. Luckily, my brother Tom was with her. But Lynch recognized my concern, and one afternoon, during a break in our schedule, we went back to the archbishop's residence where Lynch suggested, "I'll serve a mass for your mother." I stood next to him at the altar, deeply touched by the sheer humanity of this man. He is, still, one of my dearest friends.

The survey trip was followed by several months of work, during which ten days' worth of venues and 114 events were fixed. Once the schedule was established, Lynch and I set off again, to go over every detail with the visit committees in every city. When we were done with that, we did it a third time, so that everyone knew exactly how everything would be handled. Some sites were more complicated than others. The pope was going to conduct open-air masses in odd places, like the campus at Florida Atlantic University in Miami and Laguna Seca Racetrack in Monterey, California. He was also going to hold mass in the Superdome in New Orleans, Sun Devil Stadium on the campus at Arizona State University in Phoenix, the Coliseum and Dodger Stadium in Los Angeles, Candlestick Park in San Francisco, and the Silverdome in Detroit. Logistics were nothing short of a nightmare. And problems cropped up at every site. For instance, at Sun Devil Stadium, there's a huge sign bearing the stadium's name, and the question became, Would the word "devil" be left uncovered for the mass? It was. In Detroit, the agent in charge of the field office—my friend Jim Huse from the Rockefeller detail—told me that Cardinal Edmund Szoka, the archbishop of Detroit, was a very worried man. The Silverdome had recently hosted one of those world wrestling knockdown events and had filled the place with ninety thousand fans. His Eminence fretted that wrestling might outdraw the pope. Of course, it didn't.

The White House also wanted to be included in the planning because President and Mrs. Reagan would be greeting the pope when he landed in Miami. It was decided that would happen at the airport. The three would then meet privately a few hours later. For this meeting Lynch selected an impressive old Spanish estate called Vizcaya, which is now a museum.

My worry was getting the pope safely through this maze of venues and events. That also meant worrying about all of the backup that the agents needed to make these events happen safely, including hotels, meals, and transportation. My DPD staff worked on this full-time for almost eight months, fitting each part of the trip together as if it were a jigsaw puzzle. More than once during that time I reminded myself how grateful I was that Mike Deaver and Bill Henkel had taught me how to do this.

The resources we were going to devote to this trip dwarfed anything that had ever been used for anyone else, at any time, even the president of the United States. The Secret Service entourage totaled more than 750, which included three shifts of agents, Uniformed Division officers to work the magnetometers, and post standers. At each venue, we supplemented our own presence with thousands of local police.

The plane the pope would use while in the States was a leased TWA 727, configured spaciously with first-class seats, but otherwise open. There were no private compartments. Its call sign was

Shepherd One. In addition to his plane, we had two L-1011s to take the traveling entourage of the press and off-duty agents, and two sets of "advance packages," each comprising one C-5A and two C-141s, which leapfrogged so that we had identical packages in every city. Each C-5A carried one popemobile, one limousine, one follow-up car, and one tactical car. The C-141s had the UD officers, the magnetometers, and the post standers. We also had several helicopters to get us from airports into town, including a Huey presidential helicopter for the pope, which carried six people, and much larger H-53s, seating fourteen to sixteen, for the press.

We needed so many people and so much backup because the crowds we'd be dealing with were gigantic. Until then, the largest crowd I'd ever experienced was with President Reagan during a 1984 presidential campaign stop in Orange County, California. He drew just over fifty thousand people. The pope would get many times more than that. For example, at the parade and open mass in San Antonio, the crowd was estimated at two and a half million.

While Lynch and I were still working out the plans, in the middle of March, I flew to Rome to meet with the head of papal security, Michele Chabin, and his staff. They brought me along with them to a local event and what struck me, immediately, was the semihysteria that the pope generated. It was the first time that I had any inkling of what was about to happen.

Although I did not meet the pope on that trip, I did get a long look at the popemobile and decided I didn't like it. Prior to the attempt on the pontiff's life in 1981, the popemobile was open. It was little more than a Mercedes jeep with a place for him to stand. As a result of the attack, a Plexiglas cover was fitted over the back. But that wasn't much of a deterrent. I wasn't impressed with how well armored the cars were, and I didn't like the fact that there was no way to get from the driving compartment into the popemobile without climbing out of the car. Back in the States, I told Lynch, "The popemobiles need to be modified and we would want to reconfigure them."

Lynch spoke to Chabin, who personally gave me permission to do what was needed. A pair of identical popemobiles were flown to Washington and delivered to the Secret Service garage. Because the bubble was a heavy, single piece of Plexiglas, we cut a big section out of it just behind the driver's compartment, but then had to reinforce the remaining Plexiglas so the bubble wouldn't cave in. We made the opening large enough to climb through, and I spent time practicing that move. The guys at the garage were superefficient and managed the reconstruction in under three days. Later, when the pope saw his new machine, he seemed surprised. But when he realized that the agent in the front seat could now speak with him and, if need be, reach him quickly, he understood why we did it. The Vatican still uses our redesigned popemobiles.

Throughout the preparation stage, Lynch was relentless in constantly warning everyone about the emotional response of the crowds we would face. He'd go into cathedrals and churches and tell event coordinators that when the pope came down the center aisle, mayhem would reign. He would admonish them not to use ordinary ropes at the ends of the pews because people would lunge through them. He'd say, you have to block off the ends of pews with two-by-fours. He would tell organizers over and over again, "You've got to put hard barriers inside the church because nothing else will hold back the surging crowds." He made that point firmly to us, too, insisting that none of the old rules would apply. From what I'd seen in Rome, I knew he was right, and for every rope line, we used wooden or metal barriers.

Shift agents were specially selected from field offices across the country. Once we had a full complement, I brought them to Beltsville for three days' training. We worked AOPs with the popemobile, but mostly we practiced rope lines. Every Secret Service agent knows how to work a rope line, and every supervisor has his or her own technique. I always liked to be on the protectee's left shoulder looking ahead, with my hand around his waist or his back. But none of us had ever worked rope lines with crowds as big and as emotional as the ones we would get. So we practiced with crowds— hundreds of "extras" were brought to Beltsville to re-create the excitement of crowds—and we even had an agent dressed like the pope. We practiced attacks and shootings, and once we went through all of that, we started again with rope lines and crowds.

We simulated the real thing as best we could, but even then the real thing turned out to be much more than any of us ever expected. No amount of training could have prepared us fully for such raw emotion and abundant enthusiasm. We actually had people fainting in front of the pope. Talk about anomalies, confusion, and losing control. Those were dangerous situations and created serious problems for us. The pope would make his way along the rope line, reaching out, touching people's hands, and everyone in the crowd— nuns, priests, laypeople—was reaching out to touch him. Babies were being handed to him. Children were fighting to get close to him. And people were keeling over in front of us.

It was equally difficult for some of the people protecting him to remain unemotional. Policeman along motorcade routes, who were supposed to be keeping crowds back, were snapping pictures as we drove by. I even had to discipline one of our post standers in a church when I spotted him standing on a pew to take a picture. Such an outpouring of emotion never happened with politicians. I'd never seen crowds react to any single human being the way every crowd reacted to him. Nor have I ever seen anyone react to crowds the way he did. They fed off each other in a spectacular way.

Of course, all the agents were armed the same way they were for the president. We even referred to the level of protection as "a presidential package" and included CAT teams. The Intelligence Division came into the preparations and was soon working overtime. There were good reasons to worry about the safety of the pope. Not only had he been shot, but in his native Poland, the Solidarity movement was going ahead at full speed and Poland's Communist leaders were on their last legs. The Soviet Union was going through similar turmoil, and there were issues in East Germany. Throughout much of the Communist bloc, the pope—and President Reagan, too— were being held responsible for the growing popular unrest. And we had our own right-wing extremists to deal with inside the United States. Intelligence picked up threats, and agents soon fanned out all over the country to investigate and evaluate them.

I studied the attempt on the pope's life in preparation for this, but it wasn't particularly relevant. The circumstances surrounding that attempt were not going to be repeated here. In Rome the pope had been in an open car. There had been only an inner perimeter. It had been too easy for the assassin to get close. I made the decision— and there was some controversy within the Secret Service about this—that there would a "hundred-yard rule." I felt strongly that anyone who got within a hundred yards of the pope would have to pass through a magnetometer. The exception would be the big stadium events. I wasn't comfortable simply hoping that somebody sitting in the far end of say, the Silverdome—more than a hundred yards from the altar—wouldn't have a good shot at the pope. Over the course of a mass lasting three and a half hours, such a person might somehow make his way down to the foot of the altar. My solution was to require that everyone coming into every stadium would be magged. Even if that meant putting 106,000 people through metal detectors, which is what happened at the Los Angeles Coliseum, we'd do it. There were some people in the Secret Service who thought we were overreacting. I believed it was necessary, that we had the equipment to do it, and that we had the capability to do it. Finally, I knew that the director, John Simpson, supported this approach.

But not everyone did. The assistant director for protective operations had come out of the investigative side and was fairly vocal about the way I was handling things. We'd had our moments in the past when it came to protection, and now, he argued, we could be just as effective protecting the pope with fewer people. I don't think he ever realized that this assignment could not be compared to anything we had ever done before. The events were more intense, more focused, and more emotional, and were made considerably more complex by the added dynamic of colossal crowds. In emotional terms the pope was a prime target. I wasn't prepared to take any risks—I had the DeProspero training.

I knew that if someone came looking for an opportunity to create violence, the possibility existed that he could find it. What's more, there would be repetitive opportunities. If a potential assassin missed the pope in the first city, he had eight more to choose from. Moreover, the pope's schedule was public information. Anyone who wanted to know where the pope was going to be at any given time over those ten days could easily find out. Anyone looking to do him harm had 114 chances in nine cities to take advantage of that opportunity. We were going to make absolutely certain there were no opportunities. Which is why I spent almost every waking moment of those eight months preparing for this trip.

On September 9, 1987, one hour before the pope arrived, President and Mrs. Reagan landed at Miami International Airport on Air Force One. As soon as they parked, I called Ray Shaddick and asked if I could bring Bob Lynch over to say hello. He radioed back that the Reagans were looking forward to seeing us. So Bob and I walked over to Air Force One and climbed the stairs. I hadn't seen the Reagans since I'd left the detail almost a year before, and they were as gracious as always. The president kept saying to me, "You're going to take good care of the pope, aren't you?" And I kept promising him that I would.

Although I didn't say as much to him, I was nervous about this. Tens of millions of people were anxiously awaiting what would be, for many, their chance of a lifetime to see the pope. What worried me were all the things I didn't know: I didn't know the pope, and when you don't know the person you're protecting, you can sometimes find yourself walking on thin ice; I didn't know his staff; I didn't know the cardinals and didn't know if they would interfere with what I needed to do. What's more, protecting the pope is not like protecting an American president. The president is, after all, pretty much a regular guy. The pope is not a regular guy, and the protocols are starkly different. The Roman Catholic Church is a state, but with a bureaucracy that doesn't operate the way a republic does. And I didn't know how this state would react if there were unexpected conflicts.

Furthermore, being the product of Catholic schools, I'd been raised to think of the pope with reverence, but I wasn't spending ten days with him in the context of being a Catholic. I would be constantly at his side because I was the United States Secret Service agent directly responsible for his safety. To accomplish that, to maintain the highest level of professionalism, I decided that I would not do anything with him, either in public or in private, that manifested my Catholicism. I would not kneel, I would not kiss his ring, I would not bless myself. I would always be respectful, but my respect would be only displayed in secular ways. I'm not sure when the pontiff realized I was Catholic, but at no point during those ten days did he indicate in any way that my secular comportment was an issue with him.

By the time Bob Lynch and I left the Reagans, the pope's flight was on final approach. Some minutes later, an Alitalia 747—with the papal flag flying out the pilot's window—taxied to a stop and the door opened. I climbed the steps and walked aboard. And there he was. It took me a second to realize that this really was the pope. Chabin and Tucci introduced me. I said, "It's very nice to meet you. I promise that we'll take very good care of you." He said, "It's very nice to meet you, and thank you." And that was it. This wasn't the time for small talk, because President and Mrs. Reagan were waiting. I left the plane, and then the pope came down the steps to be greeted

by the Reagans. After the welcoming speeches, we all got in our separate limousines and went off to the Reagans' private meeting with
him at Vizcaya.

What was especially nice for me about the Miami visit was that
Lynch had arranged for my mother and his mother to be at the first
public event, a speech the pope was making in a small church. Naturally, our mothers were given front-row seats. When I brought the
pope into the church, he'd been briefed to greet the women in the first
pew. He shook their hands, and pictures were taken. After the visit,
the church in Miami put out a book with photographs from his visit,
and in the middle of the book there's a two-page picture from behind
the pope with Dorothy Petro and Virginia Lynch in the background.

That event was followed by a big parade through downtown Miami, with more than a million people lining the route. I was in the
front seat of the popemobile. The day ended at the very modest
ranch house that was the archbishop's residence. Because there
wasn't enough room for me inside, Lynch arranged to have a camper
put in the yard where I would sleep. It was a good idea, but I didn't
sleep very much because there was so much noise all night long,
with police radios blaring and officers talking. The next morning,
the pope hosted a series of private audiences, and Lynch again
arranged for our mothers to be there. We took them into the house
with eight or ten other people. They met the pope again and had
more pictures taken. I kept watching my mother with him, and I
knew she was thinking, "It can't get much better than this."

The second day, among other things, there was a meeting with
Jewish community leaders. The pope always did that when he visited
somewhere, because he was very conscious of the need to maintain a
close relationship with members of other faiths, both for historical and
personal reasons. I later learned that, as a young boy in Poland, one of
his best friends was a Jewish girl and, I think, that when they were
teenagers, they may have dated. She got married and had children, but
he stayed in touch, and I know that her family visited the Vatican.

The pope spoke English well, but in a very deliberate manner. His speeches were typed, double-spaced, on sheets of white paper. After the first couple of speeches we discovered—because we were counting—that it took him two minutes per page to read them. So at every speech, we'd ask Tucci, "How many pages?" If he answered, ten, we'd have a good indication of when to start preparing to leave. On that second day, the pope spoke to four to five hundred priests in a large church, and this time when I asked Tucci, how many pages, he said, "Twenty-two." But as the pope delivered his speech, the priests clapped and cheered after every line. I could see that the pope was getting a little frustrated because he knew how long the speech was. He must have been thinking to himself—as we all were—at this pace it will drag on for three hours. He plodded on, and they clapped and cheered. After the seventh or eighth interruption by applause, he held up the twenty-two pieces of paper and said, "It's a long way to Tipperary." The place went crazy. And we got out of there in under an hour.

Then came the gigantic outdoor mass in Miami. It was nothing short of breathtaking. The altar was absolutely enormous, built high enough so that three hundred thousand people could see him. Huge canvas sheets—which must have been fifty to sixty feet long—hung behind the altar on long cables, billowing in the wind like sails on a schooner.

However, as I climbed the steps to the altar with the pope, I could see a typical South Florida storm rolling in. He began the mass, and before long there was thunder and lightning off in the distance. Huge speakers were mounted on gigantic scaffolds, and we had placed countersniper teams up there, too. When I saw lightning, I made the decision to bring them down. I was also very concerned that the pope wasn't safe at the altar. By now someone was standing next to him, shielding him from the rain with an umbrella. But I was getting reports on my radio from the command post that the weather service was predicting gusts from forty to fifty miles per hour. We'd checked with the engineers, and those canvas sails behind the pope were only stressed at 35 mph. Anything more than that and they could snap. So as the pope read his homily at two minutes per page, I turned to Father Tucci and said, "We can't continue. If those cables snap, people could get injured or killed. When he finishes the homily, we are taking him off the altar."

Tucci warned, "He may not go. He has never stopped a mass in the middle."

"He hasn't started the consecration," I reminded him, "so technically it isn't a mass yet."

Tucci shook his head. "He's Polish. He's stubborn."

But I'd made up my mind. "It's too dangerous. We've got to take him off."

In addition to the hundreds of thousands of people in the field, the mass was televised, and I couldn't even begin to guess how many millions of people were watching it.

Secret Service Director John Simpson—who, as an Irish Catholic from Boston, had knelt and kissed the ring when he met the pope and had given me an odd look because I hadn't done the same thing—was standing there with us. I said to him, "If he won't agree to leave, we're going to have to pick him up and take him off."

When Simpson nodded that he understood, I told my deputy, Rich Miller, "You and I will climb up the steps to the big chair. If he won't go, you take his left arm and I'll take his right."

I'd only just met the pope the day before, and here I was about to drag him off the altar. This would be the main story on the national evening news. It was not something I was looking forward to. But the weather was getting worse by the minute. "Once we've got him off the altar," I said to Tucci, "we'll announce to the people that they should take cover."

That's when the pope finished the homily. He put his papers down. Rich and I looked at each other for a second, then started up the steps. My heart was pounding. We'd only taken a few steps when

I sensed that somebody was following me. I turned around to see John Simpson. It was his way of saying to Rich and me, if this gets ugly, the director is going to be there with you. It was a courageous thing to do, and gave me enormous confidence.

Now I was at the altar. The pope was sitting in his chair, head bent in deep thought. The rain was coming down in torrents. Rich and I slowly approached him. The pope turned to look at me, and when I was within six feet of him, when our eyes met, I waved my finger for him to follow me. That's all I did. I'm not sure why I did that, except perhaps that I couldn't think of anything else to do. He stared at me, and I kept waving my finger. I could see that he was thinking about what to do. It was a very long few seconds, while he stared. I thought to myself, I'm going to have to carry him off.

That's when he began to stand up. I quickly moved to his side and, taking his elbow, whispered to him, "We must get off the altar, it's too dangerous."

He said to me, "Are you sure?"

I said yes. He nodded and came quietly down the steps with us.

Everyone was told to seek shelter. The pope was suspending the mass but would finish it over the public address system from the house trailer placed behind the altar that was serving as the sacristy. Nobody left. Three hundred thousand people stayed in the open field, in the pouring rain, to listen to him over the loudspeakers. The storm was horrible. But almost at the exact moment that he finished the mass, the sun came out. We escorted him back to the altar, and three hundred thousand people went wild. From then on, every time we got into a limousine with the bishop or archbishop of whatever city we were in, the pope would explain what had happened in Miami. He would point to me and say, "I stopped a mass for the very first time in my life because the 'institution for security' made me leave the altar."

From Miami we flew to Columbia, South Carolina. By then the pope had changed into dry clothes. But none of the agents had anything to change into because our suitcases were already in the hold of Shepherd One, so we spent our time on the short flight trying to dry our shoes and our socks. In Columbia the pope did an ecumenical event with a congregation of Baptists, Jews, and Greek Orthodox, followed by six or seven other events, before we climbed back on the plane to fly to New Orleans. We were still in Miami-soaked clothes until late that evening. That was how the ten days started.

New Orleans featured several events in the Superdome, the first of which were relatively small gatherings with laypeople and priests in various meeting rooms. The main event was meeting the ninety-six thousand children. We'd secured a men's room for the pope—a typical stadium men's room with dozens of urinals and toilets—but his staff made it a little more attractive, if that's possible, by putting a rug and a chair in there for him. So when the private meetings were finished, Tucci suggested to the pontiff that he might want to use the men's room before going into the stadium. He said he would. Tucci, Lynch, the entourage of cardinals, the detail agents, and I waited in the hallway for the pope to come out. Two minutes went by, then four minutes went by, and we could hear the kids getting rowdy. After five minutes, Tucci agreed that this was taking longer than it should.

I offered to see if everything was all right. I left them and stepped into the men's room, only to find the pope sitting in the chair with his arms folded. He asked, "Is it time?" He'd seen the chair and assumed that after he went to the bathroom, he was supposed to sit down and wait. I smiled, "Yes, it is time."

The instant the popemobile appeared in the stadium, screaming and yelling and applause erupted. Sections of the crowd started chanting, "John Paul Two, we love you . . . John Paul Two, we love you . . ." over and over again, and it spread through the entire place. By the time we got him to the platform, the chanting was thunderous—a noise level beyond anything I'd ever heard—and it must have lasted fifteen minutes. He then walked up to the microphone and said, "John Paul Two loves you, too." And now ninety-six thousand kids erupted again in tumultuous cheering and screaming.

At the end of a very long day in New Orleans, we headed back to the archbishop's residence, which shared a property with a large seminary in the middle of a residential neighborhood. Because we couldn't cover the neighborhood with snipers and agents, we set up a tent at the entrance so that we could pull the car into it and he could get in and out safely.

We were in the popemobile because almost every route we took was a parade route, and on this evening Archbishop Hannan was in the popemobile with him. The pope's private secretary, Monsignor Stanislaw Dziwisz, had worked out a deal with the archbishop that instead of going straight into the tent, we would stop short in the driveway in front of the seminary. There we would open the window of the popemobile on the seminary side only—leaving everything secure on the side where the houses were—and the pope would speak to the seminarians. That was fine with me, as long as he stayed in the popemobile. And I was very specific when I told Monsignor Dziwisz, Archbishop Hannan, Tucci, and Lynch that under no circumstances could the pope leave the popemobile.

So we pulled up to the seminary and I got out of the popemobile and moved next to the open window, within reach of the pope. He was looking at the seminarians, who were chanting and applauding and calling out to him, when I noticed Hannan open the door on the other side, call to the pope, and invite him out. I hurried over and closed the door. But as I came back around to the pope, Hannan opened the door again. So I came back to Hannan's side a second time, and shut the door hard. I returned to the pope's side, and Hannan opened the door a third time. Now I went back there and told Hannan, "Don't open this door again," and slammed it shut very forcefully. He got the message, because it did not happen a fourth time. As I came around to the side where I needed to be, Dziwisz was saying something in Polish to the pope.

After the speech to the seminarians, we drove the short distance into the tent and went inside the residence. Before going up to his room, the pope clasped my hand with both of his, looked me straight in the eyes, and said, "Mr. Petro, thank you very much." It became a nighttime ritual that I looked forward to for the rest of the trip.

Once the pope was upstairs, I joined Dziwisz, Tucci, and Lynch in the living room. Hannan was off somewhere furious with me. After a while, Dziwisz and Tucci left, leaving me alone with Lynch.

"When you were in the middle of this confrontation with Hannan," Lynch asked, "do you know what Dziwisz said to the pope in Polish?" He grinned. "Dziwisz told the pope, do whatever Joe says."

We started each morning at 7:30 or 8:00 and often didn't finish until 10:00 or later at night. The pope would have a small breakfast by himself in his room. There were luncheons every day, and we watched the preparation of his food. He would eat very little for dinner, and never anything between meals. On the other hand, I missed a lot of meals, and a lot of sleep, too. After getting him back to his room, I'd go to mine for phone briefings with the advance agents for the next day, going over the visit site by site. I was usually in bed by midnight, but couldn't fall asleep for hours, and would be up by six. I'm grateful that the pope didn't jog.

In San Antonio, it was very hot and extremely sunny. Some agents wear sunglasses because they like the Hollywood stereotype; others say it gives them an advantage because people can't tell where they're looking. I was never one to wear sunglasses, and but I wore them in San Antonio because the sun was so bright that it hurt my eyes. I don't know how the pope got through that heat and that glaring sun.

The only unusual security incident during the entire trip happened there, while we were in the popemobile driving past the

Alamo. A woman broke through the crowd and ran toward us. The agent who spotted her, Dick O'Meara, reacted exactly the way he was expected to. He jumped off the follow-up car and stopped her. Another agent backed him up. They determined that she was just being overenthusiastic, and helped her find her place back in the crowd. At no point during the ten days were there any other incidents. Looking back, I'd like to think the reason was because we prepared properly.

At our next stop, Phoenix, something did happen that I wasn't prepared for. I hadn't seen it at the outdoor masses, and didn't notice it inside the Superdome, but at Sun Devil Stadium the very instant that the pope consecrated the host, tens of thousands of flashbulbs went off at exactly the same time. It was one huge flash of light, and for a brief second, it frightened me. Also at Sun Devil, there was a ceremony called "blessing the sick," where about fifty people in wheelchairs, on crutches, and on stretchers waited for him in the middle of the football field. The pope came down and greeted every one of them, and it wasn't just a brief hello. He put his hands around their faces and prayed with them.

What I didn't know about Phoenix until we got there is that it has a small Polish community. In fact, nobody seemed to know about it until the last minute, when the church hastily arranged a Polish event—complete with music and dancers—for the end of the day on the lawn at the rear of the residence. It was around 9:30 when we returned to the residence and went inside. The pope reached for my hand and started to say, "Mr. Petro—" I shook my head. "I'm afraid you're not finished," I said. "There's one more event." It was the only time in ten days that I saw him look tired. His head dropped as if to say, oh, no. But he immediately caught himself. We went onto the back lawn, and when he heard the sound of his native Polish, he became revitalized.

From Phoenix, we flew to Los Angeles and helicoptered from the airport to a landing pad on top of the Los Angeles police garage.

Our cars were waiting there to take us to the nearby residence. We came in without any problems, and for a few seconds, I even allowed myself to think that maybe we could leave the city without any problems. I was wrong.

The first of two problems came up at the Coliseum. While waiting in the holding room with the pope before he went to the altar, I was told by radio that one of the banks of magnetometers had lost power. As I recall, there were ten mags in a bank, and each bank could handle ten thousand people an hour. Rather than delay the mass, I told the command post—and this was controversial—just keep magging people as if the machines were working. I was sure that no one in the crowd would know that they weren't operating. If, periodically, officers pulled people out and searched them, the nonworking mags would still be a deterrent. Some UD officers were upset and thought it was a bad decision. But I felt it was a risk we could take because anyone carrying something dangerous would see the metal detectors and not try to get past them.

Interestingly enough, over the ten days of the pope's tour, putting more than a million people through magnetometers, we only turned up a few knives, some Mace, and a couple of weapons that belonged to off-duty police officers. As far as I know, no one was ever arrested.

Later that evening, we returned to the residence where the pope was going to have supper. Cardinal Roger Mahony, the archbishop of Los Angeles, escorted the pope and Dziwisz up to the third-floor dining room, but it was empty. There was no staff, so he told the pope to stay there and went to find the waiters. For some reason, we'd taken the staff off the third floor and had assembled them downstairs. I don't remember why. When Mahony couldn't locate any waiters or cooks, he went back to the dining room and by this time, the pope and Dziwisz were gone, too. He found them in the kitchen, too hungry to wait, helping themselves.

The second problem was on our way out of Los Angeles. Our

agreement with the Vatican was that, upon leaving a city, fifty people of our choosing would be permitted to stand at the base of the airplane's stairs to shake hands with the pope. It was a photo opportunity that the pope very graciously granted to thank certain people for their help with the visit. We'd have a range of local dignitaries there, such as the U.S. attorney, the chief of police, the mayor, some city councilmen, and sometimes agents with their families. But as we got to the LAPD garage, we found the helicopter landing zone filled with two hundred police officers lined up in formation. I couldn't believe it, and neither could Tucci, who ran up to me, wanting to know what was going on. I located a senior officer and was about to ask him who these people were when he asked, "Do you mind if I work the pope here?"

"To work the pope" meant to be at his shoulder on a rope line. I looked at him and said, "You've got to be out of your mind. It's out of the question. What is this?"

The pope was still in the car, and a now nervous Father Tucci was pacing back and forth, mumbling, "We don't have time for this. Our schedule is too tight. What's going on?"

The LAPD had decided, on its own, to do a photo op and chose the officers to say good-bye to the pope. Unfortunately for us, the pope had already noticed these people and, in his mind, thought this was supposed to happen. He never ignored anyone, and there was no way now that he would ignore them. Tucci wanted to get through it as fast as possible, so he leaned into the car and told the pope, in Italian, just walk through and touch hands, don't shake hands. The pope nodded, got out of the car, and quickly moved through the group of officers.

As soon as we could, we got the pope into the helicopter, lifted off, and flew to Los Angeles International, where, according to the rules, only fifty people were waiting at the base of the stairs. He shook those hands, got on the plane and we took off for Monterey. While we were in the air, I received a situation report by radio from the agent at the landing site to say that, among the people waiting to greet the pope, was the mayor of Carmel, Clint Eastwood. I was about to share the information with Tucci, who was also getting situation reports from the arrival site, when he announced that there were three busloads of police officers we had missed in Los Angeles on their way to Monterey to say good-bye to the pope. I was stunned. That's when he started to laugh and confessed that he was just kidding.

During our stop at the Carmel Mission near Monterey, while the pope was speaking to a couple of hundred people, an agent said that a nun needed to speak to me. I went outside to find ten Carmelite sisters standing behind a rope line. The head of this little group announced, "We would like to sing the Angelus to the pope."

Having grown up with nuns as teachers, my natural inclination was to help. Dressed as they were, all in white, they were angelic. But I had to inform her that it wasn't my decision. She gave me one of those looks that I knew all too well, and I promised I'd do my best. I found Lynch and urged him, "Come on, they're nuns, and the pope will love this." He didn't need much convincing and said, "It's okay with me as long as it's okay with you."

The pope believes that the Blessed Mother saved his life after the assassination attempt and prays to her all the time. The Angelus is sung in honor of her. Because I believed it was low risk, I escorted the nuns into a corner of the tent near the car. It was the only time in ten days that I permitted anyone to get that close to the pope without going through a metal detector. I stationed agents near the nuns, and as I brought the pope out to the car, they started singing. He was surprised and turned to them. They sang beautifully. When they finished, he said he wanted to thank them. I walked him to the corner of the tent and he greeted each of the nuns. Later, Lynch said he was surprised I'd allowed that. "You've been so tough on this trip."

I said, "They were Carmelite nuns. If it had been anyone else I would have said no."

"You're starting to give in." He shook his head, "A part of you is still that little Catholic boy in grade school."

For the fifty-five-minute helicopter ride from Monterey to San Francisco, I was sitting next to the pontiff. Within ten minutes of takeoff, I looked around, and everyone else—Dziwisz, the archbishop of San Francisco, and Chabin—had fallen asleep. Those helicopters have a numbing effect on people because they're much too loud to have a normal conversation, and they vibrate. Besides that, it was late, and everyone was tired. I fought to stay awake because I didn't want the pope to see me asleep. But when I glanced at him, he was looking down, lost in his own world, praying the rosary, one bead at a time. I watched him out of the corner of my eye for the entire flight. If he'd wanted to nod off, he could have. Instead, he prayed for the entire trip. I was in awe of the depth of this man's spirituality.

By the time the pope celebrated mass in San Francisco's Candlestick Park, I was running on sheer adrenaline and a lot of things were getting to be routine. Except those words he repeated to me every night, "Mr. Petro, thank you very much."

By now, too, I was starting to realize that this extraordinary experience was coming to an end. We rode around Candlestick Park Stadium with tens of thousands of people cheering and screaming—they were even doing the wave—and I remember thinking to myself, You must never forget this moment. I haven't.

From there we went to Detroit, where the visit was going to end. I'd arranged for my family to be there. For my mother-in-law, Mary Coccia, a devout Catholic who went to church every day, meeting the pope was truly momentous. At each mass, communion was distributed by hundreds of priests, stationed all over each stadium, while the pope gave communion to a hundred people in a special VIP section in front of the altar. At the Silverdome, my family was seated in that VIP section. And there are no words possible to describe the thrill of standing next to the pope as he served communion to my daughter, Michelle. Later, the Church put out a video of the trip to Detroit, and in the sequence showing communion, at the very moment Michelle was receiving the Host, the camera panned over to the pope. It is a moment I cherish.

After the mass, I escorted the pope into the holding room so that he could change. One of the agents brought my family backstage. When we came out, I introduced the pope to them. He looked at Michelle, put his hands around the back of her head, and spoke to her quietly. And there I stood, as such a proud father, watching the little girl I called "Mich-Mich" being blessed by the Holy Father.

There was no doubt, by then, that he knew I was Catholic. But throughout the trip our relationship had been purely professional, based entirely on my position as the Secret Service agent in charge of his protection. He was friendly but never got personal. Except at the very end. As we were walking to the helicopter, he turned to me and said something I will never forget: "Mr. Petro, you have a very beautiful daughter."

I left him at the base of the steps. We looked at each other. He took my hand between his. And for the final time he said, "Mr. Petro, thank you very much."

CHAPTER FOURTEEN

★ ★ ★ ★

THE QUAYLES

The Secret Service had never seen a family like the Quayles.

Dan Quayle misspelled the word "potato," and for many people, that's what they remember about him. In a very real sense, it defined his vice presidency.

He was visiting a grammar school in New Jersey, agreed to help conduct a spelling lesson, and was handed some printed flash cards by the teacher. Quayle began with a young girl, asking her to spell "president." Next came a young boy, and the word was "potato." On Quayle's flash card, it was spelled "potatoe," so when the boy wrote "p-o-t-a-t-o" on the blackboard, Quayle looked again at the flash card, decided it must be correct, and had him add an "e."

More than a half hour passed before anyone, including the press pool covering the event, realized that "potatoe" was misspelled, and it was later still before anyone found out that the flash card itself was wrong. I suppose most people would have made the same mistake. Yet the videotape of the incident was played over and again on news programs around the world.

Throughout the Bush administration, Dan Quayle was ridiculed for making such gaffes and missteps, but the Dan Quayle I saw up close for three years was a different person.

* * *

When George H.W. Bush became president, the head of his vice presidential protective division—Hubert Bell—found his team protecting Dan and Marilyn Quayle and three children: Tucker, fourteen, Benjamin, twelve, and Corinne, ten. Normally, a family with kids isn't a problem.

We'd protected lots of families with children before. But many of them were very young, like Carolyn and John Kennedy Jr., who were tots, and Amy Carter, who was just nine when her father was elected. And many of them were old enough to be considered adults, like the Johnson, Nixon, and Ford children. We didn't see much of the Reagans' adult four—Maureen, Michael, Patti, and Ron—although they occasionally visited their parents at Camp David or at the ranch. George H.W. Bush's children were also adults when he was in the White House, and the Mondale teenagers were not intensely athletic.

The Quayle kids, like their parents, were the exceptions. They were active teenagers and outstanding athletes. As a family, all five Quayles were expert skiers, played great golf, played great tennis, went scuba diving, white water rafted, rode bikes thirty-two miles down the side of the crater at Maui, and ran. The two boys were also good lacrosse players. As athletes, they were chips off the old block. Dan Quayle ran three sub-eight-minute miles almost every day, while Marilyn Quayle ran well and rode horses even better. Protecting this family presented physical challenges. The task was made all the more difficult because none of them liked being protected.

Bell's VPPD had grown used to doing things in a certain way for George and Barbara Bush, who were considerably older than the Quayles and didn't go in for a lot of physical activities. Both were relaxed with protection. The VPPD was now forced to find ways to accommodate the Quayles and to do so without compromising its responsibilities. Unfortunately, the agents didn't understand the

Quayles, and the Quayles didn't understand the agents. Making matters worse, the vice president's staff wasn't getting along well with the agents either. I was brought in to try to smooth things out.

From the moment I met the vice president in October 1989, it was obvious that there was an edge to him about protection. He was resigned to it because he didn't have a choice, but that didn't mean he had to like it. The problem is that when the people you're protecting are fighting it, agents become self-conscious. They don't want to be too intrusive, so there's a tendency to drop back just a little. And relaxing even a little can have detrimental consequences.

One of the many things that his family found claustrophobic about protection, Quayle claimed, was agents standing outside their dining-room window. Their post was actually the front door, but agents don't usually stay in one place; they walk back and forth. When the Quayles sat down to dinner, the agent would appear in the window, then disappear, then reappear again. I promised the vice president I'd look into it, and then I went to see his wife.

Marilyn Quayle argued that the residence was surrounded by uniformed guards and a fence with sophisticated alarms, so there was no need to have someone at her front door. But the agent was not there to confront problems outside, he was there to respond to an incident by coming into the house, finding the family, and getting them to a safe place. It took some negotiating, but she eventually agreed to let us create a space in the basement large enough for agents, desks, cameras, CCTV monitors, and alarms. And that way, her family never again had to eat a meal with people appearing in their dining-room window.

Being able to deal directly with her helped to improve our relationship with the entire family. But then, knowing who to talk to is one of the tricks of the trade. When it came to particularly important matters, it was often best to go straight to the spouse. It worked with Mrs. Reagan and it worked with Mrs. Quayle. In one specific instance, the vice president was making travel plans to a certain Latin American country that I felt it was too dangerous to visit. I couldn't talk him out of it, so I explained to Mrs. Quayle why I was concerned. Guys are inclined to say, I'll be all right, don't worry. But wives do worry. She told her husband, I don't want you to go, and the trip got canceled. So when I worried, I knew where to find a natural ally.

Early on in my dealings with her, the vice president's staff hired Tom Pernice to be lead advance. He'd been a young advance guy on the Reagan staff. He had been trained by Bill Henkel, and had accompanied Bill and me on several trips. Because he and I had a history, we were able to find a lot of common ground. At the same time, I had the best administrative assistant in the entire Secret Service working for me. Barbara Finn ran our office and moved mountains. So, thanks to Tom and Barbara, things began to improve between the Secret Service and the Quayle staff. Curiously, though, as those relationships improved, some people at headquarters began to think that I was being too accommodating. At the same time, the Quayles often thought I wasn't accommodating enough. That's how I knew I'd probably found just about the right level.

Although I'm not sure that the vice president ever got used to being protected, his kids were never a problem. We took them to school and kept the agents there, but they didn't follow them into classrooms. We gave them as much privacy as possible, especially when they hung out with their friends. If they wanted a little extra privacy, they soon figured out how to manage that.

But Mrs. Quayle was always pushing the envelope. On one trip through Homestead Air Force Base in Florida, as we pulled onto the tarmac, she spotted three stealth fighters parked five hundred feet from Air Force Two and asked if she could take a look. I stopped the motorcade a hundred feet away. She said she wanted to get out. We couldn't find out if the fighters were fueled or had ordinance on them, so I said no. Mrs. Quayle then made a move for the door.

I snapped, "Don't argue with me. Stay in the car." That's as close as she got to those planes.

When she learned that we practiced horseback AOPs, she asked if she could take part in an exercise. To keep the peace, I allowed her to come along with us, once, in Washington. She played the victim and we carried her off on a stretcher. It was harmless. When she heard I was taking eight agents down to St. John, in the Virgin Islands, to work AOPs with the Coast Guard, she asked if she could come along. But this was dangerous, and I refused. We scuba dived with them, and because anything can happen when you're in the water, we did a lot of specialized training. Although an assassination attempt in that environment is remote, we still practiced those. Mostly, though, we prepared for medical emergencies. I tried to make her understand that a controlled exercise in the District of Columbia was one thing, AOPs in water were something very different. I stuck to my decision. It was just as well, because on that trip we had a near-accident hoisting a stretcher onto the helicopter, and I was the one who almost got hurt.

If she wasn't trying to work AOPs with us, she was trying to sign off protection. My response was always the same: Signing off protection was not a very good idea at any time, but if she wanted to decline protection, I'd get the letters prepared. For a spouse, protection is optional. My caveat was that she'd have to sign off permanently; we wouldn't allow her to sign on and sign off at will. And there were good reasons for that, too, not least of which was the effect on agents' morale. If she could leave agents home every time she wanted to go to the mall, it wouldn't take long before agents began wondering, What am I doing here?

I also faced a situation with her that was not of her own creation. One of her agents had become too ingratiating. It reached the point where his familiarity was inappropriate. Mrs. Quayle was the innocent party, being naturally friendly and pleasant, and I think that the agent might have been reading that wrong. He never called her Marilyn in front of other agents, but he might have been doing so in private. I didn't like his body language and the way he handled himself. So I transferred him. I brought in Ed Russell to run her detail, an agent I respected. He could be tough and smooth at the same time, and the problem never recurred.

There was one time, however, when Mrs. Quayle went too far. We were in New Hampshire with the "formal" follow-up car. That's the black Cadillac convertible that was popular in the Kennedy days. A touch of Hollywood, it was a great-looking show of force, with agents hanging off the sideboards. It's not used anymore because the philosophy these days is that shift agents shouldn't be exposed like that. So today the follow-up cars are armored. But we still occasionally used the convertible for parades as late as the 1990s, and we had it with us on that trip.

At the hotel before the vice president's speech, Mrs. Quayle asked if she and her husband could ride in it to the airport. I told her no, because it was too risky. She asked if she could do it alone. I told her no, for the same reason. Later that day she asked again, and again I told her no. By the time we were ready to leave, she was still pestering me about it. I had to get her off my back, so I promised that one day I'd arrange a ride for her. My plan was to bring the car to the residence and let her ride around in it there.

That was a Thursday. On the following Monday, I took the vice president out of town for the night, got back Tuesday morning, and promptly received a phone call from the director demanding to know, "Did you authorize Mrs. Quayle to take the open follow-up car to Manassas?"

I had not. Without permission, she'd taken the car from the observatory nearly thirty miles to go horseback riding. What's more, she'd told her agents that I'd authorized it. I got her on the phone, and from the tone of my voice she knew she'd stepped over the line and began apologizing. What she couldn't have known was that her foolishness had damaged some of my credibility with certain people at headquarters. According to them, I'd allowed her to do something that was clearly inappropriate. Her escapade affected my reputation within the service for a long time.

Those matters aside, we traveled all over the world with the Quayles, and I saw firsthand how the two of them worked tirelessly as ambassadors for American interests. The vice president was actually very capable in this area, although he seldom got public credit for it. We took him to virtually every country in Latin and Central America at a time when democracy in many of those places was still developing. Despite Dan Quayle's image in the media, he had an easygoing, person-to-person style and was able to establish a relaxed rapport with several leaders, many of whom were his age. More important was his apparent grasp of the issues. In those face-to-face meetings with world leaders, he was nobody's fool.

Not that every such meeting was comfortable. In Santiago, Chile, after calling on the newly elected president, we went to see the former dictator, Gen. Augusto Pinochet. We arrived at a gated one-story house and were met by two military guards. They escorted us into a foyer and stood at attention in front of two large sliding wooden doors. Several minutes passed, and none of us knew what to expect next. Then, at some secret signal, the guards snapped back and with military precision yanked the doors open. It was like "What's behind curtain number one?" There was Pinochet, standing at attention, in full dress uniform.

On a trip to Brazil in 1991, Quayle was suddenly confronted with the dilemma of dealing with Fidel Castro. We were there for the inauguration of the Brazilian president, and at a staff briefing, Quayle was advised that Castro would also be attending. He understood that Castro would see the event as a way to embarrass the United States, and he wasn't going to allow that to happen. He said to me, "I don't want to have to be in a position where I have to acknowledge him." Quayle's worry was that, if Castro got close enough, he would try to shake hands and a photographer would snap a picture of that. Quayle said, "Help me stay away from him." So I spent that day on the radio with advance agents all over Brasilia making sure that wherever Castro went, we were someplace else. Later, at the official reception, I spent the evening jockeying Quayle around the room to keep him at a distance from Castro.

We also took Quayle to Africa, where he insisted on seeing life as it really was. Most of the time when the president and the vice president travel, they only see the opulent. Here Quayle was very much the exception. He made it a point to see the underbelly of a country, even when his host didn't want him to. On his visit to the Ivory Coast, Quayle insisted on going to an AIDS hospital, which was pretty grim. People were dying in hallways while their families were camped outside, waiting to take their bodies home. He never hesitated to see real poverty on any of these trips, and he was good at drawing attention to it.

The president of the Ivory Coast was Felix Houphouët-Boigny, who'd ruled since 1960. Having been born in the city of Yamoussoukro, he decided to move the capital there from Abidjan, and built himself a palace that comes complete with a moat filled with crocodiles. But even more spectacularly, he built the largest church in Christendom—Notre-Dame de la Paix Basilica—which is a slightly larger, but otherwise exact, replica of St. Peter's Basilica in Vatican City. And it, too, comes complete with a piazza in front.

At his meeting with Houphouët-Boigny, Quayle didn't hide the fact that he was upset with the incongruity of such excessive opulence and the stark poverty and illness he'd seen elsewhere in the country. He told the ruler that there had to be reforms and that the United States would not let up in its efforts to bring about those reforms, regardless of Houphouët-Boigny's self-interest. Quayle's message of democratic freedom and economic reform was a consistent theme in his meetings with leaders around the world. He always pressed home the fact that the United States government would support efforts in that direction, and he criticized political and economic oppression.

Those meetings were difficult and sometimes less than friendly. The trips themselves were always physically demanding. We flew to the Ivory Coast in a 707, but the runway at Yamoussoukro was too short for us to take off with the plane fully fueled for the flight back to Washington, so we went from there to the old capital, Abidjan, to fuel up. But as we were landing there, a bird hit an engine. The pilot wouldn't take off with three engines, which wouldn't normally have been an issue if it had been a presidential visit, because he always has a backup plane. But the vice president didn't. There was talk of getting onto a commercial flight, which was a really bad choice, or spending the night waiting for Andrews Air Force Base to send us a new 707. Quayle made it very clear to me that was an equally bad choice. "I do not want to spend the night here." He did not want to be Houphouët-Boigny's guest. What's more, I didn't want us to spend the night there for security reasons.

I looked down the tarmac and spotted our C-141 Starlifter. It was waiting for us to leave so that they could load up the cars and fly them back to Andrews. It's a big, noisy, four-engine cargo plane. In a flash, knowing that Mrs. Quayle would love this, I asked the vice president, "Can I interest you in a car plane?"

"Let's do it," he said. So I went over to the C-141 to tell the pilot, an air force captain who was probably only twenty-five years old, that he was about to fly Air Force Two. On the way to Africa, we'd stopped at Cape Verde so that Quayle could meet with the prime minister. Our plan was now to fly back to Cape Verde, which would take three hours, and hook up there with the new 707 coming from Andrews. We'd leave the cars in Abidjan, because it would take an hour or two to get them on board, along with enough agents to protect them. The

Starlifter could come back for the cars and the agents after dropping us at Cape Verde.

We loaded the whole entourage onto the C-141—into the cold, empty cargo hold where there were thirty seats facing backward—installed Quayle in the cockpit, and took off. A few hours later, as we were heading into Cape Verde, a diplomatic issue arose. The prime minister found out we were landing there and asked to come out to see the vice president again, so his staff had to go through all sorts of diplomatic discussions to handle that. Eventually the 707 from Andrews arrived carrying the parts to fix the engine of the 707 stranded in the Ivory Coast. The C-141 took those parts back to Abidjan while we headed home on the new 707.

Talk about physically demanding trips: In May 1991, we'd just come from Singapore and were swinging through Jakarta when word came from Washington that former Indian prime minister Rajiv Gandhi had been assassinated. The White House wanted Quayle to go to the funeral. Instead of sending the Singapore advance team home—it was headed by two of our best agents, Keith Prewitt and Mark Enright—I dispatched them along with cars to India, giving them just twenty-four hours on the ground before we arrived. When we got there, the vice president made an official condolence call on the Indian prime minister before setting off to the hall where Gandhi's coffin was lying in state.

Before we arrive anywhere, we get a site report. So three minutes before we pulled up at the Indian equivalent of a funeral parlor, Mark radioed me, "We have three hundred press uncontained, two thousand people uncontained, fourteen greeters uncontained. It's a mess. And it's not going to get any better. Come on in."

It was a mess, but there wasn't much we could do about it, so I told the shift to work in very tight. We stayed shoulder to shoulder with Quayle and, as soon as we could, got him back to the car. That's when Keith advised me there was no lead car. He said he thought the police car that was supposed to be leading us might be down the block, so he started running along the street. The motorcade followed him. Just like that, he became the lead car. He was a great athlete—he had played football and basketball at Memphis State— but even he couldn't run to the next site. Luckily, he found the lead car, we put the motorcade back together and headed out of there. We stopped at the embassy to put the vice president in his armored vest, then went to the site of the funeral pyre.

Hundreds of thousands of people were gathered there. There were some plush seats for the foreign dignitaries in front of the pyre, and our advance team managed to get our motorcade within thirty feet of it. It wasn't an ideal escape route, but it was better than nothing. We got out of the limousine to find that only three seats had been blocked off for the American delegation: one for the vice president, one for Mrs. Quayle, and, theoretically, one for the ambassador. I told Quayle, "I don't want to leave you alone. Would you ask the ambassador to sit someplace else?" He did, and the three of us sat down. Minute by minute, as they piled wood onto the fire, the sun grew more intense. It was soon close to 110 degrees in the sun, and we wound up being there for two and a half hours. More worryingly, we were surrounded by foreign dignitaries—such as Yassir Arafat and Benazir Bhutto—whose bodyguards were armed to the teeth. There were also heavily armed Indian police and soldiers wherever we looked.

Shrill music blared from huge speakers. It was a hot, noisy, and crowded situation, made all the more tense by having so many automatic weapons in the hands of people we didn't know so close to the vice president. It made us all very edgy. At one point Quayle leaned over and whispered to me, "What would you do if Arafat stood up and pulled his gun on me?"

I told him without hesitation, "I'd shoot him."

He asked, "If you did, what do you think would happen?"

I assured him, "It would not be a pretty picture."

The instant the funeral ended, we got out of there.

*   *   *   *

One thing that annoyed me about Dan Quayle was how fast he did everything. He walked faster than anybody I knew, and he ran so fast that I had trouble keeping up with him. But what really annoyed me was how fast he showered. We'd be traveling and put in a very long day and we'd end up at night in a hotel somewhere and at ten o'clock I'd walk him into his suite. He'd turn around and say, Want to run in the morning? I'd say, Okay, what time? He'd say, six. Now, that's fine for him. But it meant I had to get up at five to make sure the detail was set up and ready to run with us. Afterward, he'd take the fastest shower of anyone on the planet. In under ten minutes, he'd be dressed and out. Which meant all the agents would have to hurry back to their rooms and rush around to get ready so that we didn't have to make him wait for us. Keeping up with Quayle was always a struggle.

But then, keeping up with the rest of the family was not easy either. We used to joke that their vacations were five sports a day. Often, it was literally that. I divided their sports into two categories—observer and participatory. For agents, golf was an observer sport. We didn't have to play to protect them. Same with tennis. But skiing, scuba diving, horseback riding, running, and white-water rafting were participatory, and we had to take part with them. Fortunately, the Secret Service has such a variety of athletic people that I had no trouble finding great skiers, great riders, and highly qualified scuba divers on the detail. So we ran with them, and we skied with them—all five were double-diamond, black-slope skiers who skied from first run in the morning until last run in the evening and came down mountains at top speed—and we scuba dived with them.

But the Quayle family adventure to beat all family adventures was a trip through the Grand Canyon in a paddleboat.

This was a trip we could never have done with the president. We were going to be isolated. The president needs instant communications because he's responsible for nuclear retaliation. But the vice president doesn't have that responsibility and therefore has more leeway in where he can go and what he can do. Still, WHCA officers came with us to set up satellite dishes, so we had communications. We also had contingency plans in place if we needed to get out of there fast. To accompany the family I only took one shift and one other supervisor. I'd argue that no vice presidential family in American history had ever done anything quite like this.

Over the course of four days, we trekked and rafted from the south rim of the Grand Canyon ninety-six miles down the Colorado River. The Park Service provided four eight-to-nine-passenger inflatable powerboats and one seven-passenger paddleboat. They also set up camp for us and handled all the food. But each agent had to deal with his or her own equipment, guns, and radios. It was physically exhausting.

On the first day, we practiced flipping rafts and scrambling back in. The water was freezing. When we thought we were ready for a level-five rapids, I climbed into the front of the boat on the port side, and Quayle got into the starboard front. I put two agents on each side of the boat behind Quayle and me. We hit the rapids and the boat went under water, then popped out, launching us into the air. I'd never done rapids before and wasn't prepared to find myself, literally, in midair. As the boat dropped out from under me, boom, I went into the water. I grabbed one of the straps along the side of the boat and held on for dear life. Quayle and one of the agents pulled me back in. It was embarrassing when, that evening, Ben commented to me, "What's this, the protector gets saved by the protectee?"

In camp that night, I was faced with a very unique problem: How were we going to handle sleeping arrangements? We were at the bottom of the Grand Canyon, all by ourselves, and it was pitch dark. I was assured by the Park Service that it would be impossible for anybody to get near to us. There were sheer cliffs on one side, and rapids on the other. Nobody could go through the river at night without killing themselves. Anyway, you couldn't be in the Grand Canyon without a permit, so we knew that there was no one around for dozens of miles. My options were simple: Keep agents awake throughout the night or let them sleep. Because it had been such a strenuous day, and would be another equally strenuous day tomorrow, I opted for sleep. We put the Quayles up by the base of the Canyon, and established perimeters. The agents bedded down next to them, and the Park Service bedded down between us and the river. It was too dark to see anything, and because it was cold, everyone had his head inside his or her sleeping bag. Even if somebody could have infiltrated the camp—and I was entirely confident that was impossible—he would have had to stumble over twenty-five identical sleeping bags. There was no way he could possibly figure out who anybody was. This was not a security issue. I'm sure it was the first time in the history of the Secret Service that, at some moments in the night, all of the protectees and all of the agents were asleep.

The second night was different. Another group was camped a hundred yards away. We posted agents. The third night we were alone again, and everyone slept.

On the last day we did another big level-five rapids. Mrs. Quayle wanted to be on the boat with us, so we put her behind me and put an agent behind her. As soon as we hit those rapids, she came off the boat. I didn't see her go, but when I looked down into the water, there she was, clinging to the side of the boat. By that time, a very courageous agent, John Orloff, was in the water with her. I grabbed her by the life jacket, and we hauled her in. It wasn't as dangerous as it might have looked, but having gone overboard myself, I felt that her getting wet vindicated me a little bit. Unfortunately, the vice president never saw a thing. Years later, when he wrote his autobiography, all he said about me was that I'd fallen into the water and he had pulled me out.

*　　*　　*　　*

When the old house used by the chief of naval operations was first designated the vice presidential residence, we fenced it in. But the main gate at the observatory, the Thirty-fourth Street entrance, runs between the residence and our three-story command post. The navy controlled the gate, using contract guards. Although we were permitted to post a UD officer there, he had no authority. He couldn't open or close the gate. What concerned me was that someone could get onto the property and separate the agents at the command post from the residence. Hubie Bell tried to get it changed through channels and couldn't, and until January 17, 1991, I couldn't get it changed through channels either. The date is significant because it was the morning after Operation Desert Storm began, at the start of the Gulf War. I phoned our command post at the observatory and told the shift supervisor, "Get two uniformed officers and seize the gate."

There was a long pause on the other end. "What?"

"We're seizing the gate," I said. "Inform the station commander's office that as of nine o'clock, we are taking control of the gate because of the possibility of terrorism."

Two UD officers and a supervisor walked up to the gate and announced to the contract guards, "We're taking control." And that was that. From then on, the Secret Service decided who went in and out. I waited all morning for a phone call from the navy, but it never came, and to this day we command that gate.

Controlling access is an obvious way to protect someone. Giving the protectee access to us in an emergency situation is another. For that reason, protectees have panic buttons. It's usually a pager-type device, like the alarms many people have in their homes that are tied into a private security company. Push the button and the cavalry arrives. Among other places, we put them in the protectee's bedroom, mainly for medical emergencies. After all, we've got the room totally surrounded, so no one can get in unless we let them in. But we wouldn't necessarily know if the president or vice president was having a heart attack.

It's the Technical Service Division that comes up with these things. They are to the Secret Service what Q is to James Bond. And they're always inventing new perimeter sensors, night-vision devices, and tiny cameras to monitor hallways and stairwells. For some reason, TSD designed a panic button to look like the Washington Monument. All the protectee had to do was knock it down and the alarm would go off.

One of the first people to have one was Dan Quayle. The Quayles were on a trip, staying in a hotel, and we put one next to their bed. About half an hour after they retired, with agents on post outside the door, the alarm went off. Agents burst in, only to find a very startled Mr. and Mrs. Quayle sitting up in bed, wondering what on earth had happened. Mea culpa. I'd forgotten to tell him where the alarm was, and in the dark, he'd mistakenly knocked it over.

I later learned that TSD wanted it to look like the Washington Monument so that hotel maids wouldn't know what it was. Why any hotel maid would think that the president or vice president traveled with a replica of the Washington Monument is beyond me, but TSD sometimes thought out of the box like that. Anyway, hotel maids never get into a protectee's suite unless an agent is there, too.

Nor does room service. The president never has room service because he has his own stewards cooking for him in another room. If the vice president wants something, we order it from the command post.

The same with pizza deliveries. The Quayles ordered pizzas every now and then at home, like all families with kids, but obviously couldn't just pick up the phone and say to Domino's, "This is the vice president of the United States, please send over a large pie with extra cheese." So if they wanted a pizza, they'd place their order, and give the address of the Naval Observatory, as if it were for the guards at the front gate. When the kid taking their order asked, "Name?" the Quayles would say, "Petro."

I might not have looked all that graceful in Dan Quayle's auto-biography, falling out of the raft, but a few years ago when I bumped into him at Citigroup, he told me that, to this day, they still order pizzas using my name.

★ ★ ★ ★

CHAPTER FIFTEEN

LIFTING THE BURDEN

Leaving the Secret Service meant that I was leaving behind a big piece
of my identity, my professional history, and a great sense of fraternity.

During those years with Dan Quayle, the Secret Service resolved several long-standing problems.

The first had to do with our weapons. The Uzis, shotguns, and .357 Magnums we used were all bought off the rack. Personally, I've never liked guns and hated to shoot, but I became comfortable with the six-round .357 Magnum revolver. It was safe, you really had to pull the trigger for it to go off, it wouldn't jam, and you could reload fast. But there was a faction of agents who were "gun nuts." They'd carry two—one in a shoulder holster, the other in an ankle holster—and by the late 1970s, they faced criminals carrying guns with fifteen rounds. They were arguing that we needed to move up to 9mm semiautomatics.

So the Secret Service commissioned a study. The head of the Beltsville training facility—a fellow who knew weapons, named Don Edwards—was put in charge, and his committee looked at dozens of guns. But with every one, they always found something wrong. They tested each gun by firing ten thousand rounds, only to discover that after so many rounds the barrel cracked, or the gun jammed, or something unexpected happened. One gun after another was ruled out, and it got to be sort of a joke that no weapon could pass the test.

It wasn't a big issue for agents working protection because we had so much support around us, like CAT teams and police, but field agents doing criminal work were seriously outgunned. Many of them bought their own semiautomatics because they couldn't wait for Edwards and his committee. It took nearly fifteen years before the Secret Service settled on a weapon that became the authorized sidearm. I never qualified with it, and I wasn't alone, because a lot of older guys didn't want to give up their trusty revolver. But the struggle that the Secret Service went through became an interesting study in how you can overanalyze something to the point where the process becomes the problem.

While I sat on the sidelines of the gun debate, I got deeply involved with two problems at the Capitol. That is a different place. Because the legislature is a separate branch of government, agents accompanying the executive were treated as if we were in a foreign country. There were sacred places where we were not permitted to go.

The U.S. Capitol Police was created by Congress in 1828 to protect the Capitol and members of Congress. They are, admittedly, an older law enforcement branch than the Secret Service, and when it comes to enforcing laws on the Hill, they have jurisdiction. But we also have authority inside the Capitol, just as we have it outside the Capitol, because where we accompany the president or the vice president, we have the responsibility to protect him.

However, the Capitol Police had their "rules." For instance, there is a cross hall outside the vice president's office that is next door to the Senate Chamber. At one end of that cross hall, there's a vase and a partition where chairs and newspapers are provided for the senators. At the other end there's another little partition and another vase. The rule was, Secret Service agents could not go past those vases. So when the vice president left his office and went into the Senate Chamber, we'd have to put agents up in the gallery to watch him. But teenaged kids working as interns and pages were running around the vases. What's more, if the vice president had a meeting at the other end of the cross hall, I'd have to get somebody to go around to the other side to meet him, because the Capitol Police wouldn't allow an agent to walk across that hall with the vice president.

One day I'd simply had enough. I phoned our liaison agent on the Hill who works with the Capitol police. I said, "I don't care who you talk to over there but I am never again walking all the way around the Senate floor when I'm accompanying the vice president. The next time he walks through that cross hall, I'm walking with him."

This created a huge dilemma, putting the Capitol Police and the United States Senate on a collision course with the Secret Service. Phone calls went back and forth, but that "rule" did get changed.

The other battle we fought there was slightly more complicated. I'd accompanied President Reagan to several State of the Union addresses. When the announcement was made, "Mr. Speaker, the President of the United States," I'd walked down the center aisle of the House Chamber with him.

In 1991, I was taking Vice President Quayle to the State of the Union address. The way it works is the vice president waits in his office at the Senate while all the senators gather in the Senate Chamber. Ten minutes before the president arrives, he leads them over to the House, and they go into the House Chamber. On that particular night, the advance agent informed me, "They're not going to let you walk down the center aisle."

I wanted to know, "Who's not going to let me?" He explained that the Capitol Police were insisting I'd have to go all the way around the House chamber and meet the vice president at the base of the podium. I told the agent, "I intend to walk down that aisle with the vice president. You tell the Capitol Police, if anybody interferes, they will be arrested for interfering with a federal agent in the performance of his duty."

That night, the vice president and all the senators left their side of the Capitol and walked through the rotunda to the House. I stayed with him. When we got to the House, the doors opened and the vice president's entourage started in. I did, too. And nobody said a word. I went down the aisle with the vice president and took my place stage left. Five minutes later, I spotted the agent in charge of President Bush's detail—John Magaw—who had prepositioned himself across from me on stage right. He, clearly, was not going to accompany the president into the chamber. I was surprised. The next day Magaw called me and asked me how I was able to accomplish that. When I said that I'd firmly insisted, I heard him whisper to himself, "I guess I should have pushed harder." I felt uncomfortable that I had upstaged him.

The friction I'd inadvertently created with Magaw did not manifest itself immediately. Anyway, there were already plenty of jealousies built into our relationship. There always is between PPD and VPPD.

To improve this problem, one of the positive projects that Magaw implemented when he ran PPD was to exchange agents with VPPD. Agents on the two details did not always understand each other. PPD was looked upon as the prima donnas, and it was often joked that they carried two holsters, one for their gun and the other for their hair dryer. So Magaw came up with the idea—and I wholeheartedly supported it—that we would exchange one agent each for thirty days at a time. One PPD agent would spend thirty days with VPPD, and vice versa. We did that for a couple of years, and it really helped. Agents would return to the vice president's detail saying that it was tough on PPD; they might not travel as much, but standing post around the Oval Office is not so glamorous. We heard the same feedback from the PPD agents temping with us; the VPPD was not as easy as they imagined. I don't know whether the two details still exchange agents, but they should.

At headquarters, remnants of the Knight-Powis-Simpson battles continued. It was a sad time for the Secret Service, because it came down to victimization, or what I sometimes called the euthanasia of old agents. Too often, senior agents at the end of their careers found themselves in someone else's way. Maybe that happens in other organizations, both inside government and in the private sector, but it shouldn't happen in the Secret Service. The battle widened the schism between protection and investigation and created a parochialism that got out of hand throughout much of the 1980s and well into the 1990s. It ruined careers and caused enormous damage.

Simply put, the Secret Service had become too political. And John McGaw was one of those political characters. I'd unintentionally embarrassed him at the State of the Union address. Just before George Bush left the White House, the president rewarded McGaw by naming him director of the Secret Service. Within a few days, the new director transferred me from the vice president's detail to the Washington field office.

When I was a young agent on Edmund Muskie's detail—he was a candidate for the Democratic presidential nomination—and he went to play golf, we wore blazers with an open shirt. By the time I got to the Quayle detail, the golf course dress code had deteriorated considerably. We always wore some sort of coat, because we didn't want to display our gun or radio. But it can be hot on a golf course in the summer, so before long agents were wearing fishing vests. I always thought that outfit looked very unprofessional, and I continued wearing a blazer or some sort of wind breaker. However, I tolerated fishing vests because everybody had one. That is, until we took Quayle to a pro-am golf tournament in Fort Wayne, Indiana. As we pulled into the country club, I spotted an agent wearing a fishing vest, safari pants with huge pockets, and a pith helmet. He looked like Ramar of the Jungle. When we got back to Washington, I sent a memo to the detail decreeing no more fishing vests. The following week, we took the vice president to the Bush family summer home in Kennebunkport, Maine, to see the president. A golf game was scheduled, and while McGaw's PPD agents were in fishing vests, we were in blazers. There was a real visual dichotomy between the two details. We reflected our own pride by looking more professional, and the PPD agents knew it.

I don't know whether McGaw even recalled the fishing vest incident, but working in the Washington field office meant I could enjoy the freedom that came from no longer having to travel so exhaustively. There was no denying that I'd been moved sideways, and, in the back of my mind, I began contemplating retirement. My Irish mother always said that everything happens for a reason.

While I was thinking about what I was going to do, a call came in from an old friend, Larry Buendorf. He was the agent who'd grabbed Squeaky Fromme's gun during the 1975 attempt on Jerry Ford's life. Larry was back with Ford as the head of the former president's detail. He was calling to say, "I'm in New York, and there's a company called Primerica. President Ford is on the board, and the chairman of the company is Sandy Weill. I'm phoning from his office. He says the company is going to get bigger and they want to bring someone in to deal with security issues. Are you interested?"

My honest answer was "I don't know." I told Larry that I had a résumé and he asked me to fax it to him right away. Fifteen minutes later I got a call from one of Sandy Weill's aides, John Fowler, asking, "When can you come to New York?" I went up there the following week to meet Sandy, his general counsel Chuck Prince, Primerica president Jamie Dimon, and Frank Zarb, who was head of Smith Barney at the time. Zarb had worked for President Ford as energy czar. Sandy was very impressive, having surrounded himself with some young and very bright people. I returned to Washington thinking to myself, If I'm going to retire, this looks like the right company.

Another factor had changed my life at this point. Barbara and I had separated, and Michelle was now a freshman at James Madison University in Virginia.

As an agent on protective details, you learn the hard way that you can't make many future plans because when the time comes, there's a chance you might be halfway around the world. The reality of the job is that you are forever on someone else's schedule. It's not easy to deal with, and, unfortunately, it's not only the agents who pay the price. It also affects families. I missed many occasions to be with my daughter as she was growing up. I missed birthdays, I missed parties, I missed ball games, and I missed all those special Kodak moments. I missed a great deal of my daughter's childhood and it still saddens me.

By mid-May 1993, I had accepted the offer from Primerica and announced my intention to retire in June. On my last day in the Secret Service, I invented an old navy tradition. Someone had given me a small bottle of Jim Beam, which I'd had in my desk for years, so I invited half a dozen of my guys from the Quayle detail to join me in the "traditional emptying of the ration." When they walked into my office, they found me wearing a borrowed fishing vest.

The burden had been lifted.

I'd felt that way when I left the president's detail, and I'd felt that way as I watched the pope's plane take off in Detroit. I'd felt that way when I left the vice president's detail, and now I felt that way as I retired. I'd worked hard and had always tried to do the best I could for the people I protected and for the other agents. Twenty-three years later, it was over. I kept telling myself that going to New York might be the best career move I ever made. As it turned out, it was. The personal and professional decisions were significant and I spent a lot of time soul-searching. I had to admit that I had been extremely lucky. I am lucky to have had great role models as parents, lucky to have survived Vietnam, lucky to have had such extraordinary experiences. I may not have benefited from all the opportunities I have been given, but I am very grateful for so much.

The first call I made when I arrived in New York was to Dick Lefler, who was head of security at American Express. He'd left the Secret Service in 1985 and was one of the first agents to get a big New York job. He gave me some of the best advice anyone ever has. He said, "You've been in an agency for twenty-three years where you've been surrounded by people who mostly think as you do. There may be some disagreements on the edges but we fundamentally think about things the same way." He said, "Now you're in an organization where you're surrounded by people who do not think as you do. Be prepared for that."

He was right. Leaving the Secret Service meant losing my identity, my authority, and a great sense of fraternity. I literally had to reinvent myself. The corporate world was a whole different game, and it took me months to get accustomed to that. In a very real sense, it is the great equalizer. We are all starting over. You can see that best when former agents meet. We bond together in a natural way, even agents who had once been at loggerheads. In the end, we are brothers and sisters under the skin, suddenly forced to survive in a different arena. Many good agents have became successful in what we frequently refer to as "the real world." Many agents have failed there, too. It takes a lot of getting used to. Deceptively, the private sector can look familiar. It, too, is a bureaucracy in which personalities and egos run the gamut, from very smart to very foolish, from very humble to extremely arrogant. But in the private sector they keep score differently. I once believed that if you could survive the minefield that is the White House—where you are surrounded by and constantly required to balance conflicting interests, objectives, and egos—you could survive anywhere. But the private sector is a better breeding ground for greed, power, and arrogance. And all too often that mixture severely blurs good judgment.

In that sense, there are lessons to be learned from the public sector. One of America's great naval heroes was Commodore Thomas Truxton—a contemporary of Stephen Decatur and John Paul Jones—who commanded the USS *Constellation* in the early years of the nineteenth century. I first heard about him in officer candidate school in 1967. We were discussing leadership, and Truxton's definition was the most succinct I've ever heard. It was simply "Take care of your men."

Those five words have shaped my entire professional life. I believe that leadership can be just that simple, that caring about everyone from top to bottom—from the president of the United States to the young post stander—is what separates good leaders from bad leaders. I saw it in the navy and in combat, I saw it in the Secret Service, and I see it today in Citigroup. Truxton was right. Great organizations are no accident. They are created by and managed by great leaders.

When I joined Primerica in June 1993—a great organization created and managed by an effective leader, Sandy Weill—the problem was that nobody could tell me exactly what it was they wanted to me do. I'd just spent twenty-three years in an agency where I knew what to do, where I'd been trained in what to do, and where, if I wasn't sure, somebody would tell me. Suddenly I was in a place where none of those things existed. Chuck Prince was the one who told me, "You need to fill voids. Just keep moving until somebody tells you to stop." He had two small signs on his desk. One said, "I'm responsible," and the other, "No excuses." Both sentiments were part of our culture in the Secret Service, so I knew I could work in this world.

In July 1993, Sandy bought Shearson, which became Smith Barney Shearson. That fall he bought Traveler's Insurance, and the name of the company changed to Travelers Group. Those were followed by Aetna Life Insurance, Salomon Brothers, and eventually Citibank. As director of security for Primerica, I had no direct responsibility for any staff. Ten years later I was responsible for 2,500 guards and 750 security managers and professional investigators, had a budget in excess of $160 million, and supervised a worldwide network of people in 105 countries. I was also overseeing executive protection for a number of senior people.

And all the time I kept moving, filling voids, waiting for someone to tell me to stop.

The glacial shift came in 1998 when we merged with Citibank. Except for a couple of Smith Barney offices in Hong Kong and London, Travelers Group had very few operations overseas. But Citibank was global and had a huge security operation and so much going on internationally. That gave me opportunity to take the template I'd made at Traveler's—which combined investigations and security just as in the Secret Service—and apply it to Citibank, which had much more potential for this kind of operation.

Sandy Weill and the Citigroup board of directors have since made Chuck Prince chief executive officer. I don't think I've ever met two finer, more supportive men, particularly Sandy. He gave me a tremendous opportunity and was a terrific mentor. I will always be very grateful to him.

Another opportunity to change my life presented itself at about this time. As fate would have it, I had not seen Susan Senderowitz for more than twenty-seven years. She was my high school and college sweetheart. In 1965, we went on to pursue separate lives and had our own families. We reconnected in 1992, and it was a remarkable reunion, both nostalgic and meaningful. Susan and I were married in 1994, and began sharing our life together. I inherited an additional family of her three children, Elizabeth, David, and Peter. As I started my new career, Susan continued her interior design business and we began our "commutes" between New York and Pennsylvania.

I wish I could be as upbeat about the future of the Secret Service as I am about Citigroup. In the wake of 9/11, the Secret Service has been taken out of its traditional home at Treasury and moved into Homeland Security. The distinction between protection agents and investigative agents may soon be ended. I think that will be a sad day. Eleven years at the White House put the stamp "protective guy" on my forehead. Being at the White House that long is probably not a record, but it was almost half my career, and that is a lot. I think there are maybe only a handful of agents who spent that much time at the White House and supervised the president's detail, the vice president's detail, and the Dignitary Protective Division, too. So I was a protective guy. But I would gladly have gone back to investigations.

I've always felt that the connection between investigations and protection is largely artificial and was based on a coincidence of history. There's no logical reason why the two should be together. But there are plenty of reasons why the two should stay together in an agency that wants to attract a certain type of person. It's the combination of those two missions that has made the Secret Service much more viable, attracted better candidates, and given it the ability to do things in the field that we wouldn't ordinarily be able to do. Keeping the two functions together must be the main objective of any director. I don't know enough of the thinking behind the decision and the workings of Homeland Security to say that moving the Secret Service there was a mistake, but I think it's a shame it's no longer a part of Treasury. The Secret Service has always maintained its own identity. Incorporating it into a collection of disparate agencies has got to be disruptive. It won't put the President at risk, but it will definitely change the complexion of the Secret Service. My concern is that, as the Homeland Security Department matures, administrators will eventually move investigations out of the Secret Service into the Justice Department and limit the Secret Service to a protection function. That will be damaging.

A few years ago an incident took place that, I believe, has even more serious repercussions for the Secret Service and could seriously effect its ability to protect. During the Monica Lewinsky scandal, Secret Service agents were subpoenaed to testify about things they saw or overheard while exercising their protective responsibilities. I have always considered private conversations that I overheard to be just that—private. And I have tried very hard in this book to respect that privacy. The incidents I've written about happened to me. But in the wake of the Monica Lewinsky subpoenas, I strongly believe there must be some legally established privilege between Secret Service agents and the people they are protecting, especially the president and the vice president.

If Secret Service agents are required to testify about conversations they've overheard—which is very different from testifying about overtly illegal acts they may have witnessed—then protectees will pull away from protection, forcing agents into the untenable position of making a choice between being just close enough to protect someone and just far enough away not to overhear something. With lives at risk, no agent should ever have to guess, hope, or pray that the distance is right.

Needless to say, I am extremely proud to have been a part of such a unique agency with so many unique people. Some of us got along, and some of us did not. We had weak links, and we had immovable objects. We had good managers, and we had bad managers. We had intellectuals, and we had blockheads. We had great athletes, and we had people who couldn't tie their shoelaces. We had people who could quote Shakespeare, and we had people who couldn't read without moving their lips. We agreed with each other more often than we disagreed, but when we disagreed, it sometimes got nasty. None of us was always right, and when we were wrong, some of us made bad decisions. But in spite of all that, there was a special spirit and a unique feeling of fraternity forged by a mission that, in the end, came down to questions of life and death. In spite of our differences, and in spite of individual conflicts, it was our mission that really mattered. It was a mission that had "no margin for error."

With all its imperfections and quirky personalities, the Secret Service never loses focus on the singular role it plays. Early on, we learned that the mystique of the Secret Service is intertwined with the mystique of the presidency, that the two are connected, not just as institutions but in very human ways. Early on, too, we learned to take orders, and later we learned to give them. We were instilled with the importance of dedication to the job, and were confronted by the high cost of the sacrifices we would all have to make. We learned to work long hours and learned to outwork everyone else. We learned to balance risks against the resources needed to reduce them. We learned to make decisions and face the real dangers of indecision. We learned how to use common sense as our best guide, how to pick our battles and make a stand, how to be diplomatic when diplomacy was called for, and how to be good negotiators when diplomacy didn't work. We learned how to succeed at "the tip of the javelin."

The Secret Service taught us how to get everyone home safely.

My pride in the Secret Service knows no bounds, for all sorts of reasons, not least of them being that the Secret Service gave me a very special gift. For one small moment, I was permitted to take an extraordinary journey. That said, it is not a unique gift. Every agent has tales to tell, especially agents who have been responsible for presidents and vice presidents. In that respect, the experiences I had in the Secret Service are representative of what other agents have gone through, of what other agents will go through. We all share that special gift.

Every agent who sits in the right front seat of the president's limousine, who stands in the Oval Office, who walks with the president along the porticos of the residence, who listens to him speak with other world leaders, who jokes with him, who watches him comfort the families of fallen American heroes, who feels his joys and his disappointments, and who waits off stage with him when "Ruffles and Flourishes" begins, is granted this special gift. It is the privilege of standing next to history.

EPILOGUE

The last time I saw him was in 1991.

On Ronald Reagan's eightieth birthday, there was a party for him at the Century Plaza in Los Angeles. Vice President Quayle was invited, so I took him there. The reception before dinner was crowded, and fifty people were milling about. President and Mrs. Reagan were chatting with friends in the far corner. He had his back to the room, but she was looking around and caught my eye. She smiled and nodded and, a minute later, crossed the room. She reached her hands out to me; I kissed her hello and told her how much we missed her and the president. She asked how I was, and how my daughter was doing, and how life was back in Washington. We talked for several minutes before she returned to the president's side.

As the reception ended, and the room was emptying out, I was standing next to the vice president near the door when the Reagans came toward us. He hadn't yet seen me, and I was anxious to say hello. He was looking straight ahead, and then his face was three feet from me, and now he was looking right past me. My heart sank. There was no recognition. I thought to myself, It's been so long since he's seen me and it must be because I'm out of context.

At that very moment, Mrs. Reagan grabbed his jacket sleeve, and said "Ronnie, it's Joe." And the instant she said that, he turned to me, and his whole face lit up, and he gave me one of those big famous "Oh, hello, Joe" greetings.

I didn't put two and two together that night. Maybe I just didn't want to. It was easier to convince myself that it was because he wasn't expecting to see me there. Two years later, when I read his handwritten letter to the American people announcing that he had Alzheimer's disease, I recalled his birthday party. I wondered if that was part of what had happened that night. When she reminded him, he knew. Maybe Mrs. Reagan was doing that purposely, reminding him who everyone was. Maybe, by that time, she knew.

The day after that party, Dan Quayle went to visit the president at his office in Century City. I took him upstairs, but purposely stayed outside the office suite. I didn't think I belonged there and didn't want to put myself in the middle of the visit. I sent one of the other supervisors in.

I was waiting with the advance team near the elevators when, after about ten minutes, the president's chief of staff, Fred Ryan, came out and said to me, "He wants you to come in."

I got another one of those big greetings. Then he said, "I want a picture with the three of us."

That was quintessential Ronald Reagan—ever gracious.

His personality was so electric, so engaging. He always had great stories to tell and always loved to tell them. Often he would wind up being the object of his own jokes, like that day in July 1986 when he told a huge crowd in New York Harbor, "You know, I received an invitation that said please come to Ellis Island on July 4 for the hundredth birthday celebration of an American institution. Somebody goofed. My birthday is not until February."

His humor followed him into meetings, even serious meetings. It could be a cabinet meeting or a sit-down with the House leaders, and we'd be standing outside waiting for the meeting to end, and then we'd hear people laughing. He ended every meeting with some sort of joke. He'd say something funny, and that's how we knew the meeting was over.

He could dominate a table or a room. But when he stepped in front of an audience, the place was his.

We would be standing offstage, waiting for him to be announced. He and I would be alone, or maybe Mrs. Reagan would be there with us. As an actor waiting to go on stage, he was naturally relaxed. But then "Ruffles and Flourishes" would start, and I could see him begin to get pumped up. He would get bigger. I mean that. He would get physically larger. As soon as the music started, something magical happened. He stopped being an actor waiting to walk on stage and became the president of the United States, about to make an appearance. As soon as the music started, he took on an air about him and inflated with pride. And when he stepped onstage, he was Ronald Reagan, President of the United States.

As many times as I saw this happen, as soon as I hear that music, I always get a thrill. Even today, no matter who walks out on stage, be it George Bush, Bill Clinton, whoever, I think of Ronald Reagan. He was "Ruffles and Flourishes."

I miss my time with the Reagans.

I saw Mrs. Reagan a few years ago when she came to Citigroup to have lunch with Sandy Weill. He asked me if I wanted to stop by to say hello to her. The president had been unwell for several years, and the strain on her was evident. But she was just as warm and just as gracious as ever.

We talked for a few minutes and then I said, "I have been thinking a lot about the president."

She looked up at me with those big eyes of hers, and stared for a few seconds as tears welled up, and then she nodded.

Nothing more needed to be said.

ACKNOWLEDGMENTS

★ ★ ★ ★

None of this could have happened without my wife Susan, who not only conceived the title for the book, but ceaselessly provided encouragement and invaluable editorial guidance. Susan and I first met in high school and although our lives took us apart for a number of years, once we found each other again, she has been my source of uncensored advice, unequivocal support, and unconditional love. Her many contributions to this book and, more important, to my life, cannot be measured.

The idea for this book began in 2003 while having lunch with my old college friend, Jeffrey Robinson. We had not seen each other for nearly thirty-seven years and were reunited through the efforts of Steve Young, my Citigroup colleague in London. I agreed to do the book with Jeffrey because I trusted his judgment and experience and valued our friendship.

Two thoughts were uppermost in my mind right from the beginning. First, it was crucial that, at no point, would I compromise the protective procedures of the Secret Service or, in any way, betray the trust and unique personal access that agents have with the people that we protect. Second, while the stories in this book are mine, they are also representative of the professional and personal experiences that so many agents have had throughout their careers, especially during this period of our country's history.

For their hands-on help with this project, I would like to thank

Bob Hast, Jim Huse, Eljay Bowron, Mark Weinberg, and Jinny Swope. They each read early drafts of the manuscript and made important suggestions.

I wish to thank my New York agent Ed Breslin and my London agents Eddie Bell and Pat Lomax. It is thanks to their belief in this book and their efforts on my behalf that I am fortunate to be published by Tom Dunne and his wonderful team at St. Martin's, and to have had the privilege of working with the superb editor Sean Desmond. Also, my thanks to Donald J. Davidson for his extraordinary copyediting.

The United States Navy provided me with innumerable experiences, lessons, and friendships. I maintain a lifelong admiration for my river patrol shipmates, notably the late Lt. John Poe, Lt. Andy Arje, Lt. (j.g.) Bill Waters, and Lt. Jack Geraghty. These men, along with the other officers and enlisted men of the River Patrol Forces, demonstrated uncommon courage and played such an important role in my navy and Vietnam experiences.

Throughout my twenty-three years in the Secret Service I was fortunate to meet and to know so many people whom I respect and for whom I will always be grateful. Those include Bob Hast, Earl Devaney, Phil Kiefer, Tom Quinn, Dick Lefler, H. Stuart Knight, and Mike Weinstein.

Then there are two men who unselfishly allowed me to share so many exceptional opportunities with the president of the United States. I can never thank them enough. They are Bob DeProspero and Ray Shaddick.

And here I add thanks to a very special friend, Larry Buendorf, who introduced me to Sandy Weill and helped open the door to a second career.

One of the significant benefits of the 1987 papal trip was meeting Bishop Robert Lynch. These many years I have valued both his friendship and his wise counsel.

My years in and around the White House allowed me to work

with and get to know some truly first-class individuals. Bill Henkel, Mike Deaver, Tom Pernice, Jeannie Bull, Rick Ahern, Grey Terry, Jim Hooley, Andy Littlefair, Gary Foster, Jim Kuhn, Dave Fisher, Dan Murphy, Steve Purcell, Tom Fleener, and Craig Whitney. These are men and women who, along with many other staff and press corps members, made working at the White House such a unique experience. Many of them dedicated years away from more lucrative careers in order to serve their country. Knowing them and sharing all those unforgettable moments with them has been a highlight of my career.

Thankfully, there is life after the Secret Service. For that, and for so many other things, I am enormously grateful to Sandy Weill and Chuck Prince. I especially want to thank my colleagues in Citigroup Security and Investigative Services, most notably my good friend and colleague, Dick Steiner.

Because there have been so many people who contributed in various ways to this project or have been an important part of my life, I worry that I may forget a few. If I do, I hope they will understand.

I want to add a few words, here, about my parents, Joseph and Dorothy. Both of them, in their own way, provided my brothers and me with a loving and supportive home. Their faith in us and encouragement were always there, paving the way for us to pursue our dreams.

Finally, there is my daughter, Michelle. From the day she was born, she brought sunshine into my life. I love her and am so very proud of her.

INDEX

★ ★ ★ ★